LANGUAGE AFTER HEIDEGGER

LANGUAGE
AFTER
HEIDEGGER

KRZYSZTOF ZIAREK

Indiana University Press

Bloomington & Indianapolis

This book is a publication of

INDIANA UNIVERSITY PRESS
Office of Scholarly Publishing
Herman B Wells Library 350
1320 East 10th Street
Bloomington, Indiana 47405 USA

iupress.indiana.edu

Telephone orders 800-842-6796
Fax orders 812-855-7931

Manufactured in the
United States of America

Library of Congress
Cataloging-in-Publication Data

Ziarek, Krzysztof, date
  Language after Heidegger /
Krzysztof Ziarek.
    pages cm. — (Studies in
Continental Thought)
    Includes bibliographical references
and index.
  ISBN 978-0-253-01101-5 (cloth : alk.
paper) — ISBN 978-0-253-01109-1
(ebook) 1. Heidegger, Martin,
1889–1976. 2. Language and languages—Philosophy. I. Title.
  B3279.H49Z536 2013
  121'.68092—dc23

                      2013019223

1 2 3 4 5   18 17 16 15 14 13

foundations of sense
arise the word.

subvention by
Figure Foundation

Das Wort kommt zur Sprache,
das Seyn bring sich zum Wort.

The word comes to language,
Being brings itself to word.

—Heidegger, *GA* 74, 112

CONTENTS

PREFACE

The motivation and several ideas formative for this book have been in gestation for a while, both in my previous publications on Heidegger, language, and avant-garde poetry and poetics, as well as in my graduate teaching. These endeavors were directed toward developing the implications of Heidegger's approach to language and evolving a way of thinking *through* language in the aftermath of Heidegger's radical redefinition of philosophy. The more immediate impetus for writing this study has been the publication in German of the series of Heidegger's manuscripts from late 1930s and early 1940s that develop the insights and problems raised initially in his *Contributions to Philosophy.* Readings these newly available texts, I realized their crucial import for Heidegger's radically rethought understanding of language. The appearance of these works, in particular volumes 71 and 74 of the *Gesamtausgabe* (Collected Works), made the articulation of the innovative character of Heidegger's conception, especially its distinctness from structuralism and post-structuralism, all the more important and timely. Distinct from the linguistic turn and the post-structuralist critiques of the sign, Heidegger's approach hinges on the singular notion of the word and the relation between the event and the saying. This transition between the event and the saying is prior to and yet already related to signs and the difference between the sensible and the intelligible. My book underscores the idiomatic character of Heidegger's approach, and does so for two reasons: first, because it has not been sufficiently addressed or appreciated in more contemporary discussions of language, and second, because it offers a new way for understanding the relation between thought and language. This inventive "language" of thinking is, I believe, of crucial significance not only for future philosophy but also for gauging the import of poetic language, and not only in poetry or literature but in other arts as well.

Over the years, conversations and exchanges with my colleagues, both at the University at Buffalo and elsewhere, have contributed, in ways impossible to trace here, to how these ideas about language have evolved into the shape they receive here. I would like to thank especially Ewa Płonowska Ziarek for her advice, support, and comments on the manuscript, particularly her suggestions about the introduction. I also want to express my gratitude to Dee Mortensen, senior sponsoring editor at Indiana University Press, and to Professor John Sallis for their generous comments, advice, and suggestions during the review process for this book. Two anonymous reviewers for Indiana University Press helped make *Language after Heidegger* a better book. I am grateful to Sarah Jacobi, Michelle Sybert, and Nancy Lila Lightfoot at Indiana University Press and Deborah Oliver, my copyeditor, for their help in preparing and guiding the book through production.

I also want to acknowledge here the support from the Humanities Institute at the University at Buffalo, whose generous research grant was of great help to me in finishing the manuscript and preparing it for publication.

Nicola Del Roscio, the president of the Cy Twombly Foundation, has generously given his permission for the use of Cy Twombly, *Untitled*, 1970, for the cover.

All the translations from the volumes of Heidegger's *Gesamtausgabe* that are not yet available in English are mine. I owe special thanks to Andrew Mitchell, who read most of my translations from *GA* 69, 70, 74 and 78, and suggested important corrections and improvements. His recommendations and modifications were of great help in finalizing these translations. I also want to thank Rodolphe Gasché for his suggestions with regard to translating several sentences. Any remaining imperfections and errors in these translations are mine alone. In these translations, I opt to render the verb *stimmen* as "to tune," in part to keep playing off the translations that use "to dispose" instead (for instance, Rojcewicz in *The Event*) and in this way to indicate that Heidegger's use of *stimmen* points to how the disposing of relations from the event sets them on the way to language and gives them their "tone" or "voice." In my discussion of the relevant passages from Heidegger, I often use both "dispose" and "tune" to keep in view the relation between the "disposing" in question and the movement of language.

I have retained original emphasis (italics) in Heidegger and other quotations. In translating the archaic spelling *Seyn* used by Heidegger, I follow the recent practice of rendering it as "beyng," to preserve the "silent" distinction between *i* and *y*, which figures the attempt in Heidegger's thought to bring metaphysics to a turning point, to its *Verwindung*. For the sake of uniformity, I changed the other translation variant, "be-ing," to "beyng" in the excerpts

I cite from Parvis Emad and Thomas Kalary's translation of *Besinnung* as *Mindfulness* and from Kalary and F. Schalow's translation of "Die Armut" as "Poverty."

A few sections of this book incorporate and rework material that appeared previously:

"Giving Its Word: Event as Language," in *Heidegger and Language,* ed. Jeffrey Powell (Bloomington and Indianapolis: Indiana University Press, 2013).

"Reticent Event: Letting Things Happen," *Textual Practice* 25: 2 (2011): 245–261.

ABBREVIATIONS

Works in Martin Heidegger's *Gesamtausgabe* (Frankfurt am Main: Vittorio Klostermann, 1975–) are listed here using the conventional abbreviation, *GA,* followed by volume number.

Gesamtausgabe (Collected Works)

GA 4	*Erläuterungen zu Hölderlins Dichtung.* 3rd ed. (1991, 2010, 2012)
GA 12	*Unterwegs zur Sprache* (1985)
GA 65	*Beiträge zur Philosophie: Vom Ereignis* (1989)
GA 66	*Besinnung* (1997)
GA 67	*Metaphysik und Nihilismus* (1999)
GA 69	*Die Geschichte des Seyns* (1998)
GA 70	*Über den Anfang* (2005)
GA 71	*Das Ereignis* (2009)
GA 74	*Zum Wesen der Sprache und Zur Frage nach der Kunst* (2010)
GA 78	*Der Spruch des Anaximader* (2010)
GA 79	*Bremer und Freiburger Vorträge* (1994)
GA 85	*Vom Wesen der Sprache* (1999)

Other Works by Heidegger

A	"Die Armut"
BW	*Basic Writings*
CP	*Contributions to Philosophy (Of the Event)*
E	*The Event*
FS	*Four Seminars*

M	*Mindfulness*
OEL	*On the Essence of Language: The Metaphysics of Language and the Essencing of the Word; Concerning Herder's Treatise "On the Origin of Language"*
OTB	*On Time and Being*
OWL	*On the Way to Language*
PA	*Parmenides*
P	"Poverty"
PLT	*Poetry, Language, Thought*
ZSD	*Zur Sache des Denkens*

Frequently Cited Works by Other Authors

D	Kim, Myung Mi. *Dura*
SLT	Howe, Susan *Souls of the Labadie Tract*

LANGUAGE AFTER HEIDEGGER

Introduction

As the title indicates, this book explores both language according to Heidegger: Heidegger's idiomatic and innovative approach to words and language, and also language after Heidegger, that is, how we can think about language differently thanks to Heidegger's work. In this way, while considering Heidegger's main ideas on language, the book examines the crucial role Heidegger's distinctive language explorations and inventions play in shaping not only his approach to language but also his idiomatic way of thinking. For what is critical to Heidegger's enterprise is developing a manner of thinking *through* language, that is, thinking that opens up new avenues and discovers unexpected insights less by way of concepts or arguments than by a specific way of listening to and being guided by language and its intrinsic ingenuity.

There are several reasons why such a study is both important and timely. To begin, there is no current book devoted to tracing adequately this mutually formative relation between language and thinking in Heidegger, one that would do justice to the complex and innovative, in fact, unique, approach to language and to thinking *via* language Heidegger develops, especially as it has come into sharper focus in the texts from the 1930s and 1940s, which only began to appear in print in 1999: *Vom Wesen der Sprache, Gesamtausgabe,* vol. 85 (1999); *Über den Anfang, Gesamtausgabe,* vol. 70 (2005); *Das Ereignis, Gesamtausgabe,* vol. 71 (2009); *Zum Wesen der Sprache und Zur Frage nach der Kunst, Gesamtausgabe,* vol. 74 (2010). These volumes show that Heidegger's conception of language, known up to now mostly from his post–World War II lectures on language and poetry, collected in English in *On the Way to Language* and *Poetry, Language, Thought,* was already developed in the late 1930s and early 1940s.[1] These writings often offer Heidegger's most radical and linguistically most daring explorations, which fuse new paths in thinking with an inventive and transformed experience of language. For these reasons, we must revise what we have learned about language in Heidegger on the basis of works available before these more recent publications, and indeed radicalize our understanding.[2] This critical interlacing of language and thought aside, all too often scholarly responses either pay scant attention to language in the discussion of Heidegger's work, or such deliberations become too quickly limited to either the analysis of Heidegger's idea of language or the consideration of his engagement with poetry and art. In either case, language ends up playing "only" the role of one of Heidegger's themes rather than being explored as the "engine" of Heidegger thinking, as the way this thinking advances, escapes metaphysical determinations, or occasions critical breakthroughs. At the same time, in the discussions of Heidegger that are situated between continental and analytic perspectives, the matter of language becomes telescoped into the problematic of ordinary language or of logic or both, as though the aim was to try to domesticate Heidegger's thought back into philosophically familiar and recognizable categories and terms. As a result, the latter approaches tend to evacuate precisely the very impetus of Heidegger's thought toward a *transformation* of our relation to language, a transformation that specifically requires changing the terms and the ways in which we experience language and thinking, as well as encounter ourselves in them.[3]

Examining and developing further not only Heidegger's understanding of language but also his practice of writing and thinking through language is important for several other reasons. First, language is not simply one of the topics or issues in Heidegger's vast work but constitutes the issue *of* Heidegger's work in the literal sense: Heidegger's thinking issues *from* language, from its signature trait of having always already arrived into signs, into speech and writing, into poetry (*Dichten*) and thinking (*Denken*).[4] Though this approach is already in evidence in *Being and Time,* especially in the book's initial attempt to understand language in terms of *Rede,* or discourse, it is from *Contributions to Philosophy* onward that much of Heidegger's thought proceeds literally by way of language. What this means is that Heidegger does not simply "use" language to express or represent ideas, including his own account of language, but rather that, carefully listening to language, he allows his thinking to unfold from it and be guided by it. Quite often his thinking literally receives its impetus from the German terms he follows and develops, as is evident in his *Unterwegs zur Sprache* and even more so in *Das Ereignis* (*The Event*), published in 2009, and *Zum Wesen der Sprache und Zur Frage nach der Kunst,* from 2010. Second, language, that is to say, the philosophical and poetic German that Heidegger works with, sets the tone (*Stimmung*) for his work, lending it its idiomatic nonmetaphysical voice (*Stimme*), at once challenging and annoying to our metaphysically well-trained ears. As I show in this book, the experience of the Heideggerian thinking *from* language is irreducible to philosophizing *about* language in the sense of a novel theory or concept of language. In other words, Heidegger does not offer a philosophy of language in the conventional sense of the term, as language for him is never simply an "object" to be studied or described. Instead, his thinking about language unfolds through highly idiosyncratic and innovative mode of writing. More than presenting insights *about* language, this mode of writing enacts the event of language—and language *as* event—in order to demonstrate how undergoing an experience with language remains irreducible to assertions or theories. Thus thinking is called upon to "acquire" a poetic ear, so to speak, not for aesthetic reasons but because the ability to listen to and follow language comes to prompt and pattern the very movement of thought, allowing for the most important philosophical opportunities and openings.

The philosophical import of this way of approaching language extends to several of Heidegger's central ideas: event, world, time-space, power, relation between singularity and generality. What I mean by this is that Heidegger's key notions, whether event, world, or, Da-sein, do not come to be elaborated and then function simply as new or redefined philosophical concepts, but in fact they attain their resonance and inventive import in thinking precisely through what might be called a transformative language valence: for instance, Da-sein emerges in its breakthrough importance for the question of being through the insertion of the hyphen and the literal foregrounding and spacing of the interval marked by the hyphen as the relation of the site (Da) to being. Thus it is critical to show how Heidegger's thinking and use of language occurs within philosophy but crucially exceeds it. This book recognizes this pivotal role of language as Heidegger's way of thinking, showing the extent to which his critical engagement with the essence of technology, power, and, more broadly, the metaphysical inheritance of Western thought, is not simply tied to his rethinking of language but cannot in fact be fully understood in its innovative approach without the impetus that Heidegger's thinking receives *from* language. To this end, I examine not only the key elements of Heidegger's conception of language but, even more importantly, pay close attention to how his words and phrases work, to the critical role played by hyphens and the meshwork of prefixes in determining—in the sense of *Bestimmen*, that is, through initially setting the tone, *Stimmen*—the pathways of this thinking.

This philosophical revalorization of language by Heidegger entails several critical consequences for both philosophy and language. The first important significance comes from the fact that Heidegger's approach to language is non-Saussurean, since for him language is not primarily about signs and signification but about the tension between words (*Worte*), on the one hand, and terms (*Wörter*) and "word-signs" (*Wörterzeichen*), on the other. To put it most simply, Heidegger does not base his account on the notion of the sign (*signum*) and signification.[5] Therefore, language for him is not essentially a system of signs but rather the way in which emergence and manifesting, or being's disclosure of beings, comes *to* signs. This is why language in Heidegger cannot be thought of within the perspective of the twin metaphysical notions of *phone semantike* and *zoon logon echon*. By contrast with this non-Saussurean take on language, much of the reception of and response to Heidegger's work in English has been mediated by the work of French post-structuralist thinkers.[6] These thinkers, from Lyotard and Derrida, to Lacoue-Labarthe and Nancy, have formulated and have been themselves formed by critical responses to structuralism, both inheriting and reformulating Saussure's famous account of language as a system of signs. Placing the emphasis on the play of signification and the unstable relation between the signifier and the signified, they tend not to pay enough attention to Heidegger's distinctive account of language, especially of words, which relies on the displacement of the sign. To put it simply, Heidegger makes a crucial distinction between signs—key in different ways not only to structuralist and post-structuralist accounts of language but, more important, to the very way in which these thinkers tend to think and write—and, what he calls "words."

To flesh out the approach to language "after" Heidegger, I develop and amplify the way Heidegger plays on the divergence in German between the two plural forms of *Wort* (word): words (*Worte*) and terms or dictionary words (*Wörter*). What is critical in this context is the fact that Heidegger connects the latter plural, *Wörter*, with the notion of the sign (*Zeichen*) or word-signs (*Wörterzeichen*). This tension between the two plural forms is described most often as the withdrawal of words from signs. "Terms," "dictionary words," or sometimes "word-signs" (*Wörterzeichen*) refer to words taken as linguistic signs (*Zeichen*) and reflect an understanding of language through the prism of the play of signification. "Words," by contrast, describe a different dimension of language, one that constitutes its originative momentum, that is, the clearing (*Lichtung*) as the manner in which language opens and traverses its ways (its *Bewegung*). This momentum is the leap, the origin (*Ur-sprung*), of language, which, by giving being to beings, makes room for signification and signs. The issuing of words marks not only the origin of language but also the opening up of world, that is, of the question of being (*Seynsfrage*). In practice, this understanding of language enacts the expansion of philosophy beyond argumentation and its correlative, the statement, into a poietic practice of thinking that relies crucially on language's continual movement from words to signs. As a result, conceptuality and thought cannot be divorced from the tonality (*Stimmung*) of this movement, or distilled somehow into "purely philosophical" thought, since this tonality idiomatically designs the constellations of relations that make possible concepts and conceptual determination (*Bestimmung*). The conceptual work of thinking is tuned by *Stimmung* and thus also potentially always already put in question, interrogated, and reopened by it. In order to understand how Heidegger wants to rethink the question of being, it is necessary, therefore, to break out of the understanding of language through the notions of sign and signification and experience language through the tension between "words" and "signs," that is, through the poietic momentum of language. In this context, my claim is that no "critique," no *Auseinandersetzung* with Heidegger makes sense or makes enough sense *of* his thinking without a careful and alert consideration of Heidegger's ingenuity with language, which attempts to prompt a transformation of our relation to language beyond its metaphysical parameters of signs, differential signification, code, communication, etc.

Crucial for phenomenology and philosophy in general is the fact that in Heidegger we have two explicit articulations: of language as the event; and of the idea that the event issues (into) words in such a way that, although its occurrence is not prior to language, it is neither captured by nor signified in it. Heidegger approaches language initially not through signs (*Zeichen*) or through meaning and reference (*Bedeutung*) but from showing (*Zeigen*), which manifests from the freeing spatiotemporalizing realm of the clearing, constituting the way in which language moves—has always already moved—into signs. This unfolding of language, though requiring human participation and decision, is not animated by human beings but rather is spurred on by the nihilating momentum of being, by what Heidegger calls "the silent [or quiet, *stille*] force of the possible" (*BW*, 220, modified; *W*, 314). The event, Heidegger explains, has the momentum of *ostendere*: of manifesting and showing, and doing so not mutely but as the inceptual word, as the breaking open of language. As he puts it in volume 71 of the *Gesamtausgabe, Das Ereignis:* "The event is the inceptual word" (*E*, 145)—"Das Ereignis ist das anfägliche Wort" 170), or even more directly in *GA* 74, "The event comes to word"—"Das Ereignis wortet" (99). This last phrase needs to be understood carefully, for it is not the case that words already exist and the event comes to them, that is, becomes articulated, repeated, or represented in them. Instead, it is the event that, literally, "words," as the German phrase would need to be rendered in English by turning the noun *word* into a verb, "to word" in order to underscore the occurrence, the event, of the word. The event in one gesture issues (into) words, which means that words originate *from* the event while at the same time remaining *of* the event. In other words, the event and "its" word are neither different nor identical. To understand Heidegger's thought, it is necessary then to experience the ways in which the manifestation of phenomena, their giving from being or event—the "there is" or "es gibt" marking the event—is also the start of language, its initial opening words, which Heidegger describes as a kind of pre- or fore-word to human signs. What is thus required for undergoing what Heidegger calls "an experience with language" is both the awareness of these complex and shifting movements repeatedly underwriting language, beyond human languages and sign systems, and the attentiveness to the silent stillness (*Stille*) enveloping language. It is important to note here that dependent on this experience is not only the transformation in our relation to language, which Heidegger mentions in "The Way to Language," but also the very possibility of perhaps twisting free (*Verwindung*) of metaphysics.

In this approach, the so-called linguistic turn in philosophy gets less of an idiomatic articulation than a thorough transformation: it is not only that thought is shaped and guided by language but that, prior to words and concepts, language's saying, in its specific valence as the event of being, addresses itself to thought, and, calling it forth, disposes (*Stimmen*) it into poetic thinking. This is why Heidegger's revision of language is distinct from and more radical than the linguistic turn in philosophy: if the linguistic turn examines the way in which language constrains and influences what thought can conceive, Heidegger's language suggests going further. First of all, thinking is brought about and shaped as a listening to language. In such thinking, possibilities opened by language itself—in words and word constellations, roots and etymological connections, prefixes and the tonality they lend to words—are drawn out in attentive practice of writing and allowed to play a transformative role with regard to thinking. Concepts and meaning thus emerge from the practice of a writing that listens to language and allows this listening to guide its conceptual insight. This is clear in the case of Heidegger's idiomatic sense of the event (*Ereignis*), which, like Da-sein, is transformed and developed into the notion we now know from Heidegger's texts precisely through the insertion of the hyphen, which highlights the enactive force of the prefix *er-* and allows the multiple meanings of *eignen, er-eignen,* and *er-äugnen* to unfold into a new constellation: as propriation and appropriation, occurrence and eventuation, manifestation and seeing, further modified by the inscription of the hyphen in the word or its absence in various contexts. This constellation, with the philosophical disruptions initiated by it, is irreducible to any concept, for instance of the event, and can be heard adequately and thus thought as such only by traversing, each time anew, the poetic field of *das Ereignis*. It is certainly not equivalent to the signification of the German term *Ereignis*. In short, language for Heidegger enacts thinking and does not simply determine or convey it.

This is evident with regard to the very term for language (*Sprache*), which is not grasped in its concept or rendered transparent through description but instead comes to be experienced through the movement and the force of the constellations Heidegger draws among words with the root of *sprechen*: (*ansprechen, zusprechen, entsprechen, versprechen*) and *sagen* (*ansagen, ersagen, entsagen, zusagen, versagen*). The philosophical significance of this approach to "redefining" language can be summarized as follows: "what" language is, how it happens, is described by Heidegger first not as an idea or a concept but as the relatedness opened up in its design (*Aufriss*) by the constellation enacted by a set of prefixes. The concept thus arises from the movement of language itself, here specifically the German prefixes, and the poetic dimensionality enacted by these prefixes is never adequately defined by the *concept* of language. As I show in chapter 4, the concept of language that Heidegger elaborates, its determination (*Bestimmung*), is expanded and inflected by the *Stimmung*, marked precisely by the nonconceptualizable movement and relationality written open by the hyphen and outlined by the prefixes in play.

If the linguistic turn can be seen as consolidating the anthropological concept of language and thought by disclosing their intrinsic connection, Heidegger's approach to language breaks out of the anthropological perspective to locate the emergence of language not simply in human beings and their faculties but primarily and essentially in the event. Paraphrasing the subtitle of *Contributions to Philosophy*, one could say that language is "of" and "from" the event (*Vom Ereignis*). As such, language is never limited to human language systems but instead "says" the emergence of beings, that is, being. Human languages constitute a response to this originative saying of or from the event, providing the "translation" of this saying into signs. This response is not subsequent to the event or caused by it but needs to be understood with regard to the event and as at the same time attentive to it. In a manner befitting the turn within the event—that is, from being to the human—Heidegger makes possible a corresponding turn in our approach to language: from the notion of language based on humanity and animality (*zoon logon echon*) to language as the word of the event: "Das Ereignis wortet." What this means is that language is not human in its *Wesen*, although it unfolds toward humans and comes through them to its articulation in signs, writing, and speech. It does not mean, however, that the notion of language simply needs to be extended to animal forms of communication. Heidegger's approach is more radical: language does not begin with living beings but is granted, addressed to them, as *Zuspruch* or *Zusage,* from the event. To highlight the importance of this point, I develop the nonanthropic movement of language in Heidegger, which exceeds human speech and writing, and tie it to his critique of *Vermenschung* (humanization or anthropologization) of beings, which includes the anthropologization of language.

The overall implication of these ways of rethinking language by listening to it and by amplifying the resonance of what words, prefixes, hyphens, and compounds disclose is that the "twisting free" of metaphysics (*Verwindung*), or at least thought's preparation for the possibility of such release from metaphysical conceptuality, depends on thinking's capacity to open up its conceptual strictures to the poietic movement of language. Without transforming our relation to language, and with it of the way we deploy language in thinking, there is no possibility of twisting free of the metaphysical framing of the question of being or of changing the manner in which humans experience their existence with regard to it. Such a transformation does not mean simply a new concept or a theory of language, as another instance in the history of (metaphysical) practices of definition; instead, it allows the possibility of a nonmetaphysical experience of and with language, an experience to be carried out as "thinking," and specifically as *poetic* thinking. This poetic thinking comes to rely on the ways, sketched above, in which language moves, ways that reach beyond concepts and signs, theories and systems, into the self-designing, poietic event, *from* and *of* which language "speaks." This explains why Heidegger is skeptical about the confinement of thinking to conceptual determination alone, which neglects the crucially transformative, poietic thinking.

For contemporary discussions, the most important critical implication of the distinction introduced by Heidegger between words and signs is the unique critique of the notion of difference underpinning it, an approach that is both distinct from and, in a fashion, more "radical" than the one discussed by French post-structuralism, whether that of Derrida, Levinas, Lyotard, or Deleuze. While I explain the particulars of this approach in chapter 2, it is important to note here that for Heidegger the possibility of thought twisting free (*Verwindung*) of metaphysics hinges on rethinking difference through the prism of departure (*Abschied*). As Heidegger writes, "the essence of difference is not differentiation but the essence of differentiation is difference as departure"—"Das Wesen des Unterschiedes ist nicht die Unterscheidung, sondern das Wesen der Unterscheidung ist der Unterschied als Abschied" (*GA* 70, 73). The transformative distance marked between the prefixes *unter-*

and *ab*—from *Unterschied* to *Abschied*—offers us a hitherto unexplored, even in post-structuralism, optics on difference, where difference is thought from withdrawal, abyss (*Ab-grund,* without regard or link to grounding), and denial (*Ab-sagen*). As Heidegger makes clear in *GA 70*, at issue is an essential transformation of difference (80). This transformation is indicated not only by the fact that Heidegger on occasion holds *Unterschied* and *Differenz* as distinct—which suggests that *Unterschied* cannot be understood adequately as difference—but that the rethinking of difference (*Unterschied*) as de-parture (*Ab-schied*) indicates a fold prior to both spacing and deferral. This fold opens up the dimension of difference and the various incarnations and modifications through which it has been understood in philosophy and in critiques advanced in continental thought in the last few decades. The withdrawal and clearing, indicated by the prefix in the term *Abschied,* open the dimension for difference and its productive movement and effects. Without the characteristic retreat of being, without the de-parting of or from its event, there would be no "parting" or partition, and thus no emergence of difference. The related word *Absagen* makes clear that what makes difference possible is the "away" momentum, that is, the withdrawal that underpins and marks the saying: the *ab-* is decisive for all "Sagen" (saying), since its "back draft" moves, measures, and paces language. It is in the space opened by the withdrawal indicated by the German prefix *ab-* that any manifestation and signification of difference becomes possible to begin with, including the signification of the other. To put it plainly, for Heidegger, movement, whether spacing or temporal, with its correlative infra- or inter-relations, occurs thanks to what may be called the "back draft" of the event. What draws open differentiation is this draft, and it does so precisely by staying always on the "away" side, the *ab* side, as it were, of differences, beings, or signs. By de-parting (*Ab-schied*), it allows "parting" (*scheiden*) in the first place, while having already de-parted itself from such differentiation.

Furthermore, the distinction between words and signs on which Heidegger's language and thinking hinge affects crucially the understanding of the relation between singularity and generality. In Heidegger, it is the movement from word to signs that institutes the possibility of iteration (in Derrida's formulation), that is, the inscription of the possibility of repetition in an otherwise singular occurrence. The fact that words arrive into signs as carried by the back draft of the event, that is, as already withdrawn from and denied to—in the sense of *Abschied* and *Absagen*—signs, makes repetition, and thus the functioning of sign systems and concepts, possible. Yet this backdrafting movement of language makes meaning possible without being captured by the play of signification. In this manner, it inaugurates the space for the relation between the singular and the universal. The singular can be said, and thus opened to repetition and generalization, because it comes to be said thanks to the characteristic canceling and non-saying (*Ab-sagen*) of the always "singular" (*einzig*) and "one-time" (*einmalig*) event, where what is refused, cancelled or withdrawn is precisely the event's nonrepeatable, always one-off giving. The sole, proper, and singular way the event occurs is in calling itself off, that is, by de-parting from what comes to be through the "parting" play of the singular and the universal. In other words, the idiosyncratic "soleness" of the event's *Abschied* inaugurates the demarcation of the singular and the universal. This idiomatic Heideggerian take is explored, among other instances, in my reading of Derrida's well-known analysis of the "unique word" in Heidegger, which, as I argue, does not pay sufficient attention to the temporality (of departing—*Abschied*) marking words (*Worte*) and their movement into signs or terms (*Wörter*). Attentiveness to this characteristic and distinctive parting associated with the event makes possible being in tune with the tonality (*Stimmung*) that presets and brings about the determination (*Bestimmung*) of both the singular and the universal.

The four chapters of the book lay out the key aspects of this undertaking. Chapter 1, "Event | Language," rearticulates the question of being not only from the event but specifically from the event (as) language, highlighting the pivotal "wording" of the event. It outlines the scope of the entire book and focuses on the parameters of the transformation in the relation to language Heidegger envisions as preparatory for the twisting free (*Verwindung*) of metaphysics. Chapter 2, "Words and Signs," focuses on and develops the distinction between Heidegger's notion of words and the linguistic sign. In short, it offers an account of language "after" Heidegger that does not take its primary cue either from Saussure's approach or from its post-structuralist revisions. From the perspective of post-structuralist critiques of language and difference, as is evident in different ways from revisions offered by Lyotard and Derrida, Heidegger's approach appears insufficient with regard to the discussion of the sign, while his discussion of the unique (*einzig*) word seems to neglect difference. My response to these remarks is twofold. On the one hand, *GA* 74 (2010) provides ample discussion and explanation of Heidegger's critical approach to the sign, which explains his way of circumventing and revising the problematic elaborated by Saussure and structuralist linguistics. On the other hand, these discussions provide the foil to Heidegger's elaboration of language as the showing saying (where *Zeigen* occurs as *Sagen*) prefatory to signs. Heidegger's approach to language is, therefore, poietic, in a sense different from a certain literary or poetic inclination in post-structuralist thought, and hinges on the necessary and inceptive withdrawal of words from signs. The specifics of Heidegger's poietic understanding of language are drawn out in more detail in chapters 3 and 4. Chapter 3, "Poetry and the Poietic," engages with Heidegger's proximity to poetry, poetic language, and, in particular, the originative poietic momentum that Heidegger points to in poetry but also activates in his own language, especially in his lexical and scriptural innovations. It develops the radicalism of Heidegger's approach by looking at the poetic work of two contemporary US poets, Susan Howe and Myung Mi Kim, thus providing not only more contemporary but also more poetically innovative backdrop to Heidegger's own writings on poetry. Part of my reading "after" Heidegger is to emphasize the linguistic invention, on the one hand, and, on the other, to highlight the way in which Heidegger's own encounters with poets, primarily of romantic and neo-romantic poetics, from Hölderlin to Rilke, Trakl, and George, opens his thought to the poietic dimension of language. In order to understand the significance of Heidegger's move, it cannot and should not be limited to the German context, initially so crucial to Heidegger. Although Heidegger quickly opens up his encounter with Hölderlin and its role for the Germans to the broader problematic of the Occident and focuses on the twisting free of metaphysics in the global dimension, evident in particular in *Mindfulness* and *Die Geschichte des Seyns,* I propose going further. Here Heidegger's own inventiveness—in his twists of thinking and German language—outstrips the implications of this aspect of his work in the romantic rhetoric of Hölderlin, perhaps even in a certain ideology of romanticism. Developing the insights afforded by Heidegger's texts with regard to contemporary, "experimental" poetry, points to this limitation of Heidegger's work, thus providing a degree of critical distance. For these reasons, I am more interested in what becomes possible in the aftermath of Heidegger's encounter with Hölderlin than in the encounter itself, which has been amply documented and discussed critically in the Heidegger scholarship. Chapter 4, "Language after Metaphysics," explores the ramifications of Heidegger's call for transforming our "metaphysical" relation to language and traces the way this transformation is at issue in Heidegger's idiomatic German: from his hyphenation (from *Da-sein* to *Er-eignis, Ab-grund, An-fang,* etc.), to the root clusters (for instance, around *Sprechen* and *Sagen*), prefixes (*er-, ent-, an-, ein-,* etc.). The chapter ends with the consideration of the critique of power and violence in Heidegger and a brief reappraisal of the stakes and innovative possibilities opened up by this understanding of language "after" Heidegger.

My aim is to finally give credit to Heidegger's original take on language, distinct not only from post-structuralist accounts of language but also from other phenomenological and postphenomenological approaches, an understanding *of* language—that is, coming from the poeitic movement of language—which fundamentally departs from the notion of (human) language as a system of signs or *phone semantike*. This approach extends beyond any idea of language we can cull from Heidegger's remarks, as it evolves a unique "Heidegger" way with language, namely, an idiomatic manner of thinking and writing oriented and inspired by language. I want to emphasize and develop what I see in Heidegger as the possibility of poietically thinking *through* language, which means thinking with a view to how what Heidegger refers to as "the word 'of' being" acts both as the boundary from which language emerges and gathers its momentum and as the boundedness of the region, that is, as the clearing of the relations, folds, and crossings, which come to unfold within this movement.

ONE

Event | Language

*Was ist dann, wenn das Seiende und dessen je nachgetragene
Seiendheit (das Apriori) den Vorrang verliert? Dann ist das Seyn.
Dann wandelt sich das "ist" und alle Sprache wesentlich.*

—Heidegger, *GA 66*, 337

What happens then, when beings and the beingness (the *a priori*) that
is always appended to them lose their preeminence? *Then beyng is.*
Then, the "is" and all language transform themselves essentially.

—Heidegger, *Mindfulness*, 300–301 (modified)

Event and the Folds of Language

The key role of language in Heidegger's thinking after the "turn" of the mid-
1930s comes from his recognition, already hinted at in *Contributions to Philosophy*, that the question of being that spans the trajectory of his work is
essentially the question, or more precisely, the way, of language. This may be
why the last section of *Contributions to Philosophy* is titled "Language (Its
Origin)" (*CP*, 401), as it outlines briefly the guiding threads of Heidegger's
emerging signature approach: language and the event; language as unfolding
from silence; language and the clearing, world, and history; language as strife
and rift (*Riss*); language as both "the first and most extensive humanizing
[*Vermenschung*] of beings" and as the opportunity for the dehumanization
or, more emphatically, dishumanization (*Entmenschung*) of the human being
away from its status as "an *objectively present living being* and 'subject'" (*CP*,
401). These concerns index the reciprocity between the *Destruktion* of the
metaphysical manner of asking the question of being and the problematic of

language.[1] Just as much as Heidegger's repeated rephrasing of the *Seinsfrage* influences his writings on language, so do the evolving understanding of language and its reflection in Heidegger's writing practice impact the reformulations of the question of being from the initial prism of the ontological difference to the history of being—with Heidegger increasingly using the older German spelling *Seyn*—and the event. One of the markers of this shifting approach in the texts from late 1930s is the way Heidegger vacillates between writing about the overcoming (*Überwindung*) of metaphysics and about the need of an admittedly more radical twisting or torsion (*Verwindung*) that would bring metaphysics to a turning point. Recognizing the fact that the call for the overcoming of metaphysics remains essentially metaphysical, since it aims to open a further zone of thought "beyond" metaphysics and has a ring of finality to it, Heidegger begins to explore instead the possibility of pushing metaphysics to its edge in order to induce a turn within it that would release thinking from its metaphysical foundations and perhaps let it think otherwise, or at least allow thought to transform its own relation to thinking. In the much later "Time and Being," Heidegger goes as far as to speak of the need to cease all overcoming and to leave metaphysics to itself (*OTB*, 24; *ZSD*, 25).

This shift from overcoming metaphysics to bringing it to a turning point is also reflected in the well-known remarks from "The Way to Language" about the need for a transformation of language.

> In order to think back to the essence of language [*Sprachwesen nachzudenken:* to think after and in accordance with], in order to reiterate [literally, after-say, *nachzusagen*] what is its own, we need a transformation [*Wandel*] of language, a transformation we can neither compel nor concoct. The transformation does not result from the fabrication of neologisms [*neu gebildeter Wörter*] and novel phrases. The transformation touches on our relation [*Verhältnis*] to language. (*BW*, 424–425; *GA* 12, 255–256)

Overcoming metaphysics would be tantamount to an impossible invention of a new language, and thus to a forcible change, which would not necessarily touch at all upon that from which the transformation in question could and, in Heidegger's estimation, should spring: namely our relation to language, that is, the way we hold ourselves to and experience language's work. This is why Heidegger points instead to a shift in our relation to language that could issue in the transformation of language, a transformation that cannot be 'simply' forced or invented.[2] What would literally issue and manifest from this turn in our relation to language, is precisely the "origin" of language, its essence or essential occurrence (*Wesen* as used by Heidegger is its verbal resonance of coming to be rather than in the substantive sense of 'essence,' hence also the frequently used derivative *Wesung*) as coming specifically from the event. Approached this way, the essence of language forms the original pronouncement (*Ur-Kunde*) of the event. "For the event—owning, holding, keeping to itself—is the relation of all relations" (*BW*, 425, modified). Therefore, language needs to be experienced and considered in its specific issuing, its *Wesung* or essential occurrence, from the event: not with regard to beings, humans, or life, but to the always singular (*einzig*) and one-time (*einmalig*) clearing, that is, the coming open, of the event. Because language is (or issues) in this manner, the change in our relation to language reverberates within the event as "the relation of all relations," changing the way we think and take part in how the event unfolds. The very possibility of bringing metaphysics to its turning point, its *Verwindung,* and turning with it also the way we experience the question of being, hinges on such a transformation of language. For this transformation means a critical change in how thinking unfolds; instead of being guided by conceptual grasp and definition, it is steered and molded by what listening to language discloses, by what insights and avenues it opens. In such changed thinking, what language itself opens up or initiates comes to be amplified in writing so that it quickly acquires a transformative role with regard to thinking, in a way dictating, that is, "saying," its moves and developments. In Heidegger, this "saying" marks its turns in thought most often by way of hyphenated words and word series or constellations, through etymological connections or the networks of prefixes and the new resonances they lend to established words and concepts. In short, without transforming our relation to language, of our experience of what language is and how it guides deliberation, thinking will not be able to change, and no amount of talking about radical critique, postmodernity, or postmetaphysics, will force or manufacture the transformation at issue in Heidegger.[3]

This transformation, more critical than the linguistic turn in philosophy, points to a necessary shift from the metaphysical ways of understanding language, based on the notion of *zoon logon echon,* that is, on the concept of the human as an animal endowed with language. This dominant approach results in language being locked within the matrix of physiological, biological, and anthropological presuppositions and determinations that produce various types of metaphysical discourses "about" language—its conceptions or theories—rather than make room for an experience with and a thinking through language Heidegger is interested in. Included in this perspective is the philosophy of language, which Heidegger calls in *Zum Wesen der Sprache und Zur Frage nach der Kunst,* "metaphysical thinking 'about' 'language' (language philosophy)" (*GA* 74, 141). The fact that the German terms for *about* and *language* both appear in quotation marks in the original indicates the intrinsic objectification of language as a target of study and reflection, as though it were possible to turn language into an object and construct a meta-discourse in language 'about' 'language.' From the start, Heidegger's singular way with language calls into question and reframes the approaches to language based on physiology or biology and, today, neurobiology. Putting these determinations of language in question does not in any way invalidate these views of language. In fact, Heidegger himself would be quick to say that these conceptions are certainly correct—in accordance with the scientific paradigm of objectivity and correctness—and allow us to learn a great deal about the neurobiological processes involved in language and cognition. Yet their correctness does not mean that they lay bare the "true" way of language, as 'truth' for Heidegger is simply not graspable in terms of correctness or adequation. This is why Heidegger does not tie the origin of language to either the organs of speech or writing, just as he does not explain it with regard to the cognitive capabilities of the human brain—in fact not with regard to the human being to begin with—instead, he decisively shifts the inquiry into the domain of the event.

For the same reasons, he also distances himself from the notion that language operates as expression, turning ideality (the nonsensible) into the sensible by way of sounds and letters, since this notion relies on both the idea of the human being as the 'subject' and on the paradigm of representation. Most important, this critical stance evinced in Heidegger's texts pertains as well to the underlying anthropological assumption that language is a possession of human beings, that "man 'has' language," as Heidegger often puts it, paraphrasing the Aristotelian *zoon logon echon*.[4] To counter this prevailing metaphysical framing of language, Heidegger inverts this phrase and repeatedly states that "language 'has' man" or "the word 'has' man." "Das Wort, was den Menschen (Dasein) 'hat' (Wesung des Wortes), gründend—ab-gründig" (*GA* 74, 100)—"The word, that which 'has' man (Dasein) (essencing of the word), grounding—abyssal." And in another place, "Der Mensch hat die Sprache, weil die Sprache im Wort entspringt, das Wort aber als die Sage des Seyns den Menschen hat, d. h. bestimmt in seine Bestimmung" (*GA* 74, 122)—"Man has language, because language arises in the word; the word as the saying of beyng, however, has man, that is, defines him in his determination." The notion that human beings 'have' language assumes that language is primarily a tool, an informational instrument, which can be owned, used, and manipulated, and that as such a tool, it can be adequately described and understood through linguistics, philosophy of language, or (bio)informatics, or perhaps by the combination of the three. The fundamentally Aristotelian understanding of language is based on the conception of logos and reason, whose origin in what Heidegger calls "the attentiveness to beyng capable of holding still" (*stillhaltende Achten auf das Seyn*), remains uninterrogated and unexperienced.[5] As a result, instead of approaching language through attentiveness to being, reason (*Vernunft*) and language become mistakenly conceived as a special capacity attached to animality (*Vermögen im animal*), which renders inaccessible language in its originative relation to being.

The formulation "language has man," which occurs repeatedly in the texts on language from *Zum Wesen der Sprache und Zur Frage nach der Kunst*, bespeaks the key point in Heidegger's thinking of language. This point has not been given enough attention in responses to Heidegger's reflections on language, even in post-structuralist approaches, which are often sympathetic to at least the fundamental orientation of Heidegger's critique of metaphysics: Heidegger's continuous insistence, beginning perhaps with *Contributions to Philosophy*, that the originative moment of language cannot be explained with regard to living beings. This is the crux of the already mentioned final section of *Contributions to Philosophy*, in which Heidegger, noting the humanizing power of language, its overwhelming and pervasive *Vermenschung*, points out that, when finally experienced in its essential occurrence, language instead can "dishumanize" (*Entmenschen*) the human being, that is, break the hold that the notion of an objectively present living being continues to have on the understanding of the human. The prefix *ent-* is employed here by Heidegger in its positive sense of liberating and releasing from the ossified construal of the "human," as it is juxtaposed with the negative resonance of *ver-* in *Vermenschung*, which indicates a false turn in understanding the human and the expanding detrimental effects of such anthropomorphization. It is crucial to note that this positive, "dishumanizing" momentum of language, when it is experienced simultaneously *from* the event and as being *of* the event, does not pertain simply to the concept of the subject but, more broadly, to the notion of the living being. In other words, its import is not circumscribed or exhausted by the critique of the subject as a unitary being or as an effect of language, produced, constituted, or performed by and in it. For Heidegger, the decisive moment of dishumanization (*Entmenschung*) has to do with questioning the notion that the human being can be explained as essentially a living being who, as distinguished from other animals, is also endowed with language. It is this different understanding of language, especially its originative relation to the event, that guides how Heidegger proposes to rethink the human[6] and thus sets the stage for his critique of reason and of the notion of life. In other words, Heidegger's attempt to transform language, and through it thinking, lends its force to his critique of power, technology, and life, which began to come into focus in the late 1930s.

To consider the human being nonmetaphysically requires displacing the notion of the living being into the "wake" of the event, after and according to the event's 'language,' which means that what makes humans "human" is not their status as specifically determined living beings, as human animals, but instead their idiomatic relatedness to being. This is why Heidegger prefers to write instead in his late texts about "mortals"—written, as far as I am aware, always in the plural, *die Sterbliche,*—because the designation "mortals" sets the primary determinants with regard to language and finitude, that is, the event and its finite spatiotemporal span, and not with reference to life or living beings. What decides the scope and shape of the experience of mortality, and thus orients and forms its participants, the mortals, is the finite and historical relation they (can) have to being, that is, being-there or Da-sein. This relation transpires by way of the event's coming to word, that is, as language, and decides mortality with regard to the nothingness (*Nichts*) intrinsic to the unfolding of being, which means that neither mortality nor the nothingness at issue here can be reduced to or explained in terms of life and its end. In this way, Heidegger appears to lend the word "dying" (*Sterben*) a thoroughly idiomatic sense: not the end of life (*Verenden*) or demise (*Ableben*), but a singular attentiveness to the nothingness pulsing—in the more active sense of *Nichtung*—in being, to its wordless imprint on the event-like experience of time and space. Death thought of with regard to life understands or rather misunderstands "being" in terms of life's coming to its inevitable end and therefore does not do justice to the nothingness as the "silent force of the possible" enabling and reverberating in being.

As Heidegger explains in GA 74, "*Das Wort 'hat' den Menschen* (nicht *das Lebewesen*), sondern den Menschen als den *Vernehmer des Seienden*— vor-stellend, ver-nehmend (planend), *besorgend*" (143)—"*The word 'has' man* (not the living being), but man as the *perceiver of beings*—re-presenting, perceiving (planning), *concerned.*" Language "has" the human being because it is the word that calls forth, carries, and determines mortals as always open to deciding, as Da-sein, and thus as guardians of the truth of being (see 143). Translating the phrase *zoon logon echon* as "man 'has' [possesses] the word," Heidegger emphatically declares that his rephrasing, "the word 'has' man," which he calls the beyng-historical (*seynsgeschichtlich*) maxim,[7] does not simply reverse the metaphysical conception of language, because metaphysics, defining language through *zoe* leaves everything undecided, especially with regard to the mortal relation to being. By contrast, the possibility of being mortal and existing as Da-sein, that is, as entering and holding stance (Heidegger's term is *Inständigkeit*) in the clearing of the there (Da)—that is, in the midst of beings open to their deciding—is essential and more fundamental to what it means to be 'human,' specifically with regard to being, than living is, and it is so precisely no longer in the metaphysical sense of fundaments and essences. We must remember that Heidegger's perspective, from *Being and Time* onward, is focused on the question of being and not of life, which places the emphasis on the understanding of mortals, who, as capable of Da-sein, of being-there, fit and respond to the *Seinsfrage* in ways inaccessible and incomprehensible in terms of life or with regard to humans defined on the basis of living beings.

If one begins to understand the human being from the notions of life and living beings, it then is grasped in terms of its existence as a living entity among others, and thus with regard to its status as a being, which leaves unattended, "undecided," as Heidegger puts it, the decisive dimension of the relation to being: Da-sein. To underscore this point, *Zum Wesen der Sprache und Zur Frage nach der Kunst* makes a clear distinction between Da-sein and *Menschsein* (human being) with regard to language: the first is described in terms of stillness and silence (*Stille*), the other in terms of breaching the stillness and bringing it to words (*Lautung*) (141). While the problematic of stillness, silence, voice, and words is elaborated on later, it is invoked here to underscore the point that the essential element of language in Heidegger is nonhuman—though it is "mortal" or at least transpires with regard to mortality—and comes into the open specifically through the dishumanization (*Entmenschung*) Heidegger mentions as decisive at the end of *Contributions to Philosophy*.[8] To understand the human, or more precisely, the *mortal* relation to being, life takes a back seat and needs to be rethought from the event, from Da-sein experienced as relatedness to being, and not the other way round. For it is Da-sein that 'grounds' mortals by opening them to the *Abgrund,* to the abyss or, more exactly, to the abyssal non-ground. It is only as cut loose, in effect recurrently "de-cided" from grounding, and therefore as opened to their being as mortals, that humans can experience what it means also to live.

The phrase "language 'has' man" indicates as well that language is not limited to human language or languages. In fact, language, as much as Da-sein, is essentially nonhuman: both invite and necessarily involve reciprocal relation to humans but are neither initially delimited nor finally determined by that relation. One could put it this way: while humans, to the extent that they can experience their being as mortals, are indispensable to carrying out what Heidegger calls "the way" of language, specifically as those who bring language into words and signs, the part they play in language has to be experienced and understood from the event, not from the idea of human languages as creations and possessions of living beings.[9] This is why language as signs, signification, discourse, and speech or writing needs to be twisted away from the exclusively human and more broadly "living entities" perspective and allowed to unfold from the event; this is the only way to see which segment of the way of language becomes articulated as the system of signs, determinative of the modern way of understanding language, meaning, and communication.

In this perspective, the question of animal communication as a form of language is less important. While Heidegger acknowledges that animals communicate, he does not consider animal sounds and gestures to be language. This is not necessarily because he simply inherits the anthropocentric perspective in which humans are considered to be "higher" animals equipped with language, as opposed to other animals deprived of language; rather, he understands that communication, as determined by the neurophysiology of living bodies, is not of exclusive or "essential" import to the way of language. In this Heideggerian perspective, cognitive science cannot account for the (nonhuman) origin of language, or for how the event comes to word, since it registers neither the claim (*Anspruch*) nor the grant or award (*Zuspruch*) of the event, which calls for and prompts human language (*Spruch*) so that it comes into existence as already a response, corresponding to and fitting (*entsprechen*) the originative, nonhuman, claim. Even when we depart from Heidegger and admit—as for example, Derrida does with good reason in his repeated critique[10]—that animals communicate and in some sense have language, this inclusion of animal forms of communication does not speak directly to Heidegger's point, which he makes not from the perspective of the varied spectrum of animality to which human (animals) belong constitutively, but rather from the event and its "language," which is neither human nor animal.

Heidegger's approach to language hinges on the notion that the giving of being—its event—takes place as language, at first a word-less, that is, quiet and sign-free language of manifestation: it is a stillness and silence already breached and on the way to signs. Volume 71 of the *Gesamtausgabe, Das Ereignis* (*The Event*) makes this abundantly clear: "Das Ereignis ist das anfängliche Wort"—"The event is the inceptual word" (*GA* 71, 170; *E,* 145) and "das Seyn selbst anfänglich das Wort ist"—"beyng itself is inceptually the word" (*GA* 71, 172; *E,* 146). Human languages are part of this broader sense or expanse of language, as they come always already as a response to the giving of being—a hearing-belonging (*hören/gehören*) to manifestation that brings it into words/signs. Speech and writing come as a response (*Antwort*) to the "word 'of' being" taking place as the event; on the one hand, they function as a response to the claim of this inceptual or inceptive word, literally the answer to its getting underway as language, where language begins to speak to and at us (*an-sprechen*) and, on the other hand, as a response rendered possible by what this inceptive word grants, or literally "speaks to" us (*zu-sprechen*). As Heidegger puts it plainly: "Language is the response to the word"—"Die Sprache ist die Antwort auf das Wort" (*GA* 74, 71). The German indicates both how the word prompts and calibrates the response, as the text highlights the connection between the word and the answer (*Antwort*). This is why Heidegger can write in *On the Way to Language*: "the being [*Wesen*] of language: the language of being [*Wesen*]" (*OWL*, 94). Here it is the colon that marks the always already occasioned transition, which has moved the event as the inceptual word into the words (signs) used by human languages. The colon also indicates that the very being of language, which here means the manner in which language unfolds and comes to be language (i.e., its essential occurrence), is the language of being, that is, the wordless saying of the way being is given to be (i.e., of the event), a saying that always transpires in terms of beings and the signs used to signify them.

As though to reinforce these remarks from *The Event*, the more recent *Zum Wesen der Sprache und Zur Frage nach der Kunst*, uses repeatedly the phrase "das Wort 'des' Seyns" (the word "of" beyng), in which the genitive "of" is most often deliberately set in quotation marks to indicate its curious status as neither the subjective nor the objective genitive, nor the combination of both (see *GA* 74, 20, 127–128, 131, 135, etc.) In a parallel way, Heidegger also writes about "the saying of beyng" (*Sagen des Seyns*, e.g., 132) or of the event as *Er-sagen*, that is, as a mention or a saying that, however, as the hyphenated prefix *er-* indicates, is not representational or expressive, but instead highlights the manner in which the event brings about and institutes this saying, giving its own word and, through it, giving itself to words (see *GA* 71, 181). The sentence that best encapsulates this occurrence reads simply "Das Ereignis wortet" (*GA* 74, 99); translated literally, the phrase reads "the event words," since the German verb *worten* is intransitive. Paraphrasing, one could render the sentence into English as "the event comes to word." What is important in the way Heidegger phrases this sentence is that words do not precede the event and, therefore, the event never comes to be signified or represented in them. As the archaic verb *worten* suggests, the event itself brings about words, builds itself into them, in order to be said in them. The event issues words and, in this manner, it "speaks."[11]

That the event issues words and issues into them is also made explicit in the essays collected in *On the Way to Language* and in Heidegger's first sustained articulation of the transformation in relation to language in *Das Ereignis*, whose manuscript dates from 1941–42. The most important remarks about language in *Das Ereignis* appear in chapter 5, titled "Das Ereignis: Der Wortschatz seines Wesens"—"The Event: The Vocabulary of its Essence"—though observations on language, word, and saying are scattered throughout the volume. As Heidegger formulates it in chapter 5, "Das Ereignis ist das anfägliche Wort, weil seine Zueignung (als die einzige An-eignung des Menschenwesens in die Wahrheit des Seyns) das Wesen des Menschen auf die Wahrheit des Seyns stimmt"—"The event is the inceptual word, because its arrogation (as the unique adoption of the human being into the truth of beyng) disposes the human essence to the truth of beyng" (GA 71, 170–171; E, 145). The play of *Zueignung* and *Aneignung* signals here the way in which prefixes come to map in Heidegger's thinking the complex occurrence of appropriation and the proper (*Eignis*) characterizing the event. The prefix *zu* indicates the manner in which the event assigns itself, specifically its singular manner of essential occurrence, to the human being, and in the same move prepares or adapts human thinking to be responsive to this occurrence. This reciprocal assigning and adaptation—the event saying itself to the human and the human bringing "of" the event into words, transpires only because the event renders the human being "appropriate" (in the sense of *An-eignung*), that is, alert and attentive to the unconcealment of being. In this way the event "tunes" (*stimmt*) the humans to how being has, in the blink of an eye, always already unfolded its spatiotemporal playing field as the momentary "here and now" (*Augenblick*). Since *Zueignung* and *Aneignung* constitute the ways in which the event unfolds as inceptual word or words, they are also and in the same gesture the grant and the claim (*Zuspruch* and *Anspruch*), which open human beings to language, inviting the wording of their response. The various simultaneous vectors of 'propriation' indicated by the German prefixes that Heidegger adds to -*eignung* in *Das Ereignis* (see 147–170) are echoed by the prefixes added to *sprechen, Spruch*, or *sagen*, prefixes that in other contexts also include *er-, ver-, über-, an-*, and *ent-*, in order to throw open an expanse of the play of time-space, which Heidegger calls the clearing (*Lichtung*), where the verb *lichten* indicates breaking open as making room, as well as lighting and lightening. These dimensions and vectors at play in the clearing are opened up and bounded in a way that constitutes the idiomatic 'wording' of the event. "Clearing is never the empty, but the most originary thorough unfolding [*Durchwesung*] of the event as the carrying out [*Austrag*] of the countering and strife—the 'in-between' held unto the abyss [*Ab-grund*]" (M, 90, modified).

To think through the phrase "The event comes to word," we need first to consider the word *Ereignis* in the specific valence elaborated by Heidegger over a long period of time. As *Contributions to Philosophy* makes clear, "event" becomes the word from which "being"—and with it also "time" and time-space—is to be thought of, no longer or not simply in terms of its meaning (*Sinn*) but rather historially, that is, as the way in which history happens as event, whether or not it is recognized as such. While the late lecture "Time and Being" leaves no doubt that being (*Sein*) and time are "givens" from the event, it appears possible that "being," written with the old spelling *Seyn* to indicate an unheard (of) yet 'visible,' scripted, distinction from *Sein*, is to be thought of precisely as the event, as phrases like "the event comes to word" and "the word 'of' beyng" pointedly suggest. The word *event* (*Ereignis*) needs thus to be thought of through the prism of the scripted yet unheard fold between *Seyn* and *Sein*, the fold that would allow for *Seyn* to be understood from the event, without immediately slipping back into metaphysical thinking, which proceeds from the initial grasp of beings or beingness (*Sein* = *Seindheit*), or from the ontological difference between being and beings. In *The Event*, Heidegger provides etymological threads to indicate the parameters of his rethinking of this word, in which the emphasis falls on showing and coming into view, on the reciprocal catching the eye and catching sight of, and on eventuating or coming to pass:

> Er-eigen: er-eugen—er-äugen—ostendere, monstrare, in die
> Augen, Blick, Anblick fallen,
> erscheinen
> sich offenbaren, zu-tragen,
> be-geben.
> —erweisen—erzeigen—*lichten* (GA 71, 184)

> To show [*Er-eigen*] to bring into view [*Er-eugen*],—to catch sight
> of [*Eräugen*]—*ostendere, mon-*
> *strare*, to catch the eye, come
> into view, seize the gaze,
> to appear
> to manifest itself, carry to,
> give forth.
> —to show   —exhibit—*clear up*. (E, 156)

Heidegger underscores the link between *Ereignis* and *Augen* (eyes), so that a momentary emergence into view becomes tantamount to coming to pass (*sich begeben*), befalling (*sich zutragen*), and manifesting (*sich offenbaren*). Appearing (*erscheinen*) comes to pass as showing, pointing, or manifesting (*erweisen, erzeigen*), and these modes of showing occasion the proper domain of *lichten*, that is, of the clearing, which can perhaps be paraphrased in English as the shifting expanse or dimensionality of the event's free domain. Heidegger also points out that in *Er-eignen*, the *eu* from *er-eugnen* turns into *ei*, which leads to its etymological confusion with *eigen, proprium*, and thus also with *an-eignen* (appropriating, making one's own) and *zu-eignen* (dedicating, assigning).

Still, this apparent historical confusion does not prevent Heidegger from exploring and playing on the full extension of possibilities associated with this "false" etymology linking the event with the proper, propriation, owning, property, and so on, which suggests that Heidegger wants not to dismiss this association but rather to downplay the initial or primary explanation of the semantic scope of *Ereignis* simply or exclusively through the idiom of the proper. To this effect, he subsequently "translates" *Ereignis* primarily into the terms of the clearing rather than notions such as "appropriation" or "owning": the event thus occurs essentially by way of the clearing (*lichtend*) and as drawing into the clearing (*in die Lichtung einbeziehen*), which gives the clearing by arrogating "to it protection and preservation [*zueignen die Wahr und Hut*]" (*GA* 71, 184; *E*, 157) where the true takes place, as Heidegger indicates through the double meaning of *Wahr* as *Wahren* (preserve, keep) and *wahr* (true). Subsequently, this specific sense of *Lichtung* as eventuation comes to mean "das in die Erscheinung kommende und so zugleich sich verbergende Sich zu eigen werden"—"to come into its own of the appearing and at the same time self-concealing self" (*GA* 71, 185; *E*, 157). This bringing into the open initiated as the clearing has the aletheic valence of concealing or unconcealing, which means that any decision and separation between the true (as the correct) and the false can be undertaken only within the already opened clearing, this distinction taking place as protected and kept there (*die Wahr und Hut*), that is, literally "in view of" and thus viewed from the event, whose etymological meaning "to come into view" resonates here.

The event in the sense of *Ereignis* is not simply an occurrence, instance, or happening but rather a complex spatiotemporal expanse of relatedness in motion—the clearing—shifting and opening up projectively toward the future. Heidegger's work relies a great deal on this recurrent defamiliarization of the habitual and everyday meaning of the event, which the word *Ereignis* has in German, like the English *event*. This displacement, which retains the customary meaning of the event, repeatedly evokes the need to bring metaphysics to a turning point, its *Verwindung*, by twisting and pushing to its very limit the "metaphysical" meaning of *Ereignis* as an event or an occurrence. This refiguration of the everyday term is also echoed in Heidegger's remark in "Time and Being" that "The event neither *is*, nor *is* the event *there*"—"Das Ereignis *ist* weder, noch *gibt* es das Ereignis" (*OTB*, 24, modified; *ZSD*, 24). This formulation indicates that the event cannot be thought of in terms of its being given *as* "event," because this interpretive or constitutive structure would render the event conceivable as a "being" or a "thing." Since the event *is* not, nothing can be predicated about it. To bring into view how predication relies on the forming of being into distinct entities or beings, and thus also to call this mechanism into question, Heidegger frequently resorts to writing simply "Das Ereignis ereignet"—"The event takes place" or "the event eventuates," to retain a close etymological link present in the German phrase.

What is crucial to how Heidegger proposes to alter thinking by way of language is the fact that in this extended examination and reinvention of *das Ereignis* as a German word, the language considerations are not only a matter of etymology or meaning, since they render *Ereignis* into a critical, poietic, and nonconceptual "word" that then shapes how Heidegger thinks, deploys, or reinvents his other key terms. More importantly, this refiguration occurs precisely through how *Ereignis* is then rethought *from* the German language and its characteristic ways of building words and relations. That *Ereignis* is not a concept does not mean that it is an imprecise or a vague notion, a kind of poetic image or metaphor with multiple meanings, more evocative than defining or grasping. The phrase "the event comes to word" should be read as indicative of the fact that the event takes place as and brings itself to words, with the inclusion of its "own" name, *Ereignis,* among them, and does so specifically through the way in which the alternating prefixes added to the root meanings constellated by Heidegger span and stir the unfolding time-space of and from the event. "The event" is therefore not given as a new concept, a refurbished name, or a modified sign, but specifically through the ways in which language moves itself, writing and "speaking" in the spaces and with the beat outlined by prefixes, hyphens, etymons, and compounds. The transformed relation to language brought about by the event's coming to word, inaugurates a poietic experience with language, neither conceptual nor philosophical strictly speaking, but one that has profound consequences for how Heidegger envisions the necessary "end of philosophy." This experience with language begins the task of thinking otherwise (than metaphysics), for all the key terms in Heidegger need to be "listened to" and experienced in the manner outlined by the idiomaticness of the event. These terms come *from* the event and therefore must be allowed to resonate as such in thought, that is, as being *of* the event, part of its occurrence, without being reduced to concepts or definitions. This new poietic resonance modifies how words are experienced, guiding thinking beyond conceptual strictures and signifying practices. It perhaps can prompt thought to change from "philosophy" to "thinking," as Heidegger sets out to do in works written after *Contributions to Philosophy.*

Just as Heidegger comes to realize that metaphysics cannot 'simply' be overcome, his texts do not intend to leave behind or forget the event as an occurrence or an incident, but rather they bring the event to its linguistic verge, so to speak, and in the process they induce a twist in its resonance and in the reverberations it spreads throughout his thinking, modifying the valence of Heidegger's main terms. The idiomatic and the habitual resonances of the event, while distinct, are never separate and cannot be disconnected. Rather, the act of folding one sense into the other, together with the oscillation between the habitual and the inceptual tone of the event, outlines the active spatiotemporal movement of language. Just as there is no truth but only as (un)truth and no unconcealment without its intrinsic and constitutive concealing, there is no *Ereignis* without the customary sense of the event against which *das Ereignis* in Heidegger's idiomatic use marks its distinctiveness. Keeping the distance between the metaphysical sense of "events" and the inceptual sense of the *Ereignis* constitutes the repeated gesture of Heidegger's texts, critical to holding in view the need and the possibility of bringing metaphysics to its *Verwindung,* its turning point.

This critical change in the manner of thinking, which now proceeds not in representational fashion by way of concepts and statements, but by poetically listening to language, is what *Contributions to Philosophy* begins to approach under the rubric of a new style of thinking. As Vallega-Neu explains, this transformation of language exceeds the power of the human subject and "implies a shift away from its propositional character (based on an interpretation of language as a system of signs signifying something, i.e., the 'object' of thought) to its 'poietic' character (in the sense of the Greek word *poiesis,* which means 'bringing forth')."[12] Such a decisive transformation of style is not just a quirk of Heidegger's thinking or a result of his penchant for idiomatic use of German but arises from the task at hand: possibly to break free of the metaphysical determinations of thought and their role in the history of philosophy. The distance between the habitual sense of the event and the "Heideggerian" *Ereignis* becomes a constant reminder that the critique of metaphysics, let alone a crucial turn in it, is not possible without a transformation of thinking *from* language.

This new style of thinking prioritizes, over a definitional and conceptual grasp, our ability to "hear" language move and to hear it "speak."[13] This is perhaps why, for the most part, Heidegger often does not explain or define the ways in which his modulations occur, preferring instead to allow remarks like "Das Ereignis wortet" or "Das Ereignis ist sagend" to resonate in his texts. The latter phrase can be paraphrased in English as "the event is by way of saying," or the "event is as saying," even though these versions resort to additional prepositions absent in the German.[14] Illustrating this changed manner of thinking, *On the Way to Language* emphasizes the weave of language, which breaks open and expands as the *Riss:* as the rift or fissure that opens onto the outline or blueprint (*Aufriss*) of language taken as the strife and tension spanning the event onto its way of language. In an important note to his copy of *Unterwegs zur Sprache,* Heidegger remarks, however, that the noun *Geflecht* (weave or plait) used in the essay, hearkening back to Plato's *symploke,* is a bad choice, since it indicates only poorly what is at issue here: "der Name 'Geflecht' ist schlecht."[15] Another note, invoking the Greek *symploke,* suggests that meshwork, netting, plaiting, or braiding—the possible senses of *flechten*—should be rethought as folding (*falten*), as "das *Gefalt* | die Einfalt"—"the *co-fold* | the onefold," or "the infold."[16] While *Einfalt* conventionally means "simplicity" or "simpleness," and it is sometimes translated in Heidegger as "a simple onefold," Heidegger emphasizes, through the play of prefixes in his note, the root "fold," thus drawing attention to the double meaning of *ein* as both the particle "in" and the numeral "one." Although appearing only in a handwritten note, the remark hints at a critical distinction to be drawn out between weave or plait, on one side, and fold, or rather "co-fold," to resonate more accurately with the inventive *ge-* in Heidegger's coined *Gefalt,* on the other. This co-fold is to be conceived at the same time as a one-fold, as a gathering and a holding together well-known from Heidegger's rethinking of *logos,* on the one hand, and as the in-fold, which indicates the way in which the event in its habitual meaning, in its modes of articulation in language and thought, is always already infolded and thus one-folded, "gathered," as an array of relations into *das Ereignis.* This pull of gathering, resonated in the word *Gefalt,* suggests that *logos* becomes woven here as only one thread into this more complex account of language, which problematizes the metaphysical conceptualization of the human being as a living being possessing *logos,* or language. Though Heidegger does not develop the point, the noun *Gefalt* signals a departure from the understanding of language "simply" as *logos.*

What remains to be developed in this context is how one might understand this barely signaled distinction between meshwork and folding. Perhaps a way of making this distinction more legible is to realize that meshwork or plaiting relies on bringing together, by gathering and interweaving, distinct, apparently separate or separable, threads or strands. Likewise, terms like *mesh* or *netting* imply points of crossing and intersecting, as well as nodes or knots that are connected by the weave, that is, they are points that become part of a nexus or a network. By contrast, folds arise within one plane, as they alter it by rendering distinct various moments or sites in what, in its unfolding, remains nonetheless essentially *at one.* Not "one" as something uniform or homogeneous, or "one" as single or separate, but "at one," that is, specifically infolded as one- or single-folded, an inference that, as I began to explore in *Inflected Language,* we can evolve from the double meaning of *Einfalt.*[17] This is why it is of key importance here to elaborate carefully the distinct resonance of Heidegger's *Einfalt:* it is not first a onefold, which subsequently becomes an infold through the folds that develop within it, but rather this onefold takes place as the infold, as the German term implies. The fold at issue here is prior to the difference between the one and the many, and thus neither unified nor multiple. Instead of being seen as stitched or gathered together from separate threads, from the event in the habitual sense of incidents or occurrences interlaced with the event as *Ereignis, das Ereignis* is itself this "one-in-fold." The crucial importance of the distinction between "weave" and "fold" lies in the divergent modalities of relation indicated by meshing on the one hand and by the *Einfalt,* on the other. "Folding" as the momentum of relation does not bring together distinct, already present relata but, introducing flection, it initiates folds through which relations, spans, or proximities occur. These flections "clear"—that is, open and map—the time-space for relating, so that what is held in relation comes to unfold in this expanse in the first place.

This emphasis on emergence as relational and irreducible to beings or entities becomes indispensable to reading the idiom of the proper (*eigen*) and its complicated echoes in the noun "event." First of all, it means that any sense of the proper, the domain of what is proper (*Eigentum*), property, or *Eigentlichkeit* (authenticity or properness) needs to be explained from the event as coming to pass always *from* and *as* relation. The proper is therefore not what constitutes something in its "apparently" distinct presence as a single or "one" entity; rather, a being comes to be what it "properly" is precisely as emergent, unfolded from within its often multiple and complex relatedness. Since this emergent fold of relating transpires as the clearing of the play of time-space, the relatedness at issue here concerns the vectors of both spacing and temporalizing. The "proper" is therefore not fixed or immutable but "essentially" (in its *Wesung*) occurs as spatiotemporal. "All essence is essential occurrence [*alles Wesen ist Wesung*]" (*CP,* 53). In other words, the only way the proper can come to be proper(ly) is precisely through the singular one-in-fold (*Einfalt*), which means that it occurs as intrinsically futural and open. When the event is thought of in terms of folds, the relatedness unfolding from the event is marked by this spatiotemporal span and its intrinsic futurity.[18] The scope of such relatedness can be suggested by paraphrasing Heidegger in the following way: the onefold unfolds its singular infold as co-folds—time/space, being/language, words/signs—to suggest the reverberations of the play of *Einfalt* and *Gefalt.* The spatiotemporal event-like (*ereigni-*

shaft) momentum of the *Einfalt* as *Gefalt* indicates that Heidegger's notions of *Wesen* (essence) and *Wesung* (essencing, or essential occurrence) must be thought of as an unfolding taken in a triple sense: uncovering, unveiling, bringing out, revealing; extending, stretching out; and opening, spreading out. The uncovering at issue here, that is, the unconcealment literally issuing from the event, is not an unveiling of something existing or preexisting but constitutes instead a revealing that brings about beings by letting them be. This complex spatiotemporal vector of the "essencing" bespeaks Heidegger's idiomatic understanding of *Wesen*. The notion of bringing out highlights the aspect of springing into existence, the origination that manifests and reveals beings. It is important to note here that beings are not revealed as present, fixed, and constant—that is, in terms of essence or substance—but are instead held out into the active expanse of relatedness, which keeps spreading out spatially and opening up to the future. Thus temporalization and spacing are not aspects of or additions to this notion of "bringing" but constitute this bringing specifically as a revealing. This developed and complex notion of *Wesung* underlies and makes possible, therefore, any sense of presencing or presence. Heidegger signals this by frequently hyphenating the term *An-wesen*, showing how presence is literally brought about by the manner of occurrence indicated by *Wesen* and its derivative *Wesung*. This also means that presence has *Wesen* (essence, coming to be) always already inscribed in itself. Hence the event-like unfolding evoked here by the term *Wesen*, from which all presence (*Wesen*) and absence (*Abwesen*) spring, undercuts and revises any notion of standing or objective presence.

This is why the notions clustered in Heidegger's German around the adjective *eigen* (and its derivatives) can be understood only through the prism of *Wesen* taken not metaphysically as essence or ideality but rather as the complex, threefold unfolding outlined above. The proper in Heidegger is, therefore, never strictly speaking *of* beings—pertaining to entities or things—but rather *of* being, which means that what is proper to beings comes from their mode of being, granted from the event. What is proper in a being comes in the form of its spatiotemporal relatedness occurring within the clearing, which is never "proper" in the sense of being complete, set, or determined. Put another way, the proper never "is" but always "essentially occurs," which paraphrases here Heidegger's temporalization of essence into *Wesung*. Only secondarily or derivatively can the proper be thought of on the model of an essence, a property, or authenticity. For what can be said to belong to each being as most proper or "own" to it is its always changing and specific "is," that is, its distinct occurrence or "mode" of being. The verb *is* indicates the folds at issue here: the unfolding that takes place through the infold of thought into being, which is also their shifting and each-time recontoured onefold. The clearing, the spatiotemporal emergence from the event occurs as the infold and its spreading out yet gathered folds. The difficulty Heidegger places on thinking is reflected in the need for attentiveness to this intricate folding. It is the task of maintaining the space between the folds, maintaining their distinctness and yet keeping them in relation, the relation that needs to be recurrently traversed in its spatiotemporality, that is, by way of language. Such relation is never a binary that involves two elements existing as though "prior" to the relation; rather, it is a complex "infold" (*Einfalt*) that allows for further inflections to mark and redraft the expanse of the clearing, assigning emergent dimensions and new valences to relations arising within it. Without responsiveness and attentiveness to this folding and co-folding, thinking will not be able to help bring about the *Verwindung* in metaphysics, a twisting that would allow for a transformation of our understanding of the proper, essence, and presence.[19] The misinterpretations of the notions of *eigen, Eigentlichkeit,* or *Wesen* in Heidegger start with reading these terms in a metaphysical, conceptual manner, forcing these terms back into their neat, traditional scope that they have developed over the long period of philosophical thought in the West, instead of tracing the specific ways in which Heidegger's texts expose these metaphysical accretions, twist and fault them in an effort to transform them. This is why I have stressed how Heidegger tries to think of these terms nonconceptually and poietically, by giving full attention not simply to their meaning or conceptual significance but primarily to their inventive movement in language and its repercussions. In this way, Heidegger also tries to trace precisely the movement of language inscribed in the changed valences that these terms acquire in his writings.

This reading of *Wesen* as a threefold unfolding endeavors to make clear that in its occurrence the event does not somehow dispose of the folds, by leveling or evening them out through spreading. Rather, the spreading-out invoked by the term *clearing* (*Lichtung*) indicates that the folds are opened out into the spread that is proper and constitutive to them within the dimension and design (*Riss*) of relations. Likewise, the language fold, the *Einfalt,* which for me is so pivotal to rethinking language with Heidegger, should not be misread as closing up or confining, in the sense of shutting down. The fold is possible only as simultaneously an infold and a co-fold (*Einfalt* and *Gefalt*), which means that it "gathers" precisely in the mode of opening up, spreading out, and holding with regard to. In a sense, the fold here occurs as an unfolding, where the prefix "un-" does not signify the undoing of the fold but marks instead the event-like, spatiotemporal spread distinctive of the fold. In this idiomatic sense, the unfolding not only opens up but also maintains the fold, that is, unfolding allows the fold to obtain and hold—albeit always only for a while—its proper expanse within the spatiotemporal field.

Though the distinctness of the idiom of the fold from the vocabulary of weave, braid, or sheaf, in other words, from the notion of *symploke*, might at first appear forced or unnecessary, it is crucial to developing the workings of language "after" Heidegger. At the same time, it also provides another indication of the extent to which Heidegger's thinking through language takes a road quite different from the metaphysical presuppositions about language. What the words *Einfalt* and *Gefalt* imply is that Heidegger's reflections on language need to be kept distinct from both the notion of the weave of relations and from the echoes of naturalness in the term *sheaf*. In the first case, the idea of language as a weave or a plait patterns language on human or animal labor, which also reverberates in the term *bundle*, while for Heidegger language is neither simply "worked" nor constructed by humans. *Sheaf*, on the other hand, suggests a "natural" occurrence, as in living forms, for example, stalks of grain. Obviously, human participation is critical to language, but it does not determine or exclusively set the tone, in the sense of *Stimmung*, for how language makes its way into words. This means that the way of language in Heidegger is neither natural nor artificial; it is not something that occurs discretely within the clearing but instead traces and stirs its very unfolding—one can think here of Heidegger's idiomatic terms *bewёgen*, make way or cut paths, or *erzittern*, tremble or quiver. As a result, language, at least in its initial or originative saying, does not come "after" the clearing, as its effect or product, nor does it simply unfold within the expanse the clearing provides, but instead it eventuates and brings about this clearing: it takes place as the clearing while rendering it appropriate for language, making it "language's own," so to speak—these are among the senses of *ereignen* in German. The clearing thus occurs essentially as a matter both of and for language. Finding an idiom for this saying of language, always folded together with emerging and relating, which would be distinct from *symploke*, whether taken as a weave on the one hand or as a sheaf on the other, remains critical to the possibility of a transformation in our relation to language. Part of my intent here is to delineate the way Heidegger's own terms—for instance, the whole idiomatic deployment of *sagen, sprechen, stimmen, schweigen* (saying, speaking, tuning, holding silent), and so on, in relation to the event—try to prepare a formative change from philosophical thought to poietic thinking. In this spirit, I also try to elaborate a vocabulary, or more precisely, a different manner of thinking and wording, for instance, by having emphasized and evolved the notion of *falten* (folding) and played it off against *flechten*: weaving or meshing, in order to underscore the still largely unthought distinctiveness of Heidegger's "way of language": not just of his vocabulary but primarily of the idiomatic way in which he understands words and has thinking "listen" to them.[20]

The One-Time Singular

The poietic thinking of the event and of its senses of the proper is cued in particular to singularity and uniqueness that marks the one-time, nonrepeatable occurrence of the event's coming to word, often hinted at by the emblematic and undecidable play of the prefix *ein-*. Heidegger extensively uses at least three senses of *ein;* these three form a nexus and index how language tensions and distinctions highlighted or implied by Heidegger come to guide his thinking. The first instance of *ein* has to do with the meaning of "one" as in oneness, unity, or being at one, suggested for instance by *Einheit* (unity) and *Einfalt.* The second, already signaled in the discussion of the double play of the *Einfalt,* indicates the kinetic sense of "in" as a turning or a folding, a twist that is not accidental or posterior but constitutive of the very span and the relational tension indicated by the phrase "at one," which I specifically highlighted in Heidegger's *Einfalt:* the infold as always intrinsic to the onefold. The third sense lacing the semantic field of *ein* has to do with its function as an article, hinting at the singularity and uniqueness at issue. This threefold sense of *ein* is critical and decisive especially in terms of the notion of *Einheit* invoked by Heidegger's texts. All too easily taken for straightforward "unity" or "oneness," this term in fact needs to be thought of through the prism of the threefold *ein* that echoes in Heidegger's idiomatic use of German. The "oneness" suggested by *Einheit* is never uniform or homogeneous, just as it is not simply unified, let alone totalized. Rather, *Einheit* in Heidegger means "at one," and perhaps, pushing its use further, also signals the "at once" character of language folds, in particular the way they arise from the each-time singular onefold/infold (*Einfalt*). No oneness or sense of being at one exists in Heidegger without the accompaniment of the folds echoing through his texts, folds that happen each time singularly and therefore counteract, on the level of language segments, the unifying conceptual pull of *Einheit.* This implies that "oneness" commonly signified by *Einheit* is possible only as an inflection of the infold, in which the unitary tendency of the simple onefold gains prominence.

If the event as the way of language takes place as the *Einfalt,* then its characteristic folding repeatedly fissures and branches into further folds within the clearing, replicated by folds and fractures in the very terms employed by Heidegger. *Ein* is one of the key words, mostly in its function as a prefix, in which the originative fold of the event is reprised into the threefold play of "being at one," the infold, and singularity. Keeping in view this three-fold reverberation of *ein* in many of the key terms employed by Heidegger is, therefore, critical to tracing how language forms and guides Heidegger's insight into the matters of identity and difference. It is a matter not simply of conceptual distinctions and determinations but, instead, of the manner in which Heidegger induces folds within the terms he uses in order to forestall an all too easy slide of the terms back into their usual signification and its logic of repetition. What breaks the terms Heidegger uses, whether *Einheit, Einfalt,* or *Einmaligkeit,* out of their containment within metaphysical conceptuality is precisely this initially invisible, transformative echoing brought about among the terms Heidegger puts into play. This strategy is not defined or expressly articulated, yet its insistence and recurrence come into focus in a reading attentive precisely to how "language speaks" in the late writings. In other words, the conceptual work performed by these crucial terms becomes framed and inflected by the implicit nexus drawn among the textual occurrences of *ein.* It is language itself that provides the conduit for these connections—sometimes scripted, as in the handwritten note in Heidegger's copy of *Unterwegs zur Sprache,* sometimes not—showing the extent to which thinking along with Heidegger must become attentive to the way in which his language disposes (*Stimmen*) whatever determinations (*Bestimmen*) arise in it.

The idiom of folds discussed above plays a decisive role, for instance, in how the issues of temporality, the proper, unity, and difference can be read in Heidegger's late works. The prefix *ein* suggests that folds are indelibly marked by what perhaps must be referred to as a beyng-historical (*seyns-geschichtlich*) uniqueness or singularity, because it evinces nonrepeatable, event-like singularity (*Einmaligkeit*), which is always plural in its folds, and distinct from the conceptual play of the distinction between the singular and the universal. Without considered attention to the echoes of such *Einmaligkeit,* it is not possible to follow the nuance of Heidegger's comments on difference, words, or singularity, and thus also on the role of conceptual thought in his work. Heidegger's often-used terms *eindeutig, einzigartig,* and *einmalig* all carry the connotation of such "being-historical" uniqueness. Yet as *Contributions to Philosophy* and *Mindfulness* in particular make clear, this idiom of uniqueness is associated with Heidegger's rethinking of temporality as a futural, projective infolding of the having-been and of the possibilities opening up from the present, where the fold marks the between, or the nearness as Heidegger refers to it in *On Time and Being,* never reducible to presence, constancy, or punctuality. The one-fold of time is the nearness of its three folds, the being at one of the folds of the past, the present, and the future, whose always already "infolded unfolding" clears the room—as the clearing (*Lichtung*)—for presencing. Characteristic of Heidegger's manuscripts from the late 1930s is the thinking of the event as such an each-time singular and one-time occurrence, indicated by the words *Einzigkeit* and *Einmaligkeit*.

> Beyng's singularity [*Einzigkeit*] and uniqueness [*Einmaligkeit*, one-time occurrence] are not qualities attributed to beyng [*Seyn*] or even subsequent determinations that could result from being's relationship to "time." Rather, beyng itself is singularity, one–time occurrence, that always lets time emerge, that is, lets truth's 'free-play of time-space' emerge. The one-time occurrence does not exclude a once again, but the contrary. (*M*, 108, modified)

Einzigkeit is formed from *einzig*, meaning only, single, or sole, which suggests that Heidegger uses the term to indicate uniqueness as singleness, soleness, or "only-ness." *Einmalig* functions as an adjective signifying something unique, one-time, one-off, or unparalleled. But the root *mal* (one time, once) makes it evident that the uniqueness or singularity unfolded as *einmalig* is a one-time occurrence. This once only occurrence, Heidegger adds, is not equivalent to the notion of the "moment," the *punctum*, or of the "sudden," but points instead to an each-time unique and one-time event of the spatio-temporal play (*Zeit-Spiel-Raum*), that is, to the nonrepeatable emergence of the time-space in its encountering play: "the flaring up of the non-repeatable uniqueness of beyng"—"das Aufblitzen der einmaligen Einzigkeit des Seyns" (*CP*, 180; *GA* 65, 228). *Einmaligkeit* is not a metaphysical temporal singularity, marking the uniqueness of a time instance, open and susceptible to re-marking or repetition (as another unique moment of time). It is instead the nonrepeatable "being-historical" giving of any unique instant, which makes possible repetition, a "once again," "ein Wieder einmal" (*GA* 66, 128), as Heidegger puts it.

Employed often as a pair, this singularity and once-only occurrence (*Einzigkeit* and *Einmaligkeit*) mark the reciprocal inherence of the one-time and the unique, which means that singularity or uniqueness meant in these texts occur as each-time one-off, only one-time. As Heidegger writes in *Contributions to Philosophy*, being in the nonmetaphysical disposition of *Seyn* as event is always one-time and singular, always once and uniquely: nonpareil, alone, and unequaled. In short, being never repeats or iterates—only beings do—so that its one-off occurrence is, strictly speaking, not yet a matter of difference. This is why this event-like singularity is not conceivable in differential terms and, for the same reasons, cannot be conceived as unity, transcending or erasing difference. *"Als nichthaftes wesend ermöglicht und erzwingt es [Seyn] zugleich Andersheit"* (GA 65, 267)—*"Insofar as beyng essentially occurs as permeated with negativity, it at the same time makes possible and compels otherness."* And, a little later on, "Out of the uniqueness [*Einzigkeit*] of beyng there follows the uniqueness of its appertaining 'not' and thus the uniqueness of the other" (*CP*, 210). The uniqueness customarily associated with the existence of a being derives from the each-time one-time occurrence of being's event. This occurrence of being receives its one-time character, its "uniqueness," from the each-time one-off and nonpareil occurrence of negativity or nihilation (*Nichtung*) that characterizes the nearing folds of temporality. As Heidegger writes in *Mindfulness*, "Beyng is not only incalculable (never to be represented and produced): as the incalculable it also remains imponderable insofar as it does not let itself be put on a scale that measures only beings against beings. What is an 'other' to beyng is not even a being, beyng has no 'other' to it, for, even 'nothing' is thoroughly of the same sway [*Wesung*] as beyng" (*M*, 46). When what is other with regard to being is captured and conceived through the prism of the metaphysical sense of being (*Sein*), it comes to be constituted as a being, with the possibility of differentiation, repetition, and distinctness from other beings. Conceived in this way, the difference between being and beings assumes the valence of beingness (*Seindheit*), which repeatedly fails to do justice to the singularity of the one-time, event-like, occurrence of being. It does so because it confuses this *Einmaligkeit* with repeatable punctuality of singular moments. Scripting *Seyn* as silently distinct from *Sein*, Heidegger emphasizes his point that *Seyn* "has no other." This is the case because to think of an other to *Seyn* entails conceiving such an other as always already a being, which leads to misrepresenting *Seyn* as beingness, that is, as a kind of being, and misconceiving the relation between *Seyn* and *Seiende* as a relation between beings. The concepts of otherness and difference fail to address the idiomatic one-time occurrence of the event, to which even nothing belongs as its fold. The nothing and its negativity is neither different from nor other than beyng (*Seyn*); instead, it occurs, or "nihilates," singularly folded into and thus one-folded with being, forming the *Einfalt* critical to Heidegger's thought. The way in which being is laced or lined with the pulsing nothingness (*Nichtung*) makes for its event, giving it its unmistakable and nonrepeatable momentum of appearing—or disappearing—possibility.

To counter the inevitable oppositional pull of singularity and universality, of temporal uniqueness and repetition, Heidegger remarks that "Beyng renders itself lonesome, *is* as this lonesomeness . . ." (*M*, 46)—"Das Seyn vereinsamt sich selbst, *ist* als diese Vereinsamung . . ." (*GA 66*, 56). At issue in this quotation is *Seyn,* and specifically not *Sein,* redolent of (ontological but not only) difference. Furthermore, to make the crucial point about the need to introduce a twist or an inflection into the thinking of otherness and difference, Heidegger employs here the adjective *einsam* (lonesome, solitary, alone) and the noun *Einsamkeit* (lonesomeness or solitude).[21] Both these words hinge on the root *ein,* which is reminiscent of the three-fold working of this term in Heidegger described above. To understand what Heidegger tries to describe under the rubric of "lonesomeness," it is not enough to interpret and grasp the remarks cited from *Mindfulness.* These remarks must be read through the prism of the play of *ein* in Heidegger's work, approached not only conceptually but also in the style of thinking in tune with the one-time occurrence of the event and thus no longer relying on the metaphysical articulations of difference and identity, uniqueness and repetition. For Heidegger to write that being is *einsam* suggests conjuring up the threefold play of singularity, the infold, and the onefold, apart from which *Seyn,* "always already" metaphysically turned *Sein,* ends up being reinscribed into the play of difference (among beings), where it appears that being hypostatizes into a supra-being and thus requires a special supra-word for its designation. As *einsam,* being's event "en-lightens" and clears open, in the specific sense of *Lichtung,* that is, as the singularly and one-time infolded play of time-space. The "lonesomeness"(*Einsamkeit*) of *Seyn* highlights this indelible fold of singularity and one-time occurrence (*Einzigkeit* and *Einmaligkeit*), which become the hallmarks of Heidegger's rethinking of *Being and Time* in the manuscripts from the late 1930s.

This idiomatic valence of a one-time occurrence (*Einmaligkeit*), intimated nonconceptually through the poietic movement of language, shapes crucially Heidegger's critique of identity and difference: "Beyng [*Seyn*], as the 'between' which clears, moves itself into this clearing and therefore, though never recognized or surmised as appropriation [*Ereignung*], is for representational thinking something generally differentiable, and differentiated [*Unterscheidbares und Unterschiedenes*], as being [*Sein*]" (*CP,* 366). This is why thinking in terms of difference, even Heidegger's own initial formulation of ontological difference, fails to register being as event: "Here also lies the reason the ontological difference as such does become known: basically because the only needed distinction is between one being and another (*the being that is most eminently*)" (*CP,* 367). Ontological difference, and with it all thought of differentiation, is thus only a passage, which if taken as the goal in itself becomes a hindrance to bringing metaphysics to a turning point. This is the case because the ontological difference keeps falling back into difference as differentiation between beings and thus remains concealed. As a result, the thought of difference relies in advance on *Seyn* re-presented, that is, miscognized and repeatable, as *Sein*. In this misprision, *Sein* functions as *Seiendheit*, or beingness, and is effectively reinscribed as another being among beings. Its difference, that is, the ontological difference, becomes parallel to differences between beings, losing all its force and import. In effect, it remains unthought and cannot be raised as a question as long as difference is modeled on differentiation between beings.

With regard to this collapse of being into a being, the thought *of* and *as* difference is always already part, albeit prefatory, of representational thinking, for its practices of identity and difference are founded on the notion of differentiated beings, rather than stemming from the one-time occurrence of event, that is, from the each-time singularity (*Einmaligkeit*) of *Seyn*. Vallega-Neu points out that in *Contributions to Philosophy,* Heidegger thinks the overcoming of the ontological difference "by thinking in the 'simultaneity' (*Gleichzeitigkeit*) of being and beings without thereby re-instating a primacy of beings or slipping back into a representational mode of thinking."[22] The ontological difference cannot escape being a difference, which means that its optics remains differential and forces being to be differentiated from beings as a kind of being or beingness, failing in the end to mark its event-like singularity. When developed in the manner suggested above, the distinctive nonrepeatable singularity involved in the event, provides a critical perspective on difference, showing that even difference rethought critically or deconstructed continues to reinscribe the metaphysical pull of beingness, whose sway has always already turned being into a form of being(ness), leveling it to a being among others. "If the ontological difference which appears here is the most dangerous matter for thinking, it is because it always represents being, within the horizon of metaphysics, as a being"(*FS,* 22). This is why the thought of difference will likely fail to register being as event: with regard to difference, being will either turn into a being among other beings or, in an attempt to reclaim its uniqueness, it will become hypostasized into the highest being, supposedly transcending and thus grounding all difference, itself absolute and absolved of all relations.

My reading of the complex resonances of *Einmaligkeit* and *Einfalt* in Heidegger's texts shows the backdrop against which these texts attempt to avoid such hypostasis, and do so by turning the thought of (ontological) difference into a passageway in order to eventually sideline it. This reading hinges on the simultaneously metaphysical and poietic, nonmetaphysical, resonance of *ein, Einfalt,* and *Einmaligkeit.* The metaphysical sense of uniqueness pertains to beings, their differentiation and repetition, and even possible transcendence, thus linking uniqueness to the dream of a singular proper. Heidegger's

Einzigkeit, however, should be read, I argue, in its poietic "singularity," as one-time event refractive to the binary of the singular and the universal.

In the context of this poietic valence of singularity, singularity attendant to the event-like way of language, we must question Derrida's well-known reading of Heidegger's supposedly unique word for *being,* the reading that has influenced and shaped many responses to Heidegger's thought of being and language. In this reading, Derrida responds to a key passage in "The Anaximander Fragment," in which Heidegger points to how language and poetry shelter this each-time unique giving of being in the silence and the unsaid that come to be said alongside words. Heidegger finds this singular resonance among others in Anaximander's word *to khreon,* which connotes neither compulsion nor necessity but rather the way in which the one-fold of being and beings is also their in-fold (*Ein-falt*), thus sketching a singular relation to the nihilation intrinsic to all presencing. The force of nihilation is singular here precisely in the sense of being each time singular (*einzig*) and one-time (*einmalig*). "The relation to what is present that prevails in the essence of presencing is unique. It is comparable with no other relation. It belongs to the uniqueness [*Einzigkeit*] of being itself. In order to name the essence of being, therefore, language would have to find something unique, the unique word [*das einzige Wort*]."[23] This singular word is, however, not the unique name in the sense of the one and only word, a supra-word, as Derrida mistakenly suggests in "Différance," when he associates such word with the "hope" for the unique name: "Nevertheless I am venturing it, without excluding any of its implications, and I relate it to what still seems to me to be the metaphysical part of 'The Anaximander Fragment': the quest for the proper word and the unique name."[24]

In the context outlined above—and the discussion of Anaximander comes after the inventive texts of late 1930s and early 1940s—another more interesting and definitely more radical reading suggests itself. *Das einzige Wort* is not the unique name but rather the word—possibly each and any word, when properly attended and listened to—as each-time singular in how the event, coming to word, lets be. We must also remember that the proper (*eigen*) in Heidegger is conceived in its essential occurrence (*Wesen, Wesung*) precisely as in-folded into the one-time relatedness of the event, relatedness that unfolds in the multiple play of *er-eignen. Das einzige Wort* in Heidegger is, therefore, not the unique name (for being) but a poietic word, which originatively, each time singularly and one-time, gives being into language. The unique name for *being,* as Heidegger's readings of justice in Anaximander and of empire and imperial word in *Parmenides* make clear, would be a word "in-the-right," an imperial word, both correct (*rectus*) and just (*iustus*). The proper word would be also the "correct" word, a word operating as law (*ius*), whether legal or ethical, which would cover over the each-time singularly silent *dikē,* the one-time jointure (*Fuge*) of the event.

This is why the definite article *das* (the) that Heidegger places before what might perhaps be best paraphrased as "the one-time word," marks here not the generic resonance of a word that would always already and proleptically capture being and say, by way of veiling, each time the same, but points instead to the singularly one-time giving of the word, of words that, even though repeating the same signifying chain of letters, occur only once, and therefore are marked by the definite article *the.* This *the* is not the generic but the singular *the,* and not the singular generic of the unique name ("being": the word) but a nongeneric, one-time singular *the,* with the silent threefold resonance of the *ein* and the temporalization of one-time indicated by the German *mal.* It is this sense of nongeneric and one-time singular that merits the appellation "poietic" here, evoking the complex resonance of this term in Heidegger's work. Heidegger's use of *einzig* cannot be separated from *einmalig,* from its one-timed occurrence, since *einzig* is always folded by and in-folded into *einmalig,* pointing to singularity temporalizing as one-time. Doing precisely the opposite, that is, implicitly separating *einzig* from *einmalig,* Derrida reclaims Heidegger's rethinking of "being" for metaphysics, collapsing and evening out the pivotal fold of Heidegger's thought; that is, precisely the fold on which the possibility of *Verwindung* hinges. For the definite article in Heidegger's discussion of Anaximander gives voice to the silent—because each time only one-time and in this sense singular—giving of being to its word. The article resonates, therefore, the spectrum of plays that spans the complex and largely unheeded use of *ein* in Heidegger's language— which includes *Einfalt, Einheit, Einzigkeit, Einmaligkeit, Auseinandersetzung,* and so on—perhaps unremarked so far because Heidegger himself never thematizes it as such.

At issue in Heidegger's rethinking of *ein, Einzigkeit,* and *Einmaligkeit,* is not the unique name *for* being, a word that would, like a concept, conceive and thus grasp being. Instead, at stake is the poietically singular way in which being is given to word always only one time, in its one-time occurrence, its idiomatic *Einmaligkeit.* In question is not how a word captures being or fails to do so but, conversely, how being can come, singular and singularly, to word, thanks to and yet in spite of the repetition governing signs and signification. My position is that for being to register this way in words, what is necessary, beyond the conceptual comprehension of singularity versus universality or difference versus repetition, is precisely a transformed language experience undertaken by poetic thinking, that is, a thinking proceeding through the poietic resonance of words, prefixes, and hyphens that envelop, reverberate, and inflect concepts, signs, and meaning.

In this context, I read this silent resonance of *ein* as indicating the each-time singular way in which being gives in(to) words, and thus outlines the poietic measure of the event. Indicating therefore a difficult task for words to each time resonate singularly, despite the repetitive nature of signs and signification; a poietic task for words and language to each time think and let say the silence that marks words, each time singularly and in a flash of way-making, despite the necessary repetitiveness of meaning. A word that each time lets the jointure of the event abide singularly, stay its while: and thus a word that each time is the singular word. In the context of Heidegger's reading of Anaximander, this letting a-while is the poietic measure, the *dikē*, the 'justice' of being in its mortal and finite spanning of the play of time-space. We return in the next chapter to this specific sense of one-time as pivotal to Heidegger's understanding of *Worte* (words) in their idiomatic distinction from signs or terms (*Wörter*).

Heidegger's idiomatic phrase "Das Ereignis wortet,"—"The event comes to word"—must be thought of and evolved with regard to this specific one-time occurrence and singularity (*Einmaligkeit* and *Einzigkeit*) evoked by Heidegger. At the same time, the event's becoming word occurs as the opening up of an infold (*Einfalt*) and the traversal of its co-folds (*Gefalt*) as constitutive of the one-fold (*Einfalt*). The "lightening-like" fold described above forms, through what Heidegger terms the withdrawal or retreat of being, a kind of recess, which clears outward into the play of time-space, or in short, the *Lichtung*. Heidegger's employment of the noun *Lichtung* (clearing), actually translates well into English when folding together the English sense of "clearing" with "lightening": a path through the woods opening into a forest clearing, one of Heidegger's favorite images; a clearing of the dimension or the region (*Gegend*)—itself a kind of indentation or fold—for the countering play of time and space, world and earth (from the link Heidegger highlights in German between *gegen* [against], *Gegend*, and the verb *gegnen*, to [en]counter, to come up against); also a clearing up in the sense that evokes the *er-äugen*, the manifesting and showing at play in the event (*Er-eignis*); and finally, the lightening in the sense of rendering (being) light, in fact, almost too light for perception and words—the lightening that marks the manifestation of being as always already in withdrawal, so that "only" beings appear, while being holds back and refuses itself, that is, it either remains silent and unmarked or becomes mistakenly turned into a being. This sense of *Lichtung* is pivotal to Heidegger's thinking by way of language, since it illuminates how the event's saying (*Sagen*) occurs as the hinge, which folds back into a refusal: a

Verweigerung, which is also an *Absagen* and a *Versagen,* that is, a saying that begs off by refusing, denying, and mis-saying itself.

The Under-statement of Truth

What determines the workings of language in Heidegger is the fact that the event occurs in that it comes to word: its occurrence is its wording. Occurrence thus literally translates into words, so that one could write "Das Ereignis ereignet: das Ereignis wortet." This equivalence between the event's taking place and its coming to word requires thought to stay attentive to the distinct singularity with which the event lets be, that is, to what Heidegger calls its *Einmaligkeit.* Such thinking orients itself not through concepts or ideas but through words, which instantiate the movement of language, or, in other words, the event's occurrence into words. Juxtaposed with philosophy, poetic thinking deemphasizes and calls into question the standard vehicles of philosophical knowledge and argumentation: concepts, statements, and assertions. It calls for a transformation of both the elements and the syntax of philosophical thought, because of their rootedness in metaphysics and inattention to how thinking unfolds from the event. By contrast, poietic thinking, as Vallega-Neu shows with regard to *Contributions to Philosophy,* proceeds from the event: "The language of *Contributions* is poietic in a twofold sense: it enables the e-vent of being to appear as it appears in thinking and—in turn—it enables language and thinking to appear as events of be-ing."[25]

As Heidegger makes very clear at the end of his lecture "Time and Being," speaking in propositional statements, a metaphysical exercise of thought par excellence, is the major obstacle to twisting free of metaphysics and thus thinking being without the determining reference to beings:

> To think Being without beings means: to think Being without regard to metaphysics. Yet a regard for metaphysics still prevails even in the intention to overcome metaphysics. Therefore, our task is to cease all overcoming [*vom Überwinden abzulassen*], and leave metaphysics to itself [*sich selbst zu überlassen*].
>
> If overcoming remains necessary, it concerns that thinking that properly lets itself into the event [*das sich eigens in das Ereignis einlässt*] in order to say [*sagen*] It in terms of It about It.
>
> Our task is unceasingly [*unablässig*] to overcome the obstacles that tend to render such saying inadequate.
>
> The saying of the event in the form of a lecture remains itself an obstacle of this kind. The lecture has spoken merely in propositional statements [*Aussagesätzen*]. (*OTB,* 24, modified; *ZSD* 25)

This is one of the key passages for developing the transformation of think-ing envisioned by Heidegger. Though still invoked, the overcoming of meta-physics is assigned here a specific and limited role, namely one of breaking through the obstacles put in the way of poetic thinking by the privilege given by metaphysics to propositional statements. Seeing in propositional state-ments the locus of truth par excellence, metaphysics judges poetic thinking to speak tautologically: "to say It [i.e., the event] in terms of It about It." The capitalized "It" (*Es*) appears three times in this formulation, explicitly and properly intensifying the already tautological saying.

To measure the impact of this phrase and its insistent repetition of "It," it is worth noting that the lecture has already used the pronoun "it" in the eponymous phrase *es gibt*. The phrase serves in German the function of the English "there is," but it literally means "it gives." Like the "there" in the corresponding English phrase, "there is," the German *es* in *es gibt* plays the grammatical role of an empty subject, indicating that the event, even if scripted as it/*es*, erases any grammatical or ontological status of a being, and cannot, therefore, be captured, "said," in linguistic signs. For what the German formulation "says," it does so not by way of signs or signification but through the grammatical operation of the refusal, or withdrawal, of the "subject." The pronoun *es* and the phrase *es gibt* literally say (*sagen*) through a refusal (*absagen*) that twists and torques its very own saying into a *ver-sagen*. In fact, we have here two parallel sayings: first comes the implicit metaphysical statement about being, only to be twisted so that it leaves the metaphysical saying, here in the form of a statement, to itself. This double valence of saying is literally scripted in German through the slide from *Sagen* into *Aussagen*, lost in the English translation, which has to use different roots for "saying" and "statement." The metaphysical articulation of the saying into a statement about being performs indelibly the slide that Heidegger repeat-edly underscores as pivotal to philosophical thought in its "metaphysical" articulations: the differential thinking of being (*Sein*), while trying to mark the difference from beings (*Seiende*), ends up inevitably "stating" being as a beingness (*Seindheit*). Stating being in this manner effectively collapses the purported ontological difference, performing the reverse of what it has set out to accomplish. This is the vicious circle of metaphysical-philosophical thought. And it is vicious in the specific sense in which, purporting to state something (new) about being, metaphysics, unable to let go of its language and, even more important, its *relation to* language, continues to reproduce or repeat its original misstatement of being.

This inability to mark the distinctness of being from beings is due to the fact that metaphysical thinking in concepts and statements remains inadequate to the impetus of nothingness intrinsic to being. As Heidegger expresses it, the nothing is what is the lightest, and therefore metaphysics cannot fail but replace it, has in fact already replaced it in its approach, with a being, that is, with something with the ontological "weight" of presence. For metaphysics, there can be nothing that "is not" and thus is not a being: "Dieses aber, die einzige Wesung des reinen Nichts, wäre das Schwerste. Dieses jedoch vermag nur zu denken, wer nach der Überwindung aller Metaphysik schon in das Seyn vordenkt und das Sein nicht von Seienden her (erste Ursache) und auf das Seiende zu (als dessen allgemeinste Eigenschaft) vorstellt. Für die Metaphysik freilich scheint es und muss es scheinen, als sei das, dass Nichts sei, das Leichteste und 'eher' möglich, denn dass ein Seiendes sei" (*GA* 74, 23)—"Yet this, the unique essencing of pure nothing, would be the hardest. This can be thought of only by those who after the overcoming of all metaphysics already think ahead into beyng and do not represent being by way of beings (the first cause) and with regard to beings (as their most universal characteristic). It is true that for metaphysics the fact that nothing is, appears, and must appear, as that which is the easiest, and 'more likely' possible as well as possible 'earlier' than that there is something that is." The nothing, he remarks, "is more inceptual and more essencing (originarily more appropriative with regard to beyng) than a 'something'"—"anfänglicher und wesender (ursprünglich das Seyn er-eignender) als das 'Etwas'" (*GA* 74, 24). Therefore, the nothing(ness) is already the word of being: it does not arise from the negation or denial (*Ab-sage*) of beings but constitutes the inceptive saying of being (*GA* 74, 24). By contrast, what underpins metaphysics is an inattention to the nothing(ness), which, for Heidegger, leads to the effective lack of distinction between being and beings. In the end, repeating the slippage of being into beingness, metaphysics remains consumed with beings, indifferent to being, incapable of even raising it as a question or of seeing any point in doing so.

To this vicious circle of metaphysical "speculation," which keeps reflecting being as a being and thus reflecting thought's attention away from the *Seynsfrage*—and it would be possible to inscribe speculative, dialectical, or representational thought into this vicious circling—Heidegger juxtaposes the tautological saying of "It in terms of It about It." This remark from "Time and Being" is both a conundrum and a counterintuitive claim, which bursts the bubble of the self-importance of propositional statements, their stated self-assurance of being the proper vehicle for grasping truth. This does not mean that Heidegger rejects propositional statements and their contributions to thought on which much of Western culture relies, though he certainly discounts them, lowering the measure of truth ascribed to propositions or, stated perhaps more accurately, recontextualizing the valence of propositional truth vis-à-vis the event. His writings do so through the foregrounding of tautology, which seemingly says nothing, at least nothing worth stating, while merely circling within its own empty repetition. As if ironically adding insult to injury, Heidegger even empties out the designated "subject" of the tautology, the noted *es*/it, which turns out to be and quite literally turns into no subject at all, as though faking "something" that "is not," that is, is never present as a being. As Heidegger points out in *GA* 74, the event can never be grasped or conceived as something that stands forth or presences (*ein Anwesendes,* 25). Consequently, it cannot also be seen as something absent, hidden from view, or esoteric. This double move of the tautological operation executed on a nonsubject and thus on a nonbeing both signals being's refusal to manifest as a being, that is, as an "it," and calls into question propositional statements whose truth claims rely precisely on hypostatizing being into beings.

The need to expose and critique this pervasive hypostatizing of being (*Seyn*) into beings (by way of *Sein* and *Seindheit*) is made clear in *Mindfulness,* where, countering the "dominance" of beings in thought, Heidegger underscores the fact that only being, in the sense of *Seyn* distinct from *Sein, is*. "*Das Seyn ist and wird gleichwohl nie ein Seiendes*"—"*Beyng is and will nonetheless never be a being*" (*GA* 66, 199; *M,* 175). This remark is meant to counter the "first beginning" of metaphysical thought, within whose long shadow stretching out into the age of technology being continues to be thought of on the basis of beings: "Since then all 'is' and being arises out of beings; since then beings enjoy the preeminence of the starting point; since then beings enjoy this preeminence even there, where the 'origin' of beingness (always categorial) is displaced into the 'I think' and into its 'having been thought'" (*M,* 177). To make this point even more salient, Heidegger declares that: "It is not only disconcerting [*Befremdlich*], but remains completely unthought and uninquired that only beyng *is*, and that being as beingness is its inceptual and necessary semblance wherein what is called a being can presume to be the guise of what is properly 'a being' [*das eigentlich Seiende*]—can presume to be the guise of the actual, of that which 'is'" (*M,* 177, modified). This is perhaps as radical as Heidegger gets about saying that being is never an "it" and is thus nonrepeatable, and that being occurs intransitively, in effect rendering any supposition of a substantive existence of beings or entities into a (metaphysical) hypostatization. The quotation introduces the distinction between *das eigentlich Seiende,* what is properly a being, and "what we call a being" as the result of the metaphysical slippage from being to beingness. This means that the realization that "only beyng *is*" allows being to transform (away from beingness and beings), which in turn lets beings emerge as though for the first time as beings, when they can shed the appearance of what has come to be known as beings (conceived in terms of beingness and ontological difference) in philosophical thought. For beings "are not" in the specific sense that they are never available in the form of constancy or standing presence mistakenly ascribed to them. Thus they are neither present nor absent strictly speaking, but instead occur as continuously given to be, as futurally open and "in-constant."

An even more audacious scripting of these collapsing differences occurs in *GA* 74, where Heidegger on several occasions, turning the third person singular form *ist* (is) into an infinitive, writes: "das Seyn 'ist,' indem es das Seyn istet"(24): "beyng 'is' in that it 'is'es beyng." In effect, Heidegger invents here a new verb *isten,* or "to is" in English, trying to find a way to write the folding of being (*Sein*) into beyng (*Seyn*) and to illustrate how the verb *sein,* "to be," is already metaphysically laden and trapped into a repeated saying of beingness. In another context this new "verb" is used intransitively in the phrase "*das Seyn istet*"; "beyng 'is'es." "'Is'ing" then becomes the nonmetaphysical, poietic scripting of *Seyn,* which emerges from under the layers of metaphysical forgetting accumulated within the conventional terms "being," "to be," and "is." This invented verb is brought into the open literally through the fault between *Sein* and *Seyn.* In the same gesture, "'is'ing" becomes more resonant, more "verbal" than "being" and envelops it, I would claim, specifically with regard to the saliency given to the nothing(ness) in the coinage "'is'es": if metaphysics differentiates and separates "nothingness" from "being," thus keeping "being" and associated words separate from the momentum of nihilation, then enveloping "being" in "'is'ing" inscribes, as it were for the first time, the nothing (*das Nichts*) not only as indispensable to being but as constituting its very momentum, its force of one-time giving.

Though Heidegger in "The Way to Language" remarks that our relation to language will not be changed simply by inventing neologisms, this does not mean that neologisms and scriptural inventions are not important or useful. Rather, I take Heidegger to be saying that the transformation in our relation to language cannot be limited to inventing new words or forms, or to language play for play's sake, but must help bring about a more comprehensive change in the way we think. While interesting and playful, or, on the contrary, sometimes deliberately jarring and off-putting, neologisms are only one of the ways to prompt thinking to evolve from the mode of propositional philosophical discourse toward poetic thinking.

Perhaps an even more important way of prompting such transformation is the drawing of the distinction between metaphysical and being-historical tonalities of saying:

The metaphysical saying "being is" wants to *rescue* being as the most-being [*das Seiendste*] and as what is 'first' in relation to beings.

The beyng-historical [*seynsgeschichtliche*] saying "being is" thinks something else; it does not think the most-being as the 'first,' and in spite of saying "is," it does not at all think beyng [*Seyn*] as such a being. The beyng-historical saying says the pure unfolding [*reine Wesung*] of beyng; it says the granting of what is charged with deciding [*Entscheidunghaften*] as well as the taking back of beyng into the stillness of the abyss.

"Beyng is" says: the e-vent e-ventuates [*das Er-eignis er-eignet*] the clearing of the 'in-between' and grounds the uncommunal (*das Unöffentliche*) of the fundamental decisions and preserves its unfolding as incomparable and unapparent. (*M*, 305–306, modified)

The same-sounding phrase "being is," scripted once with *i* and then with *y*, imparts the sense of being differently: first metaphysically, where being already signifies what is most in being, that is, the highest being. Doing so, it institutes in the same gesture both the priority of beings and the requisite transcendental movement beyond them. The second time the phrase "beyng is" occurs, Heidegger claims, beyng-historically, where *Sein* folds back into *Seyn*, allowing the clearing really to unfold. The first time "being is" says itself as "being [*Sein*] is," while the second time, it says "beyng [*Seyn*] is." Though Heidegger writes about this silent yet scripted play in terms of saying (*Sagen*), this play is explicitly a matter of writing, which highlights the way in which metaphysics holds *Seyn* illegible, overwritten, and erased in *Sein*. It is evident that what Heidegger calls "saying" (*Sagen*) does not pertain simply to the register of speech but rather to the originative unfolding of language, opening onto speech and writing. To twist free of metaphysics would entail a *Verwindung* in the very manner in which being comes to be written, that is, in rewriting or understating *Sein* as always already illegibly scripting *Seyn*. The scriptural fold between *i* and *y* figures the traversal of metaphysics, preparing its turn and bringing it to the verge of release.

The innovative scripting Heidegger introduces in order to spell out the fold between beyng and being merits such a lengthy analysis because it sets the parameters for and explains Heidegger's reasons for calling into question propositional forms of thinking, which rely precisely on the "conversion" of being into a being.[26] To expose and remain attentive to this continuing slippage, thinking needs to remind itself that what can be said of *das eigentlich Seiende* is at best only the following: that as long as they exist, beings keep being given without ever being present, never really here to be grasped or represented, as they simply occur, and such one-time occurring (*Einmaligkeit*) does not have the valence of presence. To signal this problem, Heidegger insists on the burning need, the necessity (*Not*), of countering the propositional pull of thought and its allure of providing abiding and useful knowledge.[27]

Propositional statements are not obstacles in themselves but instead become obstacles to the extent they have come to monopolize truth and to discount the importance of or even deny truth to other forms or modes of thinking and saying. In German these stakes are "visible" in words themselves, that is, in the literal inscription and expression of all modes of saying (*Sagen*) into *Aussage* at end of "Time and Being." Saying submits to the claim of the superiority of the way in which truth can be captured within propositional statements. The ability to discriminate between the true and the false and the articulation of truth in terms of clarity and certainty hold sway specifically to the detriment of other ways of saying, which are regarded as either imprecise or unclear and, therefore, ultimately uncertain, or even, in the last count, untrue. The German vocabulary not only inscribes *Sagen* into *Aussage,* into the statement, but literally tries to prescribe the limits and contain the saying within the boundaries of propositions, funneling it into statements. At the same time, the prefix *aus-* spells out how the saying's "quintessence" is allegedly drawn out and captured in the statement. The scriptural enclosure of *Sage* in *Aussage* hints indeed at the letter of the prescription for how saying is to be understood as being already predisposed to deliver its semantic and cognitive core, what it really has to say, as a statement. Once again, here Heidegger lets language do the thinking—and the talking, as it were. The reason is as simple as it is difficult to communicate or say without once again forcing it to be captured in a proposition. For what I am stating here Heidegger does not articulate, instead allowing it to reverberate in the text of his speech without "saying it out" (*aussagen*) loud. More precisely, this "understatement" echoes after the lecture has ended, in the silence already invoked and induced by the theatrical claim that the lecture has spoken merely in statements. It is this pre-scription that Heidegger's texts rewrite in an attempt to provide, quite literally, the possibility of a different script for thinking.

Such possibility obviously does not mean that Heidegger proposes simply to reevaluate tautology and to prize it over propositional statements as a vehicle for a more profound or a better-articulated truth. As is well-known, the valence of truth changes in Heidegger, as the conceptions of truth as clarity, correctness, or adequation are shown to derive from the aletheic play of unconcealment. Heidegger's comments on the genesis of logic in Greek philosophy and the transformations of the notion of *aletheia* show that truth in these traditional senses is achieved or articulated at the price of suppressing the element of concealment that is necessarily at play in the event. As

Heidegger writes in "The Origin of the Work of Art," truth is in its essence (its *Wesen* or unfolding) an untruth (*BW*, 179) and thus should always be thought of as un-truth, without the possibility of ever separating, cutting of, and eliminating the constitutive dimension of concealment. The radical reappraisal of truth Heidegger proposes by going back to truth's roots as *aletheia* in the Greek beginning of philosophy, does not consist simply in admitting a degree of concealment or errancy in any delineation of the true. In a much more fundamental way, that is, pointing to how truth essentially occurs—to its *Wesung* and thus to its "essence" (*Wesen*)—it reconceptualizes truth as both unfolding from and remaining in a continuous strife with the un-true. This is why there is never such a thing as "truth and nothing but the truth," that is, truth purportedly separated decisively or cleanly from concealment. Truth "instantiates," unfolds as its instant or *Augenblick,* as suggested by the hyphen that literally marks the jointure that both distinguishes and holds together, and in this sense, de-cides, "truth" as always un-truth. The concealment is not a hidden or an inaccessible, that is, an absent, dimension that "truth" fails to articulate, but constitutes instead the projective emergence of truth within which what is true can be held in its ineliminable play with what remains concealed. Conceptions that present truth as existing separately from the untrue or the false—as clarity, adequation, or correctness—can do so only by hiding or forgetting this constitutive concealment, miscognizing what is at stake in truth's essential occurrence.

To counter the metaphysical exclusion of the un-true from the play of truth, Heidegger envelops by his way of writing statements and assertions in the aletheic *under-statement* of the un-truth. His doing so relies on the notion of the event-like temporality that underscores being's characteristic retreat behind and into beings. What the hyphen in un-truth does, in a manner similar to *Seyn* rendering legible what has been concealed in *Sein,* is to bring out the manner in which truth unfolds—its *Wesung.* It is once again a scriptural mark, here the hyphen, which instantiates the movement of Heidegger's thinking, a thinking that *with* and *in* the same mark manages to write un-truth as distinct yet ineluctably and constitutively together. Heidegger's text here, as in many other contexts and places, calls not for analysis, argument, proof, or articulation into propositions but instead for what perhaps needs to be called "typographic" or "graphemic" reading and thinking. What I mean by this is that reading Heidegger in such moments has to rely on attentiveness to his way of writing, as in the case above, to his "graphing" of truth as un-truth, which inflects the role concepts play in his texts.

Turning the spotlight on the grapheme and the graph as the novel way in which Heidegger's thinking moves, is important because often responses

to Heidegger's remarks on language and thinking tend to focus on the vocabulary of saying and speaking, downplaying the element of silence and
neglecting the key, sometimes decisive, role of scripting in his texts. While
Heidegger submits saying, speaking, and silence to frequent and extended
discussion and elaboration, he does not do so with respect to writing. But
this does not mean that his manner of writing simply discounts writing,
even though the German term for language, *Sprache,* does so, as it were,
automatically by its etymological connection to speaking. Though Heidegger writes "about" writing sporadically and even then usually briefly,
he is guided in this reflection by the terms provided by German language,
specifically by the word for language, *Sprache,* which defines language from
speaking, *Sprechen.* Because of this etymological connection of *Sprache* to
speech, when Heidegger writes "Die Sprache spricht," or "language speaks,"
one needs to paraphrase it in translation as either "language languages" or
"language speaks and writes," for obviously the *Sprechen* Heidegger names
as the "speaking" of language describes its overall unfolding into speech and
writing. Otherwise, one would have to truncate the sense of *Sprache* and
think of it only as speech, which would be incorrect, since it is clear from
the way Heidegger uses the word that *Sprache* does not mean "speech," or
for that matter the Saussurean *parole* distinguished from *langue,* but refers
to Heidegger's own idiomatic sense of the event that comes to word: "Das
Ereignis wortet."

In *Bremer und Freiburger Vorträge,* for instance, Heidegger inscribes into
the notion of saying—in the idiomatic use he makes of *Sagen*—not only speaking and talking but also writing: "Jedes Sprechen und Reden und Schreiben
ist eine Weise des Sagens, aber das Sagen ist nicht notwendig ein Sprechen
im des Gebrauches der Sprechwerkzeuge": "Every speaking and talking and
writing is a way of saying, but saying is not necessarily a speaking in the
sense of a utilization of speech organs."[28] Writing about mechanical writing
in *Parmenides,* Heidegger links the introduction of machine technology into
writing—at that time, the typewriter, and today, the word processor—with a
change in the relation of being to man and thus presumably also in the way
language comes to unfold: "Therefore when writing was withdrawn from the
origin of its essence, i.e., from the hand, and was transferred to the machine,
a transformation occurred in the relation of Being to man" (*PA,* 85). At issue is not the typewriter or the computer as means of writing but rather the
alteration of being's relation to human beings that manifests in the essence of
technology, or the *Gestell.* It is not technological products as such that pose
the problem or become the obstacle here, but a shift in the mode of acting
that is critical in Heidegger's opinion: "This 'history' of the kinds of writing

is one of the main reasons for the increasing destruction [*Zerstörung*] of the word. The latter no longer comes and goes by means of the writing hand, the properly acting hand, but by means of the mechanical forces it releases" (*PA*, 81).

Writing, as in handwriting, preserves the humans in the acting mode, because writing happens as part of responding to the word of being and as participating in the movement of language.[29] What is critical here is that for Heidegger, writing in hand does not cover over the fact that human language is not just a representation of what is already given, but it takes part in shaping the manifestation of things by responding to their appearance in an attentively tuned manner. It is in this sense that (hand) writing preserves the resonance of the word. By contrast, typing, whether on the typewriter or the computer, changes this valence, giving force to the mechanical operation whose rapidly increasing efficiency obscures the way of language and human role in it. By turning words into mechanically reproducible and set types, typing evacuates the sense of the one-time poietic occurrence and singularity associated with the word "of" being, masking it through repetition, even if differential, of the in-principle identical, that is, repeatable, type. The emphasis begins to fall on the ease of reproduction and recognition, making the script uniform and uniformly readable, which obscures the event-like occurrence of the word and of human acting (*Handeln*), figured here by the writing hand. It is not the case that Heidegger simply deplores the disappearance, by now almost complete in technologically advanced societies, of handwriting, but instead that he draws attention to the continuing obfuscation of the event's coming to word. Dismissing Heidegger's worry as nostalgia and technophobia misses the point, since at issue is not the introduction of mechanical typing but the disappearance of word as event.

Heidegger is aware that his remarks indeed seem to risk such a misreading, as he reproves his audience by saying: "The typewriter is a signless cloud, i.e., a withdrawing concealment in the midst of its very obtrusiveness, and through it the relation of Being to man is transformed. It is in fact signless, not showing itself as to its essence; perhaps that is why most of you, as is proven to me by your reaction, though well-intended, have not grasped what I have been trying to say" (*PA*, 85). What conceals itself in the obtrusiveness of mechanical typing is nothing mechanical or technological per se but instead an important change in the occurrence of language, which Heidegger dramatizes by speaking about the destruction of the word. That is why it is only by examining what Heidegger means by the word ("of" being)—see chapter 2 —and its destruction here that one can see the import of his remarks and not ascribe them too quickly to aversion to technology or writing.

One could even argue that Heidegger's reticence about writing in fact magnifies the impact of his critique of the "destruction of the word," precisely because his texts carry out this critique through scriptural marks and not by writing "about" it in propositional statements. It seems to me that what Heidegger's texts accomplish, perhaps intentionally, perhaps not, is that, by restraining writing "about" writing, they allow thinking to begin to rewrite itself. By this I mean that, while there is scant discussion "about" writing in Heidegger, there is a great deal of thinking that literally "writes itself," repeatedly spotlighting writing in its exercise, movement, or scripting. In fact, as I have already shown in the play of the prefix *ver-*, the fold between *Seyn* and *Sein,* and the hyphenation of un-truth, the turns of Heidegger's thinking, and especially his radical insights, are all indicated not by means of concepts or definitions but precisely by scriptural devices. In this context, it should also be noted that Heidegger's term for the outline or design of the movement of language, *Aufriss,* comes from the verb *reissen,* derived from the Indo-European root *uer,* which means to trace, inscribe, or write, from which the English verb "to write" also derives.[30] Seen from the perspective of its rifting or breaching outline, drawn out into the opening up of the pathways along which language moves, all of language—writing, speaking, and signs—derives from the originative "writing" of the *Aufriss* and the characteristic scribing of its unfolding itinerary (*Bewegung*). The way-markers (*Wegmarken*) of Heidegger's thought are, first of all, its scriptural gestures, which inflect and lend unique characteristics not only to signs but also to concepts or definitions. It is in this sense, as I show in chapter 3, that Heidegger's texts propose the new style of poietic thinking, which cannot be mistaken for a more imaginative, evocative, or literary way of doing philosophy. Rather, it is a stringent mode of thinking by way of the poietic register of language, its preverbal incising and writing (*reissen*). This poietic register is introduced through scriptural inventions or by holding open, most often by hyphens, of virtually all the key terms of his work. This is why it is not just the notions, such as being, Dasein, truth, or event, that must be analyzed, or the propositional "content," or even the analytic, descriptive, or argumentative side of Heidegger's texts, but their idiomatic writing. All the more so, since this way of writing becomes the way of thinking for Heidegger, which means that, without considering the style, no adequate sense can be made of Heidegger's idiosyncratic deployment of terms and concepts in his work. It is the way in which Heidegger writes his key terms that imparts their critical, nonmetaphysical tenor to them.

Let me illustrate this with regard to how Heidegger's use of tautological writing repeatedly performs the displacement of propositional statement from the primary locus of truth. Through a series of "tautological" phrases—

the world worlds, time times, space spaces, the event eventuates, "language languages" (the untranslatable *Die Sprache spricht*), and so on[31]—Heidegger critically undermines the boundary between the grammatical categories of nouns and verbs. The fraying of this limen becomes pivotal to Heidegger's idiom, precisely because it exposes and counters the hypostatizing of being into beings. Phrases like "the world worlds" and "time times" indicate that temporalization is never properly thinkable as "time," because it does not come to stand as an entity whose existence is ostensibly signified by the sign "time." Similarly, there is only "worlding," or better put, "it worlds"—*es weltet*—which comes to be hypostatized into a construct "world," which becomes graspable as an "it," as something about which we can predicate, say, that the world is beautiful, or ugly, or cruel.

Seen from the perspective of statements (*Aussage*), what sentences like "the world worlds" say is indeed tautological, merely stating and restating the world through worlding, time through timing, space through spacing, and so forth. Yet this is precisely the point, as in this manner Heidegger draws attention to the underside of statements and assertions. For what he wants to induce through this fashion of writing is for thought to no longer comprehend these phrases from metaphysical and thus logical standpoints but instead to expand the poietic resonance of the phrase, to heed what the phrase bespeaks but what cannot become accessible in a statement. More precisely, he wants to attend to what is sayable without being statable (*sagen* without the possibility of *aussagen*). Thus, phrases like "the world worlds" or "the event eventuates" mark this critical fold between *saying* and *stating*. This fold cannot be "stated," that is, defined or expressed in a proposition, which inescapably erases it, but must instead be thought by experiencing the resonance of such phrases. Thinking happens in this resonance, above and beyond propositional language.

Heidegger's emphasis on the primary importance of "lightening" in his explanation of *Lichtung* suggests that the clearing as the saying is "too light," perhaps too slight, for the "heavy" and grammatically grounded modality of statements and propositions. As such, it requires a more rigorous and stringently calibrated poietic language to register the "weight" of the clearing for thought, experience, and language. This impossibility of "stating" the clearing's opening up is not a failure of human intellect or a fault of language but a proper (*eigen*) way, as the quotation above makes clear, of letting thinking into the event. Thus what speaks in the fold between *sagen* and *aussagen* is precisely the occurrence of language, which Heidegger registers in the phrase "Die Sprache spricht." It speaks precisely by enacting the impossibility of inscribing the saying into statements.

Language as Movement: How the Event Comes to Word

Propositional statements become obstacles to conveying the saying, as "Time and Being" concludes, because the saying is less what is or can be said and more the movement through which language comes into signs. This movement is intrinsic to the event; it is nothing other than the way the event comes to word, withdrawing and refusing precisely the pathways along which it has made its way. While this movement underwrites the syntactic arrangements of signs, it tends to be obscured from view by the force of signification. Its recovery for thinking calls into question the priority of propositional statements and paves the way to granting due weight to the momentum of language, which registers neither on the level of syntax nor in signification. To display this momentum in language, Heidegger has recourse to quasi-tautological phrasings, which telescope attention specifically on the fold between subjects and predicates, or to the unusual use of the genitive.

This is why the understanding of the event's coming to word as the hinge of Heidegger's thought is indicated in multiple contexts through phrases like "the event eventuates," "the event comes to word," "the event is by saying" (*Das Ereignis ist sagend*), "the saying of beyng" (*Sagen des Seyns*, see GA 74, 132), or "the word 'of' beyng" (*das Wort "des" Seyns*). The difficulty of translating into English these idiomatic expressions so pivotal to the movement of language in Heidegger is compounded by the continuous playing of *Seyn* off and against *Sein* in Heidegger's writing. This silent play can at best be awkwardly rendered into English through a deliberate miswriting of "being," depending on the translation, as either "be-ing," using a hyphen to indicate the silently scripted fold *y/i* in German, or as "beyng," literally yet artificially replacing the *i* with a *y* in English to mirror the German spelling. In any case, the phrases that, though enigmatic and deliberately thought-provoking, come "naturally" from Heidegger's idiomatic use of German, become often impossibly artificial and stilted in English, losing precisely the language *momentum* so significant to Heidegger's way of thinking.

To underscore the priority of this momentum over the instances of articulation, that is, over the moment of *aussagen*, statement or declaration, Heidegger comes to think language in the texts gathered in *On the Way to Language* as a "way-making," akin more to the Chinese *Dao* than to the Western notions of system and signification.

> Die Be-wëgung bringt die Sprache (das Sprachwesen) als die Sprache (die Sage) zur Sprache (zum verlautenden Wort). (GA 12, 250)

> Such way-making brings language (the essence of language) as language (the saying) to language (to the resounding word). (*BW*, 418)

The idiomatically scripted and hyphenated *Be-wëgung*—Heidegger bases this scription on the transitive verb from the Alemannic-Swabian dialect for clearing a way, *wëgen*, literally "to open a way" or "to way"—is indeed a strange way-making, as it appears simply to revolve within language rather than to move anywhere or to produce anything. It repeats the word *language* three times, suggesting that language keeps shifting its shape, so to speak, where as language's essence (*Sprachwesen*) it brings "itself" (as essential unfolding) as its own saying into the articulated word. This threefold "movement has its essence in the event's taking place"—"das Be-wegen hat sein Wesen im Er-eignen" (*GA* 74, 46). As Heidegger explains, this way-making "no longer means merely transporting something on a way that is already at hand; rather, it means rendering the way to . . . in the first place, thus being the way" (*BW*, 418). As such, it is closely related to the clearing (*Lichtung*). The remark "the event comes to word" means that the unfolding of the event as the clearing is at the same time also the "way-making" of language. Its endpoint is, so to speak, the articulated word, which marks the human moment or stage of language, that is, the arrival of language, or, properly speaking, its having always already arrived, in signs. The fact that Heidegger refers to this instance of arrival as *verlautende Wort*, as a sounded word, indicates the way the word makes from its saying as event to its "sounding" in the signs of a language. The importance of this twofold sense of the word is elaborated in chapter 2.

The reference to dao in the context of the formula Heidegger provides in "The Way to Language" is not as arbitrary as it might appear at first glance, even if Heidegger elucidates dao as "alles be-wëgende Weg"(*GA* 12, 187), the way that moves all by clearing and breaking open paths for beings and relations, and thus bringing everything out into the clearing. When juxtaposed with the opening lines of *Dao de Jing*, the Heideggerian way-making appears not to be a simple or unreflected "orientalism" as it shows a crucial, often unrecognized, proximity to the dao and the relation it marks between the Way and language.

> Way-making (*dao*) that can be put into words [*dao*] is not really way-making [*dao*],
>   And naming (*ming*) that can assign fixed reference to things is not really naming.[32]

The character *dao* means not only the way or to make way, but crucially in this context, also, to say. The first line of *Dao de Jing* thus writes literally: "the *dao* that can be '*dao*-ed' is not really *dao*." That is, what can be articulated or signified of the movement of language, is not really its way-making. Knowing that Heidegger was engaged in an attempt to translate *Dao de Jing* into German makes it possible to assume, even without engaging in an explicit exploration of Daoist thought, that Heidegger's "way to language"—whether intentionally or not—appears to work through and unfold in much greater detail the twofold of dao: dao as the way-making that is also and simultaneously a saying. The key to Heidegger's thought of language, and thus of being, is the fact that the event of being transpires as language, by coming to word. In this coming to word, the event moves (as) language, in order to arrive, as its saying or "essence," into signs. Without separating Heidegger from the Western tradition or overplaying the Eastern influences on parts of his work, it is legitimate to remark that his thinking of language as the "way-making" is more in tune with Daoist thought than it is with Western, essentially semiological, approaches that define language as a system of signs. Or perhaps it would be more accurate to say that Heidegger, as I explain in chapter 2, inflects the Western understanding of signs through the notions of showing (*Zeichen* as *Zeigen*), to allow words and saying (*Sage*) to have the resonance more akin in its pathways to dao than to signs.

The opening and traversing of pathways indicated by the term *Be-wëgung* instantiates the momentum that Heidegger wants to foreground by coining the word with the hyphen from the dialectical expression of movement. The scripting is again crucial here, as both markers are literally way-markers, indicating the bestirring or agitating (*regen*) of language as it undertakes to make its way into signs (see *GA* 12, 246). This movement into signs draws up *der Aufriss*, the outline or the "rift-design," into which the essence of language is composed:

> Various modes of saying and the said permeate the rift-design, modes in which what is present or absent says something about itself, affirms or denies itself—shows itself or withdraws. What pervades the rift-design in the essence of language is a richly configured saying [*das vielgestaltige Sagen*], from various provenances. With a view to the concatenations of saying, we shall call the essence of language [*Sprachwesen*, language's unfolding] as a whole *the saying (die Sage)*. (*BW*, 409)

Heidegger explains the rift (*Riss*) by reference to a crack in the wall but also to farmers making furrows in the soil, tearing it up, rending, riving, or turning it over: "The rift-design is the totality [*Ganze*] of traits in the kind of drawing [*Zeichnung*] that permeates what is opened up and set free in language. The rift-design is the drawing of the essence of language, the well-joined structure of a showing [*das Gefüge eines Zeigens*] in which what is addressed enjoins the speakers and their speech, enjoins the spoken and its unspoken" (*BW*,

408). The prefix *auf-* suggests an opening outward of the rift and an outlining of a field furrowed or rived into relations. The key element here is that this opening out into an outline or a drawing, as Krell translates it, also evokes the advent of signs: *Zeichnung*. The opening outward of the rift as a design is simultaneously a drawing of the relatedness—the jointure and conjoining indicated by the German term *Gefüge*—marked by tears, fissures, and rends. The design or outline refers here to the way in which these tears and rends come to be drawn out and composed into signs. Its movement or agitation is nothing other than the becoming of signs (*Zeichen*), their "ensigning." The simultaneous drawing out into the open, that is, the traction of new ways or paths, the drawing back or retraction, and the drawing (of beings) into relations that give rise to signs is all indicated by the verb *aufreissen* as one conjoined and rived movement.[33] This is how "the event comes to word": as a rift rising open into a design, with its traction into a pattern of furrows related by being held, drawn together as distinctly drawn up, the event literally gives words, or more precisely, it brings words by funneling them into signs. The outline of this rifting movement of language is critical to understanding the distinction between words and signs, which is elaborated on in chapter 2.

To keep in play the tension and the agitation characteristic of language movement, Heidegger describes the way the event comes to word as a conversation (*Gespräch*). He borrows the term from Hölderlin but deploys it in a way that draws attention to the conjoining force of the prefix *ge-*, as a drawing together and into signs (*Zeichnung*) of the various modes of saying and speaking. This is why the conversation does not refer here only to human exchanges or even to speaking: "Gespräch—kein fortlaufendes Reden" (*GA* 74, 111)—"Conversation—not a continuous talking." It is also not "communication—message—instruction"—"ist *nicht* Mitteilen—Kundgabe—Unterrichten" (*GA* 74, 114). Language exchanges between and among human beings, whether spoken or written, are part of the broader *Gespräch* of language, part of how the event comes to word. As Heidegger explains in volume 74, "*Gespräch*—nicht die Mache und nicht Leistung, sondern *zugeeignet*" (108)—"*Conversation*—not something made or performed, but *delivered into ownership*"—with the implication of being assigned to human being in order to be brought into words, written or spoken. This conversation is, therefore, not a matter of human production or language practice but indicates instead the way in which the event, in its occurrence (*er-eignen*), reciprocally assigns to each other (*zu-eignen*) the sides of the conversation: the event and human language. These two sides are both language: first as the saying, here in the sense in which "the event comes to word," and second the sounded or articulated word, that is, human languages, their signs and signification. As Heidegger remarks again in *GA* 74, "*Gespräch* als Wortbehütung und Verschweigung, Er-eignung des Da als Entscheidungsspielraum des Inzwischen" (143)—"*Conversation* as caring for and withholding the word, the event of the Da as the play-space of the decision of the in-between." The conversation refers to the in-between where the relation of the event's saying and how it is brought into words is decided each time uniquely. It is only within this in-between of the *Gespräch,* as its proper outline or blueprint, that conversation or talking among humans, and with it also communication, instruction, and information, all become possible to begin with.

This co-speaking, as the essential occurrence of language, constitutes the internal conversation of language with itself, as it were, to which humans are not simply admitted but also dedicated and properly assigned. They are literally as-signed to it, that is, what the event "says" comes to be given to human beings in the shape of language signs. This explains why Heidegger can write in "The Way to Language," "Yet language *is* monologue. This now says something twofold: it is language *alone* that properly speaks; and it speaks *in solitude* [*Und sie spricht* einsam]" (*BW*, 423). We now know, in the context of *Contributions to Philosophy* and especially *Mindfulness,* where Heidegger writes about the solitude or lonesomeness of language, about its *Einsamkeit,* that this solitude has to do specifically with the way in which the event comes to word each time singularly and one-time. It is the nonrepeatable "solitude" of each moment. The solitude (*Einsamkeit*) draws together the various valences of *ein* in Heidegger's work, bringing uniqueness in its temporal sense of one-time occurrence together with the infold (*Einfalt*) as the key signposts of language. This is also why Heidegger can claim that language is at the same time a monologue and a conversation, or a dialogue, without contradicting himself.[34] For language appears as a dialogue precisely when the event's occurrence comes to be recognized as an in-fold, which brings the saying into the articulated words, that is, into human languages and their modes of expression. Yet when the event's occurrence is experienced as a one-fold, language occurs as a monologue in its singular, always one-time instantiation, which is bestirred not by human beings but by the poietic momentum of the event itself through which, in Heidegger's phrase, "the event comes to word."

The conversation is marked by the double valence of *ein* in Heidegger's understanding of the *Einfalt,* that is, here specifically as simultaneously mono- and dia-logic. The prefix *ein-* enacts the one-fold as each time an in-fold, which renders the conversation, or the dia-logue, as a mono-logue. As used by Heidegger, this prefix comes to indicate that, in its coming to word, the event as the *Einfalt* is neither one nor two, neither simply identical to itself nor differing from itself. This inventive deployment of the prefix encapsulates a novel "logic" of language and thinking, neither dialogical nor monological, and, for that matter, not strictly differential, either. The fact that the conversation happens as both flection (the event becomes inflected into words) and fault (signs mis-say the event) bespeaks the simultaneous one-folding and infolding ciphered into the German *Einfalt*, which I am elevating here, though with Heidegger's own indication in mind, to the principal term for envisaging language. This term is also pivotal to inferring how manifestation as the nonrepeatable and singular wording of the event yields signs, coming to reside and open itself to repetition in language as a human system for signification and communication. The noun *Einfalt* indicates a specific manner of holding together through infolding, which is intelligible neither as difference, that is, as a two-fold, nor identity, that is, a one-fold taken as a homogeneous unity. *Gespräch* (conversation) as *Einfalt* is, therefore, never a straightforward translation or a dictation taken from manifestation but instead a response (*Antwort*). Human language, the "sounded word," does not simply replicate what is being said in the form of the manifestation of the relatedness of beings brought into the open through the withdrawal of being, but it specifically responds to this manifestation by bringing it into words. Language signs are not copies of the word "of" being, straightforwardly transferred into speech and writing. Bringing language into words involves a response, an active encountering and a countering of the word (*Ant-worten*), which means coming toward and over against the word, and inscribing it in signs. As Heidegger remarks in *Mindfulness*, "Now, the question of being [*Seinsfrage*] questions beyng [*Seyn*], so that beyng may respond, may gift [*verschenke*] the word which says the truth 'of' beyng" (*M*, 301). While the word may be granted by being, that is, as the clearing for manifestation, human beings need to answer the claim of this word, its *An-spruch*, literally the manner in which this word addresses itself to them. In this initial answering lies the germ of acting, which means that the human answer to how the event comes to word is an active en-countering, prefatory to any deed or decision, and not a passive repetition or an inactive echoing. Furthermore, a great deal turns upon the fact that this active encountering, that is, the conversation, be measured and in tune with how being imparts its saying, that is, as each time singular and always only one-time, in short, as historial (*geschichtlich*) or being-historical (*seynsgeschichtlich*), as Heidegger puts it. For the turn of this en-countering configures the turn that is the event itself taking place.

Heidegger refers to this shift or fault that characterizes the "conversation" as the proper turning (*Kehre*) of the event. This turning is envisaged as a literal folding into word: from the word "of" being, which Heidegger describes once with an invented word *An-wort*, that is, a word prior to words, only directed at the forthcoming response or answer, the *Ant-wort*. Writing in *Das Ereignis* about keeping silent, Heidegger explains that keeping silent is paramount when, "als Antwort auf das A*n*wort des Anspruches das Wort nehmen sollte und es auch könnte und es doch nicht nimmt"—"as answer (*Antwort*) to the pre-word (A*n*wort) of the claim, is supposed to take to word, could do so, and yet does not" (*GA* 71, 313; *E*, 272, modified). Mirroring the prefix *an-* in *Anspruch*—the claim that language makes on human beings—Heidegger coins here the word "A*n*wort," where the prefix indicates that the claim makes its address by being already on the way to word—the claim is nothing other than its own specific pathway—directed toward, while not yet constituting, strictly speaking, the oncoming word. The claim becomes word only in the human answer (*Antwort*) to the pre-word averred as language's saying. The juxtaposition of the neologism "A*n*wort" with the conventional "*Antwort*" and the concurrent italicization of the prefix make clear that Heidegger forces here German in order to open up a nexus linking the claim, its being directed toward the word, and the answer to it, which comes to be given in words. This nexus is written through the prefix *an-*, which is thus made to appear invisibly, that is, as both written and unscripted as such, but that can be made to appear by overwriting the answer, *Antwort,* as A*n*twort, in order to underscore the direct echo of A*n*wort in the human response, that is, of the resonant claim of language (*An-spruch*) professed and owned up to human beings. This is why the conversation that marks the event's turn can be explained as the fold of the A*n*wort into the *Antwort,* a turn from what comes toward human language to what answers it in signs, in the "sounded word," as "The Way to Language" puts it. The key, inventive role played here by the prefix *an-* is made apparent by the fact that the only time Heidegger uses this neologism, the prefix is italicized. The italics places the emphasis directly on the momentum through which the event as a pre-word imparts itself toward word-signs in which the human response is composed. It also contrastively highlights the component *word*, pointing to the already word-like character of the event's taking place.

Another term Heidegger employs to indicate the pre-word status of the claim language directs to human beings is the standard *Vorwort:* a foreword, preface, or proem, but here cast idiomatically as a pre-word or a fore-word, which precedes and anticipates any word-signs, and meets its counter-word (*Antwort*), its literal answer, in human words. "Der Spruch ist das Wort der Antwort auf den *An-spruch* des Anfangs. . . . Das *Vorwort* in der Antwort des Wortes des seynsgeschichtlichen Denkens"—"The dictum (*Spruch*) is the word of the answer to the claim (*Anspruch*) of the beginning. . . . The fore-word (*Vorwort*) in the answer (*Antwort*) of the word (*Wort*) of the thinking of the history of beyng"(*GA* 71, 263; *E*, 227). Furthermore, Heidegger explains that both the event and the beginning (*Anfang*), which refers to the "first beginning" of philosophy in Greece and the "other beginning" Heidegger envisions for poetic thinking, are only such pre-words: "Auch der 'Anfang' und das Ereignis sind nur Vorworte"—"Even the 'beginning' and the event are only forewords" (*GA* 71, 251–252; *E*, 217). The beginning and the event are pre-words in a double sense. First, they are pre-words in the sense in which the phrase "the event comes to word" encodes precisely the encountering and the turn of the fore-word into the answer. Second, the event is a pre-word because the word is always singular and one-time, which means that any word or sign, here the term *event*, can at best only pre-word it by echoing it as a sign in its answer. As Heidegger puts it in *The Event*, the turn of the conversation from the fore-word to the counter-word (the answer) is the countering and encountering of the word "of" being by human language, that is, it is the way language makes as language (as the saying constituting its essential occurrence) into language (the sounded word, that is, speech and writing).

This complicated movement and turning can be scripted in one word, as it were, by overwriting both *Anwort* and *Antwort* into *An(t)wort*, which keeps the oscillation between the pre-word and the answering word, holding together the fissured outline of language's pathway. Without staking everything on concepts or definitions, poietic thinking heeds and tries to rewrite this overwriting and its effects of erasure, recognizing in the disappearance of the saying in propositional statements not a flaw in articulation but the fold that configures language in its conversation between words and signs. Language's folding into signs constitutes its own proper faulting: a shift and an exigent saying that always risks a missaying. Thus language makes its way into speech and writing through its proper faulting, whereby it also defaults into signs. Signs are the default position of language, the moment of language having always already arrived into what Heidegger refers to as the "sounded word."

The turns of the conversation described above are the circling through which the event comes to word. This circularity, as Heidegger signals already in *Being and Time*, even before recognizing the need to rethink being from the event as *Seyn* to encounter metaphysics properly on its terms, is not vicious, and opens out of the twisting, the *Verwindung*, in metaphysics. Perhaps the most suggestive explanation of such *Verwindung* comes in *The Event*, where it is "just the twisting up into the winding (wreath) of the event, such that beyng and its turning purely and essentially occur in the event"—"ist einmal die Einwindung in das Gewinde (den Kranz) des Ereignisses, so dass das Seyn und seine Kehre rein im Ereignis west" (*GA* 71, 141; *E*, 121). The passage pivots on the verb *winden*: to wind, twist, coil, or bind (the wreath), used three times, first, in *Verwindung* (twisting, torsion), then in *Einwindung,* a twisting into what, third, forms the *Gewinde,* the coil or the winding, which describes the event's occurrence. In this sense, the event, taken here as a wreath, configures the very rim, the circular trajectory, along which language makes its way. This circling or dancing around (*Reigen*) is the prelude to Heidegger's later idiom of the *Geviert,* the fourfold, which redescribes the event as the dimensioning of the shifting span between world/earth, mortals/divinities, and their intrinsic crossing or folding, or we could say, their *Einfalt.*

While it is easy to take issue with the "flourishes" of Heidegger's language, the point he makes remains clear: the twisting of metaphysics allows the event to turn and thus to open up its proper folds, and do so without hypostatizing being into a being, which means avoiding the syntax of predication and the grasp of propositional statements. "Die Verwindung windet nicht in das Ereignis 'etwas' ein, was diesem zuvor fehlte, sondern die Verwindung lässt die Lichtung des Ereignisses sich ereignen"—"The twisting free does not twist up into the event 'something' that was previously lacking to it; on the contrary, the twisting free lets the clearing of the event eventuate" (*GA* 71, 142; *E,* 121, modified). What is crucial is that the momentum of the *Verwindung* is the letting (*Lassen*), underscored so forcefully by "Time and Being." The twisting within the event and free of metaphysics does not add anything to the event; it does not supplement it or fill in a preexisting lack, since there is no lack in the event, without the event ever being full or fulfilled. Since the event unfolds each time singularly and one-time, its *Einmaligkeit* makes the notions of totality or fullness irrelevant. The *Verwindung* does not make, produce, or enact anything; rather, it lets the event transpire (*sich ereignen,* to eventuate, occur, or come to pass) as the clearing, that is, as the ways language opens as its traverse into signs. Metaphysics disallows the event "to clear," that is, to occur as the clearing understood in the complex sense of lighting, clearing, and making room discussed above. The event comes to word through the *Verwindung,* in coming to a turning point that can perhaps let metaphysics aside, as "Time and Being" indicates, and thus let the event make its turn or fold.

The bending and curving characteristic of the fold (*Einfalt*) can perhaps be allowed to happen by the very twist wound by poetic thinking into metaphysics. Yet this twist imparts the impression that the event forms a circle and therefore calls for tautological statements. Obviously, Heidegger's formulations deliberately tease propositional thought, from which point of view a good deal of the formulations explained here sound and look like empty or superfluous restatements. The crucial point Heidegger makes repeatedly is that these formulations need to be read doubly: metaphysically as propositions, tautological or quasi-tautological, and being-historically as poietic thinking. This repeated folding back of (tautological) statements into poietic saying recalls the play of the pre-word and the answer: the oncoming word being literally fore-worded into the words of the answer, by default given always already in signs. I use the "oncoming word" here to paraphrase Heidegger's neologism "An*wort*" in an attempt to translate the momentum of Heidegger's German, the sense of words that are about to arrive as signs, signs that encounter and answer language while maintaining the infold of the oncoming word into the response (*Antwort*) to it. Without allowing for this double play, the play that is not a matter of repetition, there is no way to encounter Heidegger's thought and its approach to language, to enter its fold, as it were, so that it can unfold its characteristic way of saying. What I have suggested here is that the way in which the event comes to word needs to begin to pattern thinking so that it comes about through the poietic pathways of language, without simply congealing into familiar syntactical forms or propositional statements. For a chance for the *Verwindung,* for preparing metaphysics for a turn, thought needs to develop a new experience of thinking by way of the transformed relation to language.

The Poietic Case of the Word "of" Being

If for Heidegger thinking is to be *of* the event, and, therefore, arise *from* the event and stay attentive to how the event comes to word, it has to learn to think being-historically (*seynsgeschichtlich*). What this means is never quite explained by Heidegger, but the cue can be taken from his remarks about the so-called being-historical genitive in the frequently repeated phrase "the word 'of' being." *Mindfulness* distinguishes between the being-historical genitive and the objective and subjective forms of the genitive: "But the fact that the enactment of beyng-historical thinking 'of' beyng can be understood neither in the sense of *genetivus objectivus* nor in the sense of a *genetivus subjectivus* indicates the incomparability of this thinking with all metaphysical thinking" (*M,* 188). Heidegger does not elaborate on this comment but makes quite clear that he has written the German genitive *des* in quotation marks to forestall its reading simply in terms of subjective and/or objective genitive. The question would be whether the discrete status of this genitive can be explained by suggesting that such a genitive can be thought of as the subjective/objective genitive, that is, a genitive that is both subjective and objective, as it is the case, for instance, in the work of Derrida. However, it seems to me that Heidegger points beyond this option, perhaps because the "subjective/objective" genitive still operates within the conventional syntax, pivoting around the categorization into subject and object and reinforcing predicative language. Furthermore, even deconstructing the operation of the genitive leaves in place the force and the momentum of generation, however complicated or reciprocal such exchange becomes in the subjective/objective genitive. It is important to note that Heidegger in fact does not describe this being-historical "of" as a genitive at all. Though it may seem audacious, his implication appears to be that this "of," even if appearing to be a genitive, grammatically speaking, is not one per se and that, furthermore, this specific case attempts to instantiate a discrete manner of relating, one that would not lead to causal, binary, or repeatable articulation. Perhaps its designation as being-historical suggests that the phrase "the word 'of' being" does not conform to the subject-object syntax and that being-historical thinking needs to learn to think with but at the same time apart from such syntactical ordering of experience and being. While beings can be readily subjected to such ordering, being experienced from the event calls instead for a poietic, and not a syntactical, jointure, one never reducible to the genitive.

What Heidegger hints at is a new relatedness, which cannot be accommodated by the existing grammatical cases and which I would like to designate here as the "poietic case," indicated by the being-historical "of." What makes this stipulation possible is the fact that what Heidegger indicates in the phrase "the word 'of' being" is not a genitive at all but rather a poietic fold through which the event comes to word without genesis or generation. The term *genetivus* suggests something inborn or having to do with being generated, and thus comes to be inscribed into the paradigm of production as well as possession contingent on such innateness or generation. Neither seems to be the case, grammatically or otherwise, in Heidegger's thinking of the word "of" being. In this particular case, Heidegger's sense of the "of" refers to the poietic movement of language, which delivers the manifestation of beings— called by Heidegger "the word 'of' being"—into signs. Signs as the "sounded word," whether in speech or in writing, remain still words of being, though they are so only as denied or missaid (*versagt*). The difficulty here is that this poietic case, when taken grammatically, "faults" into the genitive, rendering the two relations apparently identical as long as the question of being remains forgotten and unscripted. This may explain why Heidegger resorts here once again to an idiomatic scripting in order to inflect the grammatical/ metaphysical genitive into the poietic saying of "the event's coming to word."

Writing in *Zum Wesen der Sprache und Zur Frage nach der Kunst* about the essential occurrence of the word (*Die Wesung des Wortes*), Heidegger remarks that "Wort ist als Wort 'des' Seyns nicht etwa sein Ausdruck und sein Zeichen, sondern die Wesung des Seyns selbst, das als Er-eignis *stimmt* und stimmend als Stille des Ab-schieds west (die Stille der Huld)"—"The word as the word 'of' beyng is not somehow its expression or its sign, but the essencing of beyng itself, which as the event *tunes* and, tuning in this manner, essences as the quietness of the departure (the quietness of the favor)" (*GA* 74, 149). The word of being is neither its sign nor its expression, that is, such word does not occur in a genitive relation to being to begin with. Rather, the word *is* the essential occurrence of being; neither different from being nor simply identical with it, the word is instead being's occurrence as event. It is, therefore, difficult to find a way of writing for this unprecedented and always only one-time relation of word to being, which could render this nongenitive, nongenerative, and nonpossessive folding. Without stating this, Heidegger only intimates it by repeatedly placing *des* in quotation marks. This gesture recalls the particular valence of *Einfalt* as both in- and one-fold, the way it is written as neither one nor two, and, therefore, as neither identical nor different from itself. It is in this sense that one could say in English that the word comes "off" as being. I mean "off" here in a double sense: the word, thought being-historically, is not something other *to* being and yet comes "off" it as an oncoming word, while, in the human response delivered by way of language signs, it passes for and works as being.

The poietic case as I have called it here seems to me critical to understanding the manner in which thinking in Heidegger transpires as always inflected into a particular tonality. Minding this tonality opens thought, beyond its signification and propositional content to how the event's coming to word, its saying (*Sage*) can still resonate in statements (*Aussage*). Coming off the event's opening—its clearing—language already has a *Stimmung*: both a tuning or a disposition and a voicing, which reflects the particulars, the one-time character, of the clearing by bringing into its projective relatedness beings appearing and disappearing in their spatiotemporal configurations. As *Mindfulness* explains, "Therefore, grasped beyng-historically, clearing always says, already with the glow of the open, the thorough attunement. The saying of the clearing is attuned"—"Lichtung sagt daher, seynsgeschichtlich begriffen, stets mit die Erglühung des Offenen, die Durchstimmung. Das Sagen der Lichtung ist gestimmt" (*M*, 91, modified; *GA* 66, 109). The clearing opens out of the event (*aus Ereignis*) as the clearing of being, as *Die Geschichte des Seyns* indicates (*GA* 69, 144). As such, the clearing is the saying, that is, the word, "of" being. Unfolding from the event, the clearing constitutes the inceptive saying that, furthermore, is the saying that sets the pitch—one of the senses of *Stimmen*—for how and in what tonality beings come to presence. In order to delineate this setting of the tone as part the clearing's openness,

Heidegger relies on the etymological correlation between *Stimmung* (tuning, disposition, key, pitch, mood), *stimmen* (to tune or attune, to dispose), *Stimme* (voice), and the key philosophical terms *bestimmen* (to determine) and *Bestimmung* (determination).

Opening up, the clearing proceeds to resonate the tonality of relations, their disposition, which constitutes the enigmatic "voice"(*Stimme*) of being. The voice is enigmatic not because it is mystical or merely evocative but because it is soundless (*laut-los*) in a way that confounds our pattern of experiencing in terms of the difference between the sensible and the intelligible. What is more, this *Stimme* is never simply voice or speech, as it uses no speech organs and makes no sound. This is why Heidegger underscores the "soundlessness" (*Laut-losigkeit*) of this "voice" just about in all of his texts on language, which suggests that this peculiar *Stimme* is to be thought of less by way of voice than with regard to the verb *stimmen,* that is, as a predisposing or a tuning that draws out and holds open the jointure of relations. Figuratively, *stimmen* can also mean "to be true" in the sense of "to be in order," which ties Heidegger's use of *stimmen* and *Stimmung* specifically to his rethinking of truth. The term also signifies voting or balloting as well as propitiating. In particular, the two valences of *stimmen* as "disposing" and "being in order" or "tallying" strongly indicate that the emphasis in Heidegger's use of the term *Stimme* falls not on voice but, and often primarily, on the disposition that gives the tone and the pitch, lending its particular slant to how manifestation occurs. This deployment of *Stimme* complicates, therefore, any claims that Heidegger's emphasis on *Stimme, Laut,* or *Lautlosigkeit* makes his conception of language inescapably phonocentric and invites us instead to follow the turn that Heidegger induces in the word *Stimme,* which telescopes attention on the tuning and the way it inflects experience. In fact, in *GA 74,* Heidegger explicitly remarks that *Stimme* is silent, soundless, and not really a voice but the disposition as the displacement of the human being into the there of Da-sein: "'Stimme' hier in der wesentlichen Zweideutigkeit des *Anrufs*—aber des lautlosen, der gerade eigentlich stimmt, d.h. die Versetzung in das Da vollbringt" (*GA* 74, 132)—"'Voice' here in the essential ambiguity of the *call*—but of the soundless one, which precisely tunes properly, that is, accomplishes the displacement into the Da." *Stimme* in Heidegger is to be thought of in quotation marks. As such it is less about *phone* than it is about the design, the drawing-out and scripting (*Aufriss*) of the relatedness constitutive of beings as they are brought by language to words. *Stimme* resonates primarily as *Stimmung,* which means that it becomes less a (speaking) voice and more the predisposing of what arrives into the clearing, by imparting it on the way to words.

A key passage from *The Event* instantiates this critical turn in the word *Stimme* and illustrates how Heidegger reframes the notion of experience (*Erfahrung*) through the prism of language: "Was ist das Wort? Die laut-lose Stimme des Seyns. / Was heisst hier Stimme? Nicht 'Laut,' sondern das *Stimmen*, d.h. Er-fahren lassen"—"What is the word? The soundless voice of beyng. / What is called voice (*Stimme*) here? Not 'sound' but, instead, dis-posing (*Stimmen*), i.e., to let experience" (*GA* 71, 283; *E*, 246). The passage can be translated only with difficulty, because it hinges on the etymologi-cally inflected turn Heidegger brings about in the word for "voice": *Stimme* is rendered here directly dependent on *Stimmung* rather than the other way round. If this critical shift remains unacknowledged, the formulaic tendency to read *Stimmung* (tonality or attunement) in terms of *Stimme* and *phone* sets in. But it does so at the risk of missing the point and crucially misreading Heidegger. It seems to me that the numerous passages in Heidegger's *oeuvre* devoted to the discussion of *Stimmung* as a predisposing and tuning of the relatedness of beings, which allows for their perceptual and conceptual de-termination (*Bestimmung*), leave no doubt that this is how Heidegger intends *Stimmung* to be rethought. What is more, *Stimme*, voice, and *Laut*, sound, are precisely to be reconceived from the originative sense of *Stimmung* as such a predisposing. The passage from *Das Ereignis* makes this turn unequivocal, since Heidegger writes directly that *Stimme* is not sound (*Laut*) and there-fore not a (speaking) voice to begin with but instead *Stimmen*, a disposition or, more actively, a disposing that in its occurrence lets there be experience (*Er-fahren lassen*). As such all voice and speaking arise from and become forms of *Stimme(n)*. In *GA* 74, Heidegger explains again that "'Stimme' aus Stimmen als eröffnende Versetzung in das Da / und *erst deshalb Sprache* als Verlautbarung" (153)—"*Voice' from tuning* as the disclosing displacement into the Da / and *therefore only then* language as vocalization." Only from this displacement into the Da, and from the way relations come to be disposed or redisposed with regard to this site of the experience of being, that language in the sense of articulation into speech and writing comes into play.

This originative sense of *Stimmung* helps us understand why in the be-ginning of "The Essence of Language" Heidegger emphasizes undergoing an experience with language as imperative for opening up the way to language. Undergoing an experience with language as critical because language, its "tone," lets experience transpire at all. It does so because it lets experience open up as "ex-perience" (*Er-fahren*), that is, as being on the way (*fahren*), in the specific sense of relations being disposed and beings dispatched on their way to signs. This relation to language shows why experience is neither subjective nor objective but, prior to this difference, engages with the influence that the movement of language exercises on the relatedness of beings. When Heidegger writes about the "voice" (*Stimme*) of being, at issue is not some mystical voice addressing us but being's characteristic way of disposing (*Stimmen*) what is given to be and how it comes to be experienced. Like the being-historical "of," this disposition or tonality is neither subjective nor objective. Rather it bespeaks the historiality of being, the essential occurrence (*Wesung*) of history as tantamount to the shifting and contextually inflected disposition of experience, what each time allows experience to get underway and make its way to language. In other words, the way language makes to signs, before it arrives into voice (*Stimme*) and sound, into speech and writing, is indeed already such a disposing (*Stimmen*). Without this disposing of relations, there would be no experience, no language in its human senses of speaking and writing, no voice or sound, no letter or writing. This is why all of language, all articulation, whether in speech or in writing, is always *gestimmt:* tuned, disposed, inflected.

As the *Stimme* inscribed and resonant within the *Stimmen* of being, this disposition lets there be experience in the specific sense of manifesting beings and showing what comes to be. Therefore, phenomenologically speaking, showing also "says" what appears, originating its movement into word-signs. In the formulation offered by "The Way to Language," "we understand the saying in terms of 'to say' in the sense of 'to show' (*Zeigen*)" (*BW*, 410); and "*What unfolds essentially in language is saying as pointing* [Das Wesende der Sprache ist die Sage als die Zeige]" (*BW*, 410; *GA* 12, 242). This showing, Heidegger explains, is not credited to human doing, since it is not yet perception or representation but instead a self-showing that arises from being's letting be:[35]

> However, in view of the well-joined structure of the saying, we dare not attribute showing either exclusively or definitively to human doing. Self-showing as appearing characterizes the coming to presence or withdrawal to absence of every manner and degree of thing present. Even when showing is accomplished by means of our saying, such showing or referring is preceded by a thing's letting itself be shown. (*BW*, 410)

This quotation describes the way in which "the event comes to word" by letting things show themselves. This showing is not a mute manifestation or a wordless appearance, but, disposing what comes to show itself, it is a *Stimmen:* the showing already has a tone, a reverberation, which soundlessly carries over into all articulated language, sound or writing. As *Stimmen* the showing is already language, specifically, language on the way to words.

This manner of showing is not a human doing, since human activity comes into play the moment this already tuned showing is brought into signs and rendered meaningful. Because this showing disposes what shows itself by moving it toward language, eventually bringing it into speech and writing, it is a saying: "The saying is a showing" (*BW,* 413). Showing accompanies saying, so that both share the same element, or provide each other with their element. This is why Heidegger frequently writes about the showing saying (*zeigende Sagen*), making both words form a sort of a compound, or perhaps a fold, where showing shows only to the extent that it says and the saying says precisely through showing. This showing saying marks every coming to presence or withdrawal to absence, which means that such showing saying clears the room for presence and absence and, as its *Stimmen,* sets the tone for relations and beings that obtain as present. Because this originative showing "says," that is, tunes and disposes on the way to articulation, Heidegger can write about it as "the word 'of' being." "The word 'of' being," in its being-historical amplitude irreducible to the meaning of the genitive, means the peculiar *Stimme* within the *Stimmen* of being.

Heidegger's claim that showing is saying hinges on the reversal of the metaphysical priority of *phone* with regard to the disposing of language and experience, and therefore critically undermining phoncentrism. For this tonality (*Stimmung*) is nothing other than the pre-word dispatched "of" and "from" the event to language. Speech and writing, on the other hand, appear in its aftermath as part of the answer, in which the word or pre-word, while still being the word, appears differently, that is, as a sign. Words and signs are therefore neither different nor identical; their complicated, event-like relation is indicated in German by the fact that both *Anwort* and *Vorwort* (foreword), on the one hand, and *Antwort* (response), on the other, are versions of *Wort:* the word remains the same in them yet is dislocated, faulted or defaulted into signs, where it resonates another way. One is tempted to say, playing between English and German, that what Heidegger calls the showing saying (*zeigende Sage*) as the oncoming word is indeed a kind of pre-sage, or a pre-saying, of what becomes articulated in language.

The enigmatic phrase "the word 'of' being" echoing through Heidegger's texts produces an idiosyncratic dislocation away from signs, syntactic connections, and propositional statements, inviting us to rethink the relation between the event and language in terms of a certain topology of the word.[36] The experience with language Heidegger's texts unfold for us is neither systematic nor fully explicable in differential terms, nor is it even thought of primarily in relation to humans or living beings. To convey the idiomatic sense of language disclosed in this experience and its crucial implications for the transformation of thought, Heidegger deploys an array of terms, concepts, scriptural marks, and even graphs in order to lay out and prescribe the region proper or owned up to what he understands as the showing-saying movement of language. This topological way of encountering language in terms of how it cuts and clears pathways through a region open to experience is foregrounded in "The Essence of Language": "In thinking there is neither method nor theme, but rather the region [*die Gegend*], so called because it gives room and free reign [*gegnet, freigibt*] to what it gives for thinking to think" (*OWL*, 74, modified). What pertains to language in Heidegger are not concepts, ideas, or themes, but the region in which language makes its way, opening a free reign for beings and forming their relations as both countering and encountering. All this is suggested in Heidegger's use of the verb *gegnen,* which recasts thinking in topological, or perhaps more accurately, topographical terms.

This topographic sense of language as a region is marked in Heidegger's shift from *Geflecht* to *Gefalt* in the remarks handwritten in his copy of *Unterwegs zur Sprache.* There the conception of language as *symploke,* with its array of terms for weaving and interlacing, is abandoned for the sake of understanding language in a tectonic, and eventually, topographic, manner, as a matter of folds: infold, cofold, and onefold, determinative of the defaulting of words into signs. Perhaps the most obvious yet neglected signal of this change is the assignation of language to a region that is never simply or exclusively human but maps the shifting contours of the unfolding world. The distinction between saying as showing and saying as signs makes this re-dimensioning of language ostensible. As the famous formula from "The Way to Language" manifests, the human space of language—its system of signs, speaking, and writing—forms the articulated, "human" part of the broader region for the way of language. What brings about this shift from *symploke* to topology in thinking about language is the understanding of the event's occurrence in terms of the clearing. Once Heidegger begins to explain the momentum of the event as the clearing, it becomes evident that the way "the event comes to word" is to be understood in terms of the opening, closing, and shifting regions or fields, within which relations come to be configured through rifts and fissures. The clearing is an open, cleared, and gathered region or locale.[37] It reflects the situatedness or the locality of language, that is, the fact that language unfolds from and into a "site" that is both open and bounded. The boundary here, as Heidegger remarks on several occasions, is the limen from which something can unfold as what it is, and in this sense constitutes an origin and not an end or a terminus. The clearing is also a boundedness, because it unfolds (into) the way of language as the relatedness of beings, with its folds and crossings opened and held forth futurally into the overall outline of language's movement. This movement contours the world, as if coming off the landscape and its paths.[38] This is why the world is never a substantive or a being but simply "worlds." When seen topologically the notion of the *Aufriss*, the "rift-design," and the various senses of *reissen* that Heidegger deploys in "The Way to Language": *umreissen, aufreissen, zerreissen, entreissen,* and so on, come to have a particular bearing with regard to the nonmetaphysical notion of world and language Heidegger tries to develop.

The critical vocabulary of folding added to the topology of the clearing and the "rift-like" design of language comes to weigh also on Heidegger's critical refiguring of thinking in relation to *logos,* for instance, in the repeatedly discussed fold of *legein* and *noein* in Parmenides. I have expanded this vocabulary here by drawing on the meaning of the English "fold" as fault, which also suggests the possibility of a flaw or an error, in order to draw out the constant overlaying of the saying—its de-fault—as showing and as signs. There are, of course, also Heidegger's explicit references to *Ort* and *Ortschaft,* to site and sitehood, and to the locality, that is, to the historial, spatiotemporal emplacement of language and world, abounding in particular in later texts. Even the framing of Heidegger's inquiry into language is essentially topological: thinking needs to open the way *to* language, that is, to traverse the history of the metaphysical forgetting of this path to language, specifically in order to render itself on the way, that is, literally underway (*unterwegs*), to language. The event itself is, strictly speaking, a topological event, an *Einfalt,* folding and assigning (*aneignen*) human language to respond to what is being imparted (*zugeignet*) within the event. Finally, this Heideggerian topology of language is entailed by the tectonics already implicit in the question of "beyng" (as *Seynsfrage*), which can be opened up only through a shaking open and a displacement of the inescapably metaphysical and differential *Seinsfrage.*

These various strata of terms, shifts, and displacements in thought and language come to evolve through the course of Heidegger's work a topographic of their own, relying on a style of thinking that performs shifts in metaphysical thought in order to repeatedly bring us back almost full circle to the initial problematic of the turning point (*Verwindung*) in metaphysics. The German *Verwindung* in fact evokes a topological or tectonic fault, which would in-fold metaphysics into the first beginning in order to break open and disclose the possibility of the other beginning. In this way, the mid-1930s turn from the interpretive priority of the ontological difference to a new way of thinking "of/from" the event and the concomitant shift from "overcoming" to "twisting free" of metaphysics come to be reflected in the changing language register in which Heidegger thinks the question of being: the initial understanding of Dasein as being-in-the-world gives place to

Da-sein as the site of the clearing and subsequent unconcealment; new terms that increasingly come into play become evocative of spatiotemporal and topological occurrence: event (*Ereignis*), clearing (*Lichtung*), the play of time-space (*Zeit-Spiel-Raum*), fourfold (*Geviert*), placehood or locality (*Ortschaft*). With time, Heidegger begins to emphasize the fact that the event happens as sited or emplaced, which means that it opens (onto) a locality that is spatiotemporal and historial (*geschichtlich*) in the specific sense of being a history-in-the-making. As Françoise Dastur explains, the verb *schicken* has not only the temporal dimension of sending or destining but also the spatial sense of making room (*einräumen*), indicating that historiality (*Geschichtlichkeit*) involves spatiotemporalization.[39] In this evolving context, the appointed task of thinking consists in inflecting the question of being in terms of the clearing and the way-making movement of language, where both come to foreground the unfolding spatial-temporal-historial locality (*Ortschaft*) of the event. This may be the sense of Heidegger's term *Er-örterung* taken as a thinking that, as an alternative to explicative and grasping thought, instead "localizes" being, that is, attends to the way it opens up always in terms of a region or a locality proper to its singular and one-time event.[40] At this point, at issue would no longer be simply the understanding of the play of unconcealment but rather a new attentiveness to the complex tuning or disposition (*Stimmen*) of thinking from the event, so that thinking could allow the event's play to unfold in its specific nonrepeatable "locality" and remain attentive to its changing expanse or dimensionality.

The overall displacement that Heidegger's thought works out from overcoming to twisting free of metaphysics entails a veritable tangle of small shifts in words and terms, changes often scripted inventively with the use of hyphens. The intensive hyphenation to which Heidegger submits numerous German words happens in sync with the complex charting of the plays of prefixes as well as etymological relations between word sequences based on the same roots: from *eignen, halten,* and *reissen,* to *sprechen, sagen, weisen, zeichnen,* and so on. Because of the distinctive and decisive role of scripting, which I have emphasized in Heidegger's texts, the topology he mentions in his late thought can be better thought of in terms of a topographics. This is specifically the case because these regions, fields, and dimensions of language, together with their folds and faults, are often less stated or described by Heidegger than they are marked though scriptural notations and word displacements. Formulas such as the one cited from "The Way to Language," approaching or at least simulating definitions, are much less frequent in Heidegger than insights signaled by his idiomatic writing gestures and his often-idiosyncratic use of words. In many cases, Heidegger literally uses graphics to illustrate some of his points about language, being, and the event, which is especially his practice in the works he wrote for the drawer as well as in the notes and sketches for various lectures and courses.[41] Some of the short sections or paragraphs characteristic of Heidegger's initially unpublished works from the mid-1930s on are attempts to draw or graph the complex relations that obtain not only from the event but also in the critical tension between the first and the other beginnings. Several of these in fact consist of whole pages of graphed relations, shifts, and changes in word or concepts.

To underscore the nonpropositional and originative movement of language, Heidegger on occasion ventures to graph the outline of language, as he does for instance in *Zum Wesen der Sprache und Zur Frage nach der Kunst*, where the graph is topped with the term *Ereignis* (event), followed by *Wort* (word), and then *Wahrheit* (truth, 111). In turn, two slanted bars open "truth" on both sides toward *Erde* (earth) and *Welt* (world), only to close subsequently the rhombus with two more slanted bars leading from earth and world to *Sprache* (language), which rounds out the graph. The constellation incorporates spatial and temporal vectors: the rhomboid spacing of truth, earth, world, and language indicates the spatiality of the clearing, its instantiation through the rift and strife of sheltering (earth) and unconcealment and openness (world), which span the unfolding of being as language. Truth in this graph becomes topographic: not propositional, conceptual, or ideational but "cleared" (in the sense of the *Lichtung*), aired out, opened, lightened, and illuminative. The term *language* closes off the rhomboid spatiality of the graph, which suggests that it both can stay open to its own origin in the event's clearing and yet foreclose it within the play of signification. On the other hand, the vertical sequencing or spacing of the graph enacts its properly temporal vectors. The spatiotemporal expanse and span of the graph locate the site for meaning and representation in language, while graphing the way-making that brings signification about and into the open. What is most interesting is that the words inserted into the graph and forming its contours, though indicative of the gestures and relations happening simultaneously as the breaching movement (*Be-wëgung*) of language—that is, a movement that clears new paths for words and thinking rather than simply retraversing the already existing ones—are less important in forming the contours than the textual spaces, markings, and vectors that compose them. I have in mind here the spaces holding together in sequence the various terms Heidegger employs and the slanted bars outlining the forking of truth into world and earth on the way to language. These spatial indexes try to chart the unfolding of the clearing, while indicating with the top two words, *Ereignis* and *Wort*, that the relatedness presented visually in the graph tries to draw the dynamic of the phrase "the event comes to word" (*Das Ereignis wortet*) together with what is rendered manifest by this movement.

These literally "topographic" strategies and scripting moves should not become overshadowed by references to topology, which continues to emphasize *logos* and possibly also its association in the Western tradition with the priority of *phone,* speech, and reason. The word *topology* refers to the study of geometric properties and spatial relations as well as to the understanding of the way in which constituent parts are interrelated or arranged. The component term, *logos,* emphasizes either the knowledge resulting from the study or the logic of the topological arrangement or design. While the word is employed by Heidegger himself as well as by his commentators, it must be noted that the topology at issue in his texts is a curious one, as it emphasizes explicitly the movement, the kinetics, underscored again and again by various terms, formulations, and figures Heidegger employs to evolve the thinking of the other beginning. Let me mention here three such figures, all of pivotal importance to language. The first one is the notion of the event, which, as Heidegger makes clear, must be thought of and experienced as a turn (*die Kehre*). This turn is not simply internal or intrinsic to the event, but the event constitutes itself a turn—or, better yet, one should say that the event turns. Heidegger describes this turning most often as the way in which the clearing opens up as the site, the Da, in which being's relation to humans becomes possible and imparts itself to words. This turn is scripted as the hyphen that transforms the customary German word for existence, *Dasein,* into the between of being's relation to human beings: *Da-sein* or even *Da-seyn.* The hyphen not only indicates the turning of the metaphysical notions of being and existence, *Sein* and *Dasein,* into the nonmetaphysical sites of thinking and relation, but it also becomes the marker of the each-time singular and one-time turn of the event, which, unfolding the between of its relation to humans, forms a pre-word calling for human response. This active or actuated "in-between" scripted by the hyphen and replicated and intensified by numerous other instances of hyphenation in Heidegger, marks the poietic momentum of the event.

In a short and most unusual of the texts in *GA 74,* titled simply "Das Wort"—"The Word"—Heidegger speaks about the way in which language "houses" the human being in terms of the spatiotemporal dwelling in the "while" and the "width" (*Weile* and *Weite*) of the event: "Die Sprache behaust den Menschen, indem sie dem Gedächtnis das Wohnen in der weilenden Weite des Ereignisses gewährt" (*GA 74,* 43)—"Language houses man by granting to memory dwelling in the lingering expanse of the event." The "width" is explained in terms of "the fostering nearness of the lighted remoteness" (*die hegende Nähe der gelichteten Ferne*), and the "while" as "the sparing hesitation of the lightening arrival" (*das sparende Zögern der lichtenden Ankunft*), as well as the nearness and farness. The references to the lightening or clearing make it evident that these phrases, characteristic of Heidegger's late idiom of sparing and foregoing, or, in short, of letting (*Lassen*), describe the event as the clearing of the play of time-space, or here as the while and the width delineating the event's region. All these gestures and motions concatenate into what should perhaps be called more fittingly a topo-grapho-kinetics in order not to confine Heidegger's idiosyncratic scripting marks to static graphs and drawings but instead to emphasize the whole palette of its graphic and mobile way-markers. Although, Heidegger's explanation of the *Seynsfrage* as the matter of language unfolds indeed in terms of scripting a topos: a region or a dimension, this scripted dimension comes to be instantiated as a "kinetic," even tectonic event, that is, as the event's de-faulting into words. The combination of the three terms to indicate the "site" (*topos*), the breaching of pathways (*kinetics*), and their writing (*grapheme*) indicates here the need to conceive Heidegger's phrases like "the event comes to word" and "the word (or the saying) 'of' being" in terms of such a complexly mobile topographics.

Approaching language in these terms illustrates the way in which language closely maps the world here, projecting open into the future a configured relatedness of the world as the event's clearing. Language both comes off the opening world and carries this opening into signs, while nonetheless holding it open to the future. In a way, language befits the world in a reciprocally molding relationship. Language is "of" the event, necessitating human participation in carrying itself into signs, while not being limited to or explainable through human language. In this fundamental sense, language is not human for Heidegger, that is, it is not human in its essential occurrence (*Wesung*), which gives the entire world its contours while designing the suitable site for the specifics of the human relation to it, or, in other words, Da-sein. It is easy to see why for human beings language appears simply to unfold from this site, that is, in terms of Da-sein, humanizing this site and forgetting its emplacement within the larger topographic of the event and its word or saying. Only when our relation to language becomes transformed through a radical *Entmenschung* or dishumanization—from its anthropological orientation to its being embedded in the language of the event—can the metaphysical moorings of language be loosened and changed.

This de- or dis-humanization of language is the main cue we can take from Heidegger's thought. Its significance is certainly not limited to language, as it has to do with remapping the notion of the world, the manner of its experience, and, of course, the redefinition of the human with regard to the event. Through the dishumanization of language, human beings become mortals, as mortals are experienced as occurring essentially in terms of the relation to being and to the event: this means that, with regard to being, mortals happen first of all as Da-sein and only then, secondarily or supplementally, if you will, as living beings. The world is experienced not in terms of a representable collection of entities but as the event-like showing that addresses itself to human beings. This showing calls to human beings to bring it into words. Disclosed with regard to this call, the world sheds any appearance of an entity—a globe or a planet, for instance—and comes into experience in terms of a language mapping: charting the vectors of relations, diagramming the pull of "the future," that is, of the projective, opening possibilities, and drawing up the emergent relatedness of beings. It is this realization of the bearing of language and world that transmutes our relation to language so that language is no longer "a nexus existing between man and language," an anthropocentrically limited idea of language. In the transformed relation, language "is not a mere human faculty. Its character belongs to the very character of the movement of the face-to-face encounter of the world's four regions" (OWL, 107). In this sense, language becomes, "as world-moving saying, the relation of all relations" (OWL, 107, modified), always more than human, irreducible not only to human terms or affairs but also to the broader problematic of living beings. Language is of the world, so that it moves the world while bringing it to words, relating and maintaining the encounter of the world's regions as their "showing saying."

This world is always borne (out) with regard to things, nonliving, inanimate beings, or produced objects. If indeed, as Heidegger suggests, things carry the world, they play a critical role in how language occurs, for language can map the world only by way of the world's relation to things. Therefore, things are never simply named or signified in language, so that they can become an intrinsic part of the world unfolded through language. The way in which things bear the world, rendering the world possible and holding it open in the first place, must be—even if Heidegger does not say this—the very bearing of language: its course and orientation, its impact on experience, but also its support or carry. Carrying out the world, things invisibly underwrite the movement of language, lending it their support and bearing. The saying of the world, the manner in which language "shows" the world as an oncoming word, has its scaffolding in things. If we can say here that there would be no world without language, then we should add that there would also be no world without things. This scaffolding implies much more than the notions of materiality or sensibility can carry: a more fundamental, world-wise bearing of things, so far not really adequately considered in philosophy. Conversely, without language and the "dishumanized" experience of its way, things remain too easily reducible to objects, materials, or resources, available precisely for the purpose of being disposed of.

It is the role of living beings, in particular animals, that remains underthought in Heidegger's approach to event, world, and language in the texts following *Contributions to Philosophy*. When Heidegger orients the dishumanizing—in his idiomatic sense of *Entmenschung*—rethinking of the "human" being through Da-sein, he separates this aspect, that is, the relation to being, from the domain of living beings. Thus, the place of animals within the Heideggerian topographic of the event would have to be thought of in terms of the role that "living" plays in the unfolding of the world. Defined in the context of the essay on Rilke, "What Are Poets For?," animal and plant living has to do with the experience of the Open and not world, which, within Heidegger's terminology, opens up only from the site of Da-sein.[42] On the other hand, the Open of animal and plant life has the benefit of never running the danger of being reduced to materials or resources, contrary to the way humans tend to objectify their relation to it. Given these distinctions, animal forms of communication or "language" would arise from the Open and thus would be distinct from the way in which language tropes the event's coming to word. This would entail a difference between the way "mortals"— when dishumanized of their metaphysically defined humanity—and animals experience signs: perhaps the same signs but nonidentical ways of experiencing them. One related to world, event, and word, the other transpiring with regard to the Open. In the last count, though, within the experience of the world there is no direct access to, and no experience properly speaking of, the Open. It remains other, animal, perhaps overwhelmed by the shifting historial dynamics of the clearing. At best, even this distinction between the world and the Open is the human projection alongside the animal, trying to grasp what is ultimately never open to human beings.[43] Just like things, whose essence lies in their nondisclosing themselves to human grasp, animal way of being remains inaccessible.

The difference between the world and the Open pivots on the sense of the beginning (*Anfang*) and, more precisely, on the characteristic inceptiveness (*Anfänglichkeit*) of world and word. The way the event comes to word is each time singular: its essential occurrence (*Wesung*) that is essential precisely in its properly being one-time. In this specific sense, the event and its coming to word are inceptual. This sense of inceptuality is what, to my mind, crucially determines the experience of language in Heidegger and makes his approach stand apart from other modern accounts of language. This nonrepeatable, inceptive *Einmaligkeit* institutes signification and repetition and yet singularizes the event and its word beyond the possibility of repetition brought about by signs. It is indicated by Heidegger's language through the connections established by means of the prefix *an-*, which brings into a constellation a number of key terms, which Heidegger characteristically inflects to draw their connection to language and the event: from *Anspruch* (claim), *Anblick* (sight, aspect), *Anmut* (grace, charm), or *Anstimmen* (to pitch, to intone) to what I would suggest is the hinge between *Anfang* (beginning, inception) and the coined *Anwort*, a kind of emergence toward or with regard to the coming words. The momentum generated in Heidegger's writings by the prefix *an-* does not conform to the characteristic play of difference and repetition but instead marks its onset, its *Anwort* or *Vorwort*. It is this sense of inceptuality encoded each time into the oncoming of the word, which holds *Einmaligkeit*, the one-time occurrence, apart from the difference between the singular and the universal. It is, therefore, perilous to translate *einmalig* as singular, for it is not thought of by Heidegger in distinction from the universal but rather by way of the nonrepeatable inceptuality of the event. At issue here is less uniqueness than the inceptive force that gives to be, each time one-time in the manner in which it initiates possibilities and lets relations emerge. This inceptive giving is another way to understand the poietic here: the poietic way of language, distinct from any sense of poetry or poetics, bestows its stamp of inceptiveness, the nonrepeatable momentum of emergent possibilities, to the seemingly recurrent world and its phenomena.[44] The poietic momentum conveys the onset of the "word 'of' being," its initial stirring up, already bringing it to signs. It is this giving, with its *Einmaligkeit* astir in language, that registers as the event coming to word.

TWO

Words and Signs

In der Sprache und ihren Wörtern, im Sagen, ist dem Menschen
das Wort *gegeben, ist ihn* ver-sprochen *das Seyn.*

In language and its signs, in the saying, the *word is given*
and being is *promised* to the human being.

—GA 74, 113

Ungesprochen ist das Wort.

Unspoken is the word.

—GA 74, 60

The Quiet, Un-signed Words

In most approaches to language, words are regarded as essentially linguistic
signs. Their use and valence come from their place in the system of signs,
their meaning is circumscribed by the play of signification, their definitions
are to be found in dictionaries. In Heidegger, however, words (*Worte*) are not
just distinct from language terms (*Wörter*) or signs (*Wörterzeichen*): Heidegger's entire account of language, as well as his characteristic practice of
poietic thinking, pivots on this distinctness of words from signs and their
irreducibility to them. Because it is not based on the notion of the sign, Heidegger's approach, in the context of twentieth-century accounts of language,
is non-Saussurean.[1] In fact, it provides an alternative way of understanding language, whereby signs come to be enveloped within the movement of
language, since they come into play only when language's event-like saying
articulates itself into the spoken or written signs. As the dynamic envelope of

the sign, the word accomplishes the giving of the phenomenal saying of the relatedness of beings and the world to the play of signification. Heidegger's account provides, therefore, a crucial and not yet adequately explored inflection of the current philosophical discussions not simply of language or signs but also of the correlate problematic of difference and otherness.

To understand the particulars and develop the consequences of this distinction between words and signs, it is necessary to examine how language, what Heidegger calls its saying (*Sagen*), unfolds, in tandem with the manifestation of beings, from the event. Heidegger's claims that "the event comes to word" (*Das Ereignis wortet*) or that "the event is by saying" (*Das Ereignis ist sagend*) adumbrates a distinction between the saying as showing (*Zeigen*) and the saying as signs (*Zeichen*). The showing, which Heidegger discusses at length in "The Way to Language," equates the originative saying with the showing that points to what emerges and assigns it to its proper nexus of relations and differences. The discernment of this double valence of the saying as showing and as signs underpins the way of language and becomes the prerequisite not only to understanding what Heidegger means by "the word 'of' being" or "the saying 'of' being," but, above all, to situating his rethinking of language in relation to the differential notion of signs and signification as well as with regard to approaches to language based on these notions.[2] Writing about a Heideggerian topographics at the end of chapter 1, I underscore Heidegger's critical extension of the region of language outside and beyond not only human speech and writing but also animal forms of communication, extension that points in fact beyond the notion of life and living beings. This critical expansion of the field of language beyond the domain of the living beings and their highly differentiated modes of language, communication, and signage, is a prelude to resituating language in the conventional sense of the system of signs with regard to the notion of the saying. This important change is signaled by Heidegger's comment on signs in "The Way to Language": "*What unfolds essentially in language is saying as pointing*. Its showing is not based [*gründet*] on a system of signs. Rather, all signs arise from a showing in whose realm and for whose purposes they can be signs" (*BW,* 410, modified). To render this *saying as showing* distinct from ordinary and linguistic notions of saying or speech, on the one hand, and mere showing or appearance, on the other, Heidegger uses the old terms *die Sage* (the saying) and *die Zeige* (the showing). The saying is tied to *Sagan,* which "means to show, to let something appear, let it be seen and heard" (*BW,* 409). The letting appears as part of the movement of language, as its intrinsic monstration, making room for saying in the customary sense of speaking or signifying.

The decisive point here is that language in the sense of the event cannot be accounted for as a system of signs and cannot, therefore, be confined to the differential play of signification, which has its basis in the distinction between the sensible and the intelligible, and the signifier and the signified. "Darum ist auch die Sprache unendlich anderen Wesens als jenes, das die Metaphysik kennt, wenn sie das Wort zusammensetzt aus dem sinnlichen Leib des Lautes und dem übersinnlich Geistigen der Wortbedeutung" (*GA* 74, 51)—"Therefore, language as well is of an infinitely different essence than the one that metaphysics knows, when it pieces together the word from the sensible body of the sound and the supra-sensible intelligibility of its meaning." For Heidegger, signs neither play the originative role in language nor constitute its culmination, its single most important part, but instead arise from the showing saying. As such, they make up the form that this saying obtains, through human articulation, on its arrival into signs or "dictionary words" (*Wörter*). De-emphasizing the notion of the sign, Heidegger insists that language must be conceived in its essential occurrence, its *Wesung*, from the event, so that it can be experienced in terms of the event's coming to word and not simply as human language or meaning. What Heidegger terms the "way-making" (*Be-wëgung*) movement of language provides the context or, topologically speaking, the region, from which all signs and signification unfold. This is why language must be thought of initially on the basis of the showing and only secondarily with regard to signs, even if from the temporal point of view and from the customary experience of language the showing has already entered signs and become circumscribed by them.

> The saying is a showing. . . . It lets what is coming to presence shine forth, lets what is withdrawing into absence vanish. The saying is by no means the supplementary linguistic expression of what shines forth; rather, all shining and fading depend on the saying that shows [*in der zeigenden Sage*]. . . . The saying joins and pervades the open space of the clearing which every shining must seek, every evanescence abandon, and to which every presencing and absencing must expose itself [*sich hereinzeigen*] and commit itself [*sich einsagen*]. (*BW*, 413–414)

The signature differentiation between presence and absence arises within the fold of the saying that shows (*die zeigende Sage*), so that all presencing and disappearance is already disposed, tuned, (*stimmt*) and informed by this saying. Like presence and absence, signs too arise from this originary saying and should be explained with regard to it.[3] Fleshing out the implications of this approach entails the rethinking of signs and signification through the distinction between the saying showing—"the word 'of' being"—on the one hand, and the saying articulated as signs, on the other, or between words and word-signs.

The understanding of the import of this distinction for how Heidegger understands the event, the other beginning, thinking, technology, or power requires a careful piecing together of remarks from many familiar texts, as well as those published since 1989. Already in *Contributions to Philosophy,* Heidegger's approach to language evidences a striking shift from the conception of *Rede* briefly outlined in *Being and Time,* as his new emphasis on transforming our relation to the word emerges. This transformation highlights the word's momentum of giving being as distinct from the differential economy of signification. "The word fails us; it does so originally and not merely occasionally. . . . The word does not yet come to word at all, but it is precisely in failing us that it arrives at the first leap. This failing is the event as intimation and incursion of beyng [*Seyn*]" (*CP,* 30, modified). When the word fails, when it does not reach dictionary words—that is, signs—the word, as it were, also escapes and frees itself from signs. This escape marks the opening of the interval between signs and words, and as such it constitutes the hint of being, that is, the intimation of how what has been endowed with being has been so by being brought to word. This interval provides the hint of the spatiotemporal play that opens being into its always already given site, that is, its *Da,* its here or there. It is the leap-origin, and that is why the word, in not failing to come to word, that is, to come into signs, fails originarily, that is, in its characteristic ur-leap (*ursprünglich*). To be word, the word needs to fail "originarily," which means "fail" or get away in the very moment in which it gives rise to and appears to enter terms. The paradox of the word is this ambiguous rise into signs conceived as terms, which is at the same time also its escape from them, that is, the word's "failure" to be contained in or limited to language signs. By working as a leap and not primarily as a sign, the word, rather than signifying beings, abides in being, which unfolds and grounds by leaping, by having always already brought us "here and now." This is why words taken as terms—*Worte* taken or mistaken as *Wörter*—and conceived first and foremost in relation to the differential play of signification tend to obscure the way in which the word unfolds as a leap that endows with being. What becomes necessary in order to open up this poietic momentum—that is, the way that words as giving being) have traversed into dictionary words (as signification)—and to keep it astir in speech and writing is nothing short of a deracination of the conception of language as a system of signs. More specifically, it requires a constitutive and radical resituation of the sign with regard to Heidegger's idiomatic notion of the word.

This crucial displacement of the primacy of the sign and its differential play is better visible in the texts published since 1989—the publication of *Beiträge zur Phiosophie*—in part because in those texts Heidegger consistently deploys the distinction between *Seyn* and *Sein,* linking his notion of "the word 'of' being" to the possibility of twisting thought away from the meta-physical ideas of being and beingness. In the texts on language and poetry published during his life, Heidegger writes in a more conventional manner, spelling being as *Sein,* which does not immediately foreground the fold be-tween beyng and being(ness) so pivotal to his most inventive texts. Taking the scripted distinctness of *Seyn* from *Sein* as our lens makes it possible to recognize the fact that the sign-based conceptions of language, explaining language as the differential economy of signification, categorize language into the terms of being (*Sein*) already cast as beingness (*Seiendheit*), because of the unspoken primacy of beings (*Seiende*) and its influence on the no-tion of the sign. The sign-based approaches begin with the notion of beings, signs, and their constitutive elements, as well as beings or objects that signs signify and refer to. Language is thus understood as itself a kind of a being, say, a system or a code. Thought's predilection for folding and erasing the difference between being and beings back into beingness makes accounts of language dependent on the notion of beings. The formative role played by the notion of beings renders it impossible, in Heidegger's view, to gain access to a thinking of language that would proceed not from beingness but from being, that is, from the event. We can infer that such access will not be opened through critiques of language as a system of signs but instead must be initiated through the critique of being, that is, through its transformative inflection into *Seyn.* In the perspective opened up by Heidegger, the under-standing of language through signs and signification remains inescapably metaphysical. In Heidegger's sense of the word, metaphysics cannot escape thinking being within the perspective of beings, which means that being remains effectively no different from beingness and beings. Language based on signs is unable, therefore, to hear the distinctness of being as event. What is required is a departure from this optics and a novel approach "from the event," which hinges on the distinctness of words from signs as the index of what we might call the simultaneous nearness and farness of *Seyn* from *Sein,* nearness that cannot be experienced or grasped in differential terms. Just as Heidegger proposes to counter metaphysics by displacing and enfolding *Sein* into *Seyn,* he also indicates that signs must be displaced from the priority they hold in understanding language, and come to be resituated and rede-fined with regard to his nonmetaphysical notion of the word.

In *GA* 74, in the longest section that Heidegger devotes to the discussion of signs, he begins by declaring the need for thinking of "the event-related origin of signs"—"der ereignishafte Ursprung der Zeichen" *GA* 74, 79). When signs and their systemic relations are reconsidered from the event, what can unfold is precisely the decisive distinction between word and sign, as well as the continuous passing from one to the other that marks the movement of language as it occurs "prior" to and yet constitutes the very opening of signification. This traversal of words into signs reveals that "the originary word is the event-related showing"—"Das ursprüngliche Wort ist ereignishaftes Zeigen" (*GA* 74, 85). The word in this originative sense is distinct from signs in the specific way in which the "showing saying" is demarcated from the saying as articulated in signs in *On the Way to Language*. This idiomatic valence of the word in Heidegger cannot be explained with the notion of the sign, and cannot be derived, therefore, from either speech or writing: "Aber das Wort lässt sich nicht aus den Wörtern denken, die zunächst als Laute und Schrift genommen werden, wobei diese als Signale dienen" (*GA* 74, 85)—"The word cannot be thought on the basis of terms, which are taken as sound and writing to begin with, whereby these serve as signals."

Several elements in this remark are of critical importance to our consideration here. First of all, the verb *lassen* emphasizes the fact that it is the word itself that does not let thought approach and grasp the word's function through the notion of the sign as the "dictionary word." Second, this observation makes evident that Heidegger does not simply disregard or devalue writing, which is here mentioned in parallel with sound. It is not the case, therefore, that the distinctness ascribed to the word in Heidegger could be evolved from the analysis of either speech or writing, and that it is Heidegger's explicit and "detrimental" focus on speaking, saying, or sounding, that leads him to neglect writing. This is why the emphasis on sound in Heidegger's choice of terms needs to be counterbalanced by reference to his consistently inventive re-scripting of his key insights through hyphens, colons, prefixes, verbal roots, etc. The key terms *Laut* (sound, tone) and *Verlauten* (announce, make known) with which Heidegger describes language's arrival in signs, or word-signs as he sometimes calls them, as the "resounding word," cannot simply be equated with sound or speaking. They refer, instead, to the manner in which words announce beings by bringing them to signs, whether spoken or written. As Fynsk explains, *Verlauten* "is an intransitive verb meaning 'to spread about' or 'to give to understand,'"[4] which means that the series *Laut, Verlauten, Verlatubarung* is not about making audible but about what the word gives to understand through signs, whether spoken or written.[5] Further on in the same volume, Heidegger in fact emphasizes the scriptural dimension of the sign, the role that both the sound and the writing perform in signifying: "But the *sound* and the *stroke* (sign), the *letter* [literally, the book-stroke], litera"—"Aber der *Laut* und der *Stab* (Zeichen), *Buch*-stab, litera" (*GA* 74, 106). Even though Heidegger's reflections on language offer relatively few explicit remarks on writing, when we remember that *Laut* is always bound with *Schrift* and *Buchstab,* just the way the written and spoken signifiers are in relation to the sign, then Heidegger's extensive commentary on *Laut* and *Verlautbarung* can be linked directly to his fundamental point: words in their event-like (*ereignishaft*) momentum cannot be evolved out of the understanding of signs, which means that they cannot be comprehended through reflection on speech or writing or the relation between them. What is more, the comments on the relation of both "sound" and "letter" to his idiomatic notion of the word, indicate that Heidegger's account of language is, strictly speaking, neither phono- nor grapho-centric but focuses instead on the nonhuman register of the pathways of language.[6] Finally, the weight and scope of this comment, especially its stipulated departure from the "metaphysical" notion of language—whether as sign, speech, writing, expression, communication, representation, and so forth—depends on developing the decisive role of the distinction between *Wort(e)* and *Wörter,* that is, between event-like words, on the one hand, and word-signs, on the other.

In fact, *GA* 74 makes this change of relation to language explicitly dependent on the transformation of the word:

> *Wenn das Wort—Wort "des" Seyns, dann nur aus der Wahrheit des Seyns zum anderen Wort, und so Wandlung des Bezugs "zur" "Sprache"—nicht mehr "über" das Wort, so wie über die Sprache—sondern?* / Hinweisungen. (*GA* 74, 155)

> If the word—the word "of" beyng, then only from the truth of *beyng* toward the other *word,* and so the transformation of the relation "to" "language"— no longer "about" the word, nor about language—but? / *Advertencies.*

This fragment makes the transformation of language hinge on the crucial distinction between the word in its customary or linguistic sense and "the other word," that is, the word "of" being in its being-historical register. This other word is not something one can talk "about," just as little as one could talk "about" this transformed language, as neither is reducible to or graspable as an object that could be described or comprehended conceptually. The fact that Heidegger puts the transformed "language" in quotation marks indicates perhaps that it can no longer be even thought of *as language,* if one continues to hold on to the metaphysical notion of language and the conception of humans as *zoon logon echon.* At the same time, Heidegger acknowledges the difficulty of this transformed relation to language, indicating that only hints are discernible and therefore a patient attentiveness to these intimations is called for.

In his postwar lectures and essays, Heidegger on occasion explicitly engages this distinction between words (*Worte*) and terms (*Wörter*), which, since they both function as plural forms of *Wort* (word), means that the word in Heidegger is essentially double, or better, twofold: words (*Worte*) and dictionary terms or signs (*Wörter*) can be seen as two dimensions of the complex event of the word. In his *On the Essence of Language* seminar, Heidegger illustrates this twofold by writing: "*Das Wort—Die Worte / Das Wort—Die Wörter / Wie Worte zu Wörtern werden*" (GA 85, 56, OEL, 46). The English translation correctly renders the first two lines as "The word—the words." On both lines, the plural indicates "words," though the first time with regard to the event-like word, and the second, as signs or dictionary terms. That is why the third line should read in translation: "How words become word-signs," in order to render the distinction between the two German plurals.[7] The way Heidegger composes these remarks makes clear that the question of this difficult and easily erased distinction is marked scripturally in German: for *Worte* are literally inscribed and echoed, but also "dissembled" and overwritten, in *Wörter,* by the addition of the umlaut and the final *r*. One is tempted to say that *Wörter* are indeed *Worte,* except written and spoken slightly differently. Yet it is this slight graphic and phonic divergence that figures the most important turn in Heidegger's thought, on which the possibility of bringing metaphysics to a turn hinges.

This distinction, which has been given scant attention in commentaries and responses to Heidegger, emerges as indisputably the pivot of his thinking also in the 2010-published *GA 74*. It replicates and takes various forms in Heidegger's texts: words/terms (*Worte/Wörter*); words/word-signs (*Worte/Wörterzeichen*); word/sign (*Wort/Zeichen*), showing/sign (*Zeigen/Zeichen*); the word "of" being/words or terms (again *Wörter*); or word/resounding word (*verlautbare Wort*); it is also signaled in the contrast between saying (*Sage*) and statement (*Aussage*) as well as in the distinction between the unsaid and the said. Still, it is the unfolding of the German *Wort* into its double plural that best figures this decisive parting or folding of the word, which underwrites the path-breaking movement of language in Heidegger.

When one realizes the scope and the degree to which this distinction, though not always explicitly articulated, pervades Heidegger's work, not just on language but with regard to his key terms—event, world, power, thinking, and so on—it becomes possible to claim that this mostly overlooked variation provides in fact the impetus for much of Heidegger's innovative insight. For instance, with regard to truth, Heidegger explains in *GA 74*, "The word names the event as the welling truth of beyng"—"*Das Wort nennt das Ereignis als die quillende Wahr-heit des Seyns*" (54). The issuing of words from the event is not just a matter of language, since it marks also the opening up of world, which emerges from the clearing. As Heidegger puts it in his *On the Essence* *of Language* seminar, *"The word grounds not only 'world,' but is of being (des Seyns) and preserves discretely the clearing of the there.* / Meaning and sounding and script only shoot up to it and are not the 'essence'" (*OEL*, 46).[8] While signs signify or refer to the world and to beings within it, words, by contrast, are "of" being, they are world-like or wordly, never separated from the world or (re)connected to it. As the clearing of the *Da*, which gives being to beings by opening up world, "the word [is] *essentially* richer than language" (*OEL*, 46; *GA* 85, 56) and more expansive than language understood as a system of signs. Meaning, speech, and writing do not exhaust the originative momentum of the word, and the differential play of signs does not convey the world-like occurrence of the word. This is why the word taken idiomatically as opening up the world should not be understood as simply the singular form of terms (*Wörter*) or signs (*Wörterzeichen*), or as a specific single word, but needs to be approached instead as constituting *"naming, speak-to, address* and before that and essentially word of being (*des Seyns*)—that is? Silencing of the deliverance [Austrag] (event), original clearing"* (*OEL*, 46; *GA* 85, 56). With regard to the sign-based conceptions of language, the word in Heidegger opens—in its originative momentum—the clearing of the there, where signification and signs can arise to begin with. As this enactment of the world, the word is to be understood as *"the tuning silence"—"Die stimmende Stille"* (*OEL*, 60; *GA* 85, 70), and this reticent, self-silencing stillness becomes audible, as it were, only when words, this time understood as linguistic signs, reach their limit and break up, opening onto silence. As Heidegger writes again in *On the Essence of Language:* "If the word does break—being (*das Seyn*) denies itself [*versagen*]. But in this denial it reveals itself in its refusal—as silence, as 'in between,' as there" (*OEL*, 62; *GA* 85, 72). This foregoing of being at the exact point when words (*Wörter*) break up and open onto words (*Worte*), that is, at the point their so far unacknowledged originative momentum—which imparts being to beings—constitutes only seemingly a refusal, for, happening as the necessary missaying of the word "of" being into signs, it in fact reveals itself as giving being—as *das Gebende*—to recall the essay "Words." This is the case because the (mis)saying marks a specific sense of nearness to being, a *Wesensnähe*, that is, the nearness to the disposing stillness of the words (*Worte*) with which being unfolds.

Since a new language cannot simply be invented or creatively fabricated, this decisive distinction within the word can instead be intimated by trying "to say the language of beings as the language of beyng" (*CP*, 62). At issue specifically is a transformed way of saying that would open a decisively altered, newly disposed or tuned, nonmetaphysical relation to the word. This relation to the word, recognizing its force of saying—manifest in its leap or origination into signs—is neither simply immediate nor requires mediation. "We can never say beyng (event) immediately and therefore not even mediately in the sense of the heightened 'logic' of dialectics" (CP, 63). This is the case because the event opens—in its word—the very space for the immediate and the mediated, inaugurating this very distinction, its vicissitudes, movements, sublations, and so on. The word here is idiomatic, naming not an already ex-isting being but instead instantiating the movement through which a being is first given (to) its being. As Heidegger explains in his essay "The Word," the word endows a thing with being (OWL, 141), and thus it conditions the thing, it literally be-things (be-dingt) it, by letting a thing be a thing.[9] It is this minimal and yet all-opening momentum—the incipient momentum of language granting being and world—that Heidegger calls "word" (Wort).

Because of this decisive change in our relation to the word (GA 12, 228), one can no longer relate to words in the same way in which one comports to and understands signs or linguistic terms. For language signs are in a certain way "things" or beings, and one can therefore state that they "are" and ascribe predicates to them, which makes possible describing their manner of be-ing and analyzing their functions. As Heidegger clarifies this dependence of signs on the notion of being(s): "signs themselves—formally objective, thingly representation"—"Zeichen selbst—formal gegenständliches, dinghaftes Vor-stellen" (GA 74, 69). Or in another place, "In objective-technical representing, we perceive everything as object, even the word in the figure of terms [auch das Wort in der Gestalt der Wörter]" (GA 74, 71). The notion of the sign is underpinned by the idea of representational thinking (Vorstellen), whereby the sign is a thingly entity, formally conceived as an object. Furthermore, signs or terms are understood as having been "made up" or created by speak-ing human beings, specifically in order to designate and describe (Bezeich-nen) objects. This representational, descriptive relation between objects and signs—both beings, although in different ways—is in fact what constitutes the sign in terms of its characteristic features of "signifying" and referring to an object. As a result, the prevalent sign-based understanding of language is predicated on the existence of signs as beings equipped with distinctive signifying properties.

The word, on the other hand, is not something thing-like, in fact, it is not a being to begin with, since it does not pertain at all to the domain of beings but has to do instead with being (Seyn). "Thus the poetic experience with the word gives us a meaningful hint. The word—no thing, nothing that is, no be-ing; . . ." (OWL, 87). One cannot say, therefore, that the word "is," only that it gives being, that the word means nothing other than this specific originative way of letting be. "If our thinking does justice to the matter, then we may never say of the word that it is, but rather that it gives—not in the sense that words are given by an 'it,' but that the word itself gives. The word: the one giving [*Das Wort: das Gebende*]. What does it give? To go by the poetic experience and by the most ancient tradition of thinking, the word gives: being [*gibt das Wort: das Sein*]. . . . Our thinking, then, would have to seek the word, the giver which itself is never given, in this 'there is that which gives'" (*OWL*, 88; modified/*GA* 12, 182). The poietic momentum reflects the way words project open a relation, namely the relation of beings to their being, which makes possible the existence and functioning of signs. "The word itself is the relation which in each instance retains the thing within itself in such a manner that it 'is' a thing" (*OWL*, 66). As Fynsk describes it, "*Es gibt*, then, names the manner in which language essences (*west*) as it gives a relation to what is—which is also to say that it names the mode of being of the relation between the word and the thing the word holds in being by granting the is, for the word itself is the relation."[10] Since this relation brings about signs while obscuring the experience of the word, Heidegger can remark: "Plenty of terms [*Wörter*, i.e., signs], and not a single word [*Wort*]. Because a dictionary [*Wörterbuch*] can neither grasp nor keep the word [*Wort*] by which the terms [*Wörter*] become words and speak as words [*zum Wort kommen*]" (*OWL*, 87). Words are thus secreted in language signs, both sheltered there but also obscured and even erased by the primacy of the play of signification.[11]

When Heidegger comes to the moment of "defining" the word, he deliberately avoids predication, since the word "gives" to be but never "is," whether as a being, a thing, or a sign. This is why the text marks the relation between the word and what it does through a colon twice: "The word: the one giving" and "the word: being." This colon is unfortunately erased both times in the English translation, replaced the first time with the copula "is" and the second time omitted, reintroducing the syntax of predication that the word in Heidegger's approach expressly eludes. This translational intervention countermands and mutes Heidegger's insistence on the unsuitability of predication with regard to words, because words do not happen to be beings, things, or signs. Rather, apart from and prior to predication, words happen by giving, which means that they happen as the relation of giving and therefore do not have an existence as signs do. The word constitutes the giving but never *something* given, for the word never "is" as a something or a being. Hence neither the word as *das Gebende* nor the fact that what gives (is) simply the "giving" can be signified, as Heidegger's deliberate use of colons makes evident. These colons in the original German mark precisely the force of giving which occurs as the word; they indicate the idiomatic way the word lets or gives something to be without being itself given as an entity or a being. That is why nothing as such can be predicated about the word, because the word in Heidegger's understanding of it opens up predication by letting be, that is, by making room for the "is." And this traversal, the force of giving and making room, can only be scripted by colons without ever being signified or given over to the functions of the sign. Since the word gives to be by making room for the "is," it is in the wake of the word that signs first appear and that things can be said "to be," that is, that an "is" can be ascribed to anything at all. The word holds open what *is* in an emphatic sense, that is, it holds a being to the possibility of its being, or it holds this being forth into its "to be." This silent holding forth of beings into their possibilities is the way language brings itself into signs or terms, into *Wörterzeichen* or *Wörter,* that is, into words in their habitual, dictionary sense. The word thus eventually functions as a linguistic sign, yet this semiological function attaches to the word only because the word initially "gives" through its poietic force.

Because the word "gives," it is the word *of* being in a double sense: it both gives "of" being, that is, it lets something be, but it also is itself "of" being in that it issues from being as the event's coming to word. Being issues (into) language while language provides the issue for being—its event—into signs and meaning. This is why "we can first experience how being donates itself in the word, when the word is thought of in terms of the event"—"Wie im Wort sich das Seyn verschenkt, erfahren wir erst, wenn das Wort ereignishaft gedacht ist" (*GA* 74, 70). Experienced event-like, the word gives to be, and, spending itself in this giving, never occurs or registers as a being. This is why the word is neither present nor absent, and thus has no status with regard to the copula "is." Unlike the sign, the word does not "mean" or signify but occurs essentially as the clearing of being: "Das Wort 'bedeutet' nicht und die Bedeutung zeigt nicht, sondern das Wort ist die Lichtung des Seins selbst" (*GA* 74, 72)—"The word does not 'mean' and meaning does not show, rather the word is the clearing of being itself." The sign can appear only within the word occasioning the clearing of being, which, holding beings to their being, makes room for meaning and reference.

Another explanation of the word as the momentum of giving (of the relation to) being is provided in *GA* 74: "nicht der Wortlaut bedeutet den Gegenstand mit Hilfe einer irgendwoher zufliegenden 'Bedeutung,' sondern das Seyn be-deutet (ereignishaft) das Seiende als solches, so dass es in das Deuten und Zeigen der anfänglichen Zeichen ereignet und das Ereignete ist, demzufolge erst das Wort zunächst und nur nach dem blossen Schall genommen und dann mit der 'Bedeutung' ausgestaltet werden kann" (122)—"It is not the sound of a word that signifies [*bedeutet*] an object with the help of a meaning flown from who knows where, but beyng that indicates [*be-deutet*] (appropriatively) beings as such, so that they take place in the pointing and the showing of an inceptual sign and are thus appropriated. As a result the word can for the first time be seen as mere sound and be furnished with 'meaning.'" The initial pointing that lets be is performed by being, so to speak. Only when a being is eventuated, let be in this manner, can it be signified and given meaning. This instantiation of signification is the *phenomenal* pointing out, that is, the bringing into the open and the showing, or manifestation, of beings. Before the word-sound, the spoken signifier, can signify, being points to—in the sense of *be-deuten*—by letting be. Only when the word is mistakenly taken within the register of the sensible as mere sound (*Schall*), or, we can add, as mere letter, can its scope be limited to signs and their signifying play. Heidegger draws a demarcating line here between *Laut* and *Schall*, and while both words mean "sound" in German, *Laut* in Heidegger's idiomatic use is not only inclusive of script and the written signifier but is also employed to describe the way in which words are imparted into signs. This difference suggests that Heidegger wants to distinguish between the sounded and scripted sign, on the one hand, and the originating, the "sounding," of the sign out of the word, on the other.

The first, much longer part of *GA* 74, devoted to the essence of language, provides multiple illustrations of this doubling of the word into words and terms (*Worte/Wörter*), while explaining the difficulty inherent in marking this distinction as a result of the fact that, among the array of concepts and approaches evolved in the long history of metaphysics, it is precisely the metaphysical understanding of language as *phone semantike* that is the most difficult one to overcome. Because metaphysics keeps itself and language (the sign) between *phone* and *noemata*, "Hier ist die Überwindung der Metaphysik am langwierigsten und schwersten" (*GA* 74, 102)—"Here [that is, when it comes to language] the overcoming of metaphysics is most protracted and most difficult." It is the sway of the metaphysical understanding of language as a system of signs within the public domain, including philosophy and linguistics, that reinforces the understanding of language with regard to terms: "they [beings] strive after publicness and everywhere force the word into language terms; [it] gives the appearance that the essence of the word can only be questioned by starting from this"—"erstrebt es [das Seiende] die Öffentlichkeit und verzwingt überall das Wort in die Wörter der Sprache; erweckt den Schein, als könnte nur von dieser her das Wesen des Wortes erfragt werden" (*GA* 74, 127). This is why the fact that "the word appears first as language belongs to the same history which brings with it every interpretation of beingness in all its stages, reifications and mix-ups"—"Dass das Wort zuerst als Sprache erscheint, gehört in dieselbe Geschichte, die alle Auslegung der

Seiendheit in ihren Stufen, Verfestigungen und Vermischungen trägt" (*GA* 74, 127). This remark pinpoints Heidegger's decisive claim: the word in his idiomatic sense appears first as signs and signification because of a metaphysical semblance, which forces the impression that words need to be inquired about as to their essence within the differential framework of language signs. By contrast, to give the word its proper resonance, the word needs to be initially separated from language, since language is still understood primarily in terms of signs, signification, and difference. In other words, the word needs to be separated from the idea of *phone semantike* to which metaphysics clings, conceiving the word as language (speech) product, shape, or structure, all possible senses of *Gebilde* in the remark: "Die Metaphysik hält sich an das Wort als Sprachgebilde (φωνη σημαντική)" (*GA* 74, 127–128)—"Metaphysics holds on to the word as a speech construct (*phone semantike*)."

While signs can indeed be seen as both products and forms of language, that is, as components that arise within the field of the language system and constitute its proper operation, the word needs to be rendered initially distinct from *phone semantike*. The reason for this divergence of the word from the sign comes from the fact that the metaphysico-anthropological notion of language, whose origin is frequently associated with the Stoics, moves language away from manifestation toward designation and thus establishes the initial split between words (as signs) and things, both understood ontologically as separately existing beings.[12] Heidegger's distinction of words from signs intends to undermine the prevalent notion that the word is an existing "being" or "entity," substantive and present, and thus ontologically comparable to the thing it designates. What is crucial is that this distinction does not register in and cannot be accomplished by representational thinking: "Yet being does not allow itself to be grasped in representational—neither 'ontological' nor 'ontic'—thought but can only be said in the word 'of' beyng": "Das Sein aber lässt sich nicht im vorstellenden Denken—weder im 'ontologischen' noch im 'ontischen'—fassen, sondern nur im Wort 'des' Seyns ersagen" (*GA* 74, 128). This remark should leave no doubt that what Heidegger calls "the word" is never simply phonocentric and should not, in fact, be thought of at all in terms of *phone* but needs to be approached instead as *Stimmen* "prior to" any voice or speaking, that is, as the disposition of the clearing, where sound and voice come into being in the first place.

The reversal of the derivation of voice (*Stimme*) and disposition or tuning (*Stimmen*) anchors Heidegger's critique of the metaphysical explanations of language through physiology and anthropology based on the notions of sound and signifying: "The mere physiologically biologically anthropologically understood outfitting with the capacity for language, which man takes metaphysically from animal rationale as the original one, means nothing for the meditative thinking [*Besinnung*] on the essence of language, as it in fact walls off any entrance into the meditative thinking of the essence [*Wesensbesinnung*]."[13] Because of their metaphysical frame, also logical-grammatical conceptions of language as well as aesthetic-psychological explanations have to be called into question. To bring into question the priority given by metaphysics to signs and signification in understanding language and thought, Heidegger insists on the double reading of the phrase "to have the word," through which he renders the Aristotelian *logon echon*. The first sense, dominant in the Western tradition, is that of the audible expression of the perception of beings. In the second, thoroughly other sense (*ganz anderen Sinne*), this phrase indicates that it remains the human decision whether "man" simply belongs to beings and belabors them or whether the human being ventures, as Heidegger puts it, "the grounding of the truth of beyng" ("die Gründung der Wahrheit des Seyns wage," GA 74, 144). The word in this context is not thought of in terms of the signifier or the signified but instead as the unfolding of a decision: "Das 'Wort'—hier Entscheidungswesen—aus dem seynsgeschichtlichen Wesen des Wortes, d. h. nicht der Mensch 'hat' das Wort, sondern das Wort 'hat' den Menschen" (*GA* 74, 144)—"The 'word'— here the essence of decision—from the beyng-historical essence of the word, that is, not the human being 'has' word but the word 'has' the human being." The second, nonmetaphysical sense of the word discloses how the word is never set or determined the way signs are differentiated and constituted as part of a language system with its semantic and grammatical registers, but is instead each time a matter of deciding. What is not only open to but invites, even necessitates, this decision, is the word's momentum of giving to be. It does so because its letting be means the emergence of possibilities brought out in the opening of the clearing, the emergence that calls for a decision. How beings are given to be and how the valence of this giving, and with it the "meaning" of being, become apparent or not is precisely the essence, the occurrence of the decision that prompts the wording of being in particular ways. The sign plays and can be played with, the word decides and undergoes decision through human participation. On the movement of this decision depends how and if the clearing opens up in its complex topographic, as well as how the ontological difference is decided and parsed: beings in their relation to being or beingness, in short, forgetting or, by contrast, remembrance (*Gedächtinis*) of *Seyn*, which Heidegger emphasizes repeatedly in *GA* 74. What comes up for decision in the unfolding of the word are thus the parameters of the world, of the manner one dwells and acts in it. In this way, language inheres in and de-cides the very manner of thinking.

This is why "The *word of beyng* and language as the echo of beings are immeasurably different"—"Das *Wort des Seyns* und die Sprache als Widerhall des Seienden sind abgründig verschieden" (*GA* 74, 128). Here we have one more indication that in its being-historical momentum, the word "of" being is not a matter of sound (*Hall*), that is, the word does not recall or echo beings but instead lets them be. In fact, the word is neither *phone,* nor is it a matter of signifying (*semantike*), but instead charts the topographic of the clearing: "Word not a sign (*semeion*), the signification of beings, but the clearing of being"—"Wort nicht Merkmal (σημειον), Bedeutung des Seienden, sondern Lichtung des Seyns" (*GA* 74, 132). Signs or markers signify *beings,* which means that they ineluctably collapse the ontological difference into a mere distinction between beings and beingness, and make it impossible to raise the *Seynsfrage,* which in turn prevents access to how language occurs, to its "way-making." A few pages later, Heidegger again underscores this key point: "The 'word' / is not an instance of marking—the *objectivation* of beings / *The intoning of the clearing of beyng*"—"Das 'Wort' / ist nicht Mal des Merkens—der *Gegenständigung* von Seiendem. / *Anstimmung der Lichtung des Seyns*"(*GA* 74, 135). The sign's signifying is bound to beings and relies expressly on their objectivation. Though themselves never simply objects or things, signs in fact depend in their signifying work on beings disclosed as objects or presences, and on the signs themselves conceived as things capable of marking, signifying such objects—this is why Heidegger repeatedly writes about *Zeichendinge* (sign-things) and *Zeichenzeuge* (sign-tools).

The function of signs in language, their existence as tools for signifying, pivots on this double encoding of beings and signs themselves into objects. Yet this objectivation covers over and assigns to oblivion from where the signs taken as tools arise in the first place: "'Zeichenzeug' erst aus Zeugnis—Weltnis von Welt—Ereignis dem 'Gedächtnis,' / darum 'Sprache' nicht zu denken von signum und signal her" (*GA* 74, 165)—"'Sign as tool' first from testimony—worldness of the world—event to 'memory'—therefore 'language' not to be thought of in terms of signum and signal." Signs need to be reconceived from the perspective of the event, as its testimony to the worlding of the world, which means that language cannot be defined on the basis of the notion of the sign (*signum*) or signal. While the sign relies on relations among objects and other signs, the word is the agitation of the clearing, its breaking open—literally its *Anstimmen,* intoning or initial tuning—that is, the initial disposition of the clearing's topographic, whose onset and emergence is indicated by the prefix *an-*. *Anstimmen* recalls here the imparting of words into signs, which Heidegger indicates through the coined "An*wort,*" or "oncoming word." The onset of words is not simply a matter of language—as a system of signs—but instead pertains to the disposition (*Stimmung*) of beings and relations within the topographic of the clearing.

Because of its relation to *Stimmung* and to silence/stillness (*Stille*), the word has a completely other way of unfolding than the sign: "Die ganz andere Wesung des Wortes—jene aus dem Seyn, d. h. der Er-eignung" (*GA* 74, 134)—"The completely different essencing of the word—from beyng, i.e., from the happening of the event." The relation of word to silence has critical implications for thinking: the transformed relation to language means a style of thinking that takes its cue not from concepts and statements but from alertness to silence and stillness, which remain astir in the proliferation of signs. *Zum Wesen der Sprache und Zur Frage nach der Kunst* describes this important link between word and stillness/silence, with both senses quietly resonant in the German word *Stille:* "Das erste Wort ist, weil Wesen des Wortes die Stille, das Ungesagteste und im Sagen Unbestimmte—*das Seyn.* / Das Wort 'des' Seyns"—"The first word is, because the essence of the word is silence, the most unsaid and in its saying indeterminate—*beyng.* / The word 'of' beyng." And on the same page, "*Wort*—entspringt aus dem Seyn, / besser: Seyn *west als Ursprung des Wortes*—Er-*schweigung*" (*GA* 74, 135)— "*Word*—originates from beyng / better: beyng *essences as the origin of the word*—keeping *silent*." In the first remark, the word's essence, its unique manner of unfolding, is identified as *die Stille:* silence, but in the specific sense of quietness and stillness. This, in essence, quiet word is not mere muteness or simple absence of the word or of any saying; rather, it is what says itself quietly as the most unsaid, as Heidegger indicates here through the superlative "das Ungesagteste." Only human speaking can be rendered mute; the saying of being is always quietly eloquent, always silently sending itself toward signs.

This stillness, however, is not to be misapprehended as motionlessness; on the contrary, it marks here the breaking open of the clearing and the incipient movement along the opening pathways of language. In the second remark, Heidegger reinforces the verb *schweigen,* to be silent, with the prefix *er-,* which not only marks this specific silence as intrinsic to the *Er-eginis,* hyphenated to underscore its sense of occurrence, but also indicates the need for thinking actively to hold silence as the index of the onset of words. This reticence enfolding the stillness, its refusal of signs, is the proper holding silent of the eventuation (*Erschweigung der Stille,* or of the Er-*eignung, GA* 74, 132–135). For Heidegger, it delineates the manner in which the answer to the quiet word should be carried out and decided in thinking: "Erschweigung ist die Verant-wortung des Wortes" (*GA* 74, 135)—"Holding silent is the bringing into the response of the word." Hyphenating *Verant-wortung,* Heidegger leaves no doubt that the silent onset of the word resonates in the response, among the signs that articulate it in human language. The answer takes place as ensuing response—"wording" of the silent word "of" being.

Another way in which Heidegger brings out this critical distinction between word and sign is by demarcating the "silent" or "quiet" word from the saying word, that is, from the word that literally strives to say and keeps this saying in its "strife": "Das *wesende Wort* als stimmende Stille (das stille Wort). / Das *streitbare Wort* als *Sage*, Ver*laut*barung. / Das stille und das streitbare Wort je verschieden einig" (*GA* 74, 154)—"The *essencing word* as the tuning silence (the silent word) / The *conflictual word* as *saying*, resounding. / The silent and the conflictual word ever unified in difference." "*Das streitbare Wort*" is "polemic" in the sense of *polemos*, as it refers to the strife of world and earth, familiar among others texts from "The Origin of the Work of Art." The German phrase indicates that the word strives both to articulate the inseparable distinctness of world and earth and to keep this distinctness always alive, in continuous strife. This is why the word is also called by Heidegger "die Stille des Risses" (*GA* 74, 136), the quiet or stillness of the rift, where the rift marks the struggle between encountering and strife, which being itself places in the abyssal non-ground of its clearing. "Hieraus entsprigend kann das Wort im Zwischen der Entgegnung zum *Gespräch* und aus diesem im Zwischen von Welt und Erde zur Sage und Aussage werden. Beides erscheint zunächst gern als Verlautbarung" (*GA* 74, 136)—"Emerging from here, the word can become, in the between of the encounter, a *conversation* and from it, in the between of world and earth, it becomes saying and statement. Both appear at first as a sounding." Stillness describes the expanse of the outline of the entire span of language in its quiet way as the conversation between the saying and the stating. This sounding (*Lautung*) of language in word-signs arises as the echo of the rift of the clearing: "Die Lautung—der Widerhall—oder Er-hall des *Risses der Lichtung* (stimmend)" (*GA* 74, 138)—"The sounding—the echo—or the re-verb of *the rift of the clearing* (tuning)."

In a characteristic move, Heidegger thinks here by resonating connections among various German terms for sound and sounding: *Verlautbarung* becomes part of the *Lautung* (sounding) or echoing (*Widerhall*), literally the re-verb or the re-sound (*Er-hall*) of the rift of the clearing. The hyphenation in *Er-hall* implies the event-like (*ereignishaft*) character of this re-verb, and, when rendered this way into English, opens up an interesting play between a reverberation and a "re-verbalizing," that is, a re-wording, which words undergo upon their entrance into signs. This "re-verb" gives the proper tuning (*Stimmen*) to all the "announcing" of language in speech and writing, to its statements and their meaning. Rather than providing a definition or a more detailed description of how "sounding," which re-verbalizes words in signs, works, Heidegger lets the German words, specifically the multiplying links among them, carry and stage his insight. The way Heidegger writes out this sounding of language into word-signs through a full array of German terms for sound: *Laut, Hall, Schall, Klang,* and, of course, *Stimme,* tends to envelop this phonic spectrum within the dispositve or tuning momentum of the word, its *Stimmung.* All the words for sound Heidegger uses arise always in response to and in tandem with the clearing and thus by way of *Stimmen.* As Heidegger puts it succinctly, "The *word* is the ringing light of the event"— "Das *Wort* ist das klingende Licht des Ereignisses" (*GA* 74, 102). The word constitutes the momentum of the event opening into the registers of light and sound, which are aspects of the clearing, and thus part of the playfield of time-space. Therefore, the "sound" in Heidegger is never simply, nor even primarily, *phone* but instead *lichten* (lightening, clearing, lighting) and *stimmen* (disposing). *Laut* is never mere sound (*Schall*), and this is why the sound proper to language, so to speak, is the echo of what is always quiet, silent, and still. The sign, its sound and its "silent" script, all echo this quiet word, together with its "lighting" inception of the world.

For all these reasons, "As the word 'of' beyng, the word is not somehow its expression or sign, but the essencing of beyng itself, which, as the event, *tunes* and, so tuning, essences as the silence of the de-parture (the silence of the favor)"—"Wort ist als Wort 'des' Seyns nicht etwa sein Ausdruck und sein Zeichen, sondern die Wesung des Seyns selbst, das als Er-eignis *stimmt* und stimmend als Stille des Ab-schieds west (die Stille der Huld)" (*GA* 74, 149)—In its event-like resonance, the word is precisely the disposition of be-ings and relations that lets what is be present or absent, and so exist in its proper valence. But as such a disposition, the word retreats and withholds, that is, it parts from beings and departs from signs. The distinctness of words from signs is not simply a matter of difference but instead a complex de-parture (*Ab-schied*), which, erasing the tracts of its way to signs under the pressure of speech and writing, can either hold the word properly quiet or, much more commonly, cover it over with meaning. The word in this specific sense is, therefore, not "about" being and does not "signify" any object—for example, being as a being—just as it is also not a word "from" being, that is, the "subjective" expression or appearance given by being. The genitive in "the word 'of' being" is being-historical, not grammatical: "Der Genitiv ist seynsgeschichtlich—Wort gehört in die Wahr-heit des Seyns selbst. / Das Wort 'stimmt'; ist nicht 'über' und nicht 'aus'; Seyn west als Er-eignung der Lichtung, und dieses ist das Stimmen der Stille" (*GA* 74, 149)—"The genitive is beyng-historical—the word belongs to the truth of beyng itself. / The word 'tunes'; it is not 'about' or 'from'; being unfolds as the event [*Er-eignung*] of the clearing, and this is the tuning of silence." The word neither signifies nor expresses but unfolds (as) the eventuating of the clearing, which is the quiet disposing of stillness. In its poietic momentum, the word actuates the outline of language's movement, its quiet traversal into signs.

This traversal is described on several occasions as a splitting or a falling apart (*Zerfallen*) of the word upon its utterance. As Heidegger argues, the word should be thought of not in terms of adequation or *homoiosis* (151) but, conversely, in terms of a constitutive fissure into word-signs: "Das Wort zerfällt als ausgesprochenes in Wörter und Sätze. Diese werden als vorkommende zusammengenommen als seine 'Sprache'" (*GA* 74, 136)—"Uttered, the word falls apart into signs and sentences. As they appear, these are collected together as a 'language.'" And "Ein *Wort—der Zerfall eines Wortes in 'Wörter'—die Sprache spricht Wörter*" (*GA* 74, 138)—"*A word—the falling apart of a word into 'terms'*—language speaks terms." What is mostly muted and rarely apparent in the essays and lectures on language published during Heidegger's lifetime is stated here with the emphasis on the disintegration intrinsic to the word's falling into signs. If every word is singular and one-time in its onset, its movement occurs as an instantaneous breakup along the rifts and furrows that chart the clearing. This falling apart constitutes the proper momentum of the word, which transpires as the poietic emergence of possibilities and decisions. In order for the word to be uttered, "stated" in speech or writing, it needs to rupture into the constituent elements of what is customarily seen as "language." In fact, this breakup of the word is nothing other than language's rifting movement (*Riss*), its proper fissuring that clears the time-space of the event into which beings and their relations unfold.

This breakup of the word becomes the shorthand for the language formula Heidegger later discusses in "The Way to Language": the way of language as the bringing of its event-like occurrence into signs. The breakup indicates the exigent silencing of words into signs, which requires in turn that we listen attentively to words as signs in order to hear and trace the word's "reverb" in signs, both its reverberation and its rewording. This is why undergoing an experience with language means primarily undergoing an experience with this silence or stillness, which here means a practice of alertness to the hints and echoes of the silent breakup of the word still reverberating in speech and writing. Words are only answered in a "language," that is, responsively reworded (*verant-wortet*) as signs and sentences, recast semantically and grammatically, which is also why words remain linguistically inapparent. As Heidegger remarks, language speaks (in) signs, and it speaks and writes only signs, which makes the task of making the "words 'of' being" audible or visible very difficult, requiring less conceptual or propositional exactness than a poietic rigor and stringency.

If signs bespeak and talk about beings (*GA* 74, 121) and thus constitute what Heidegger often calls *das Besprochene,* that which is spoken about, then this poietic rigor of thinking expressly attends to what conceals itself in the conversation: "Gleichwohl aber verbirgt sich im Gespräch noch ein Gesagtes, was nicht ein Besprochenes ist. Gerade dieses zuletzt genannte Wort 'ist' sagt 'etwas,' was nicht ein 'Seiendes' ist;—das Wort nennt das Seyn" (*GA* 74, 121)—"Yet at the same time a said, which is not something spoken-about, conceals itself in the conversation. Rather this just mentioned word 'is' says 'something' that is not a 'being';—the word names beyng." The word refers to the momentum of language that cannot be spoken about, that cannot, strictly speaking, be put into words, but that still comes to be said sometimes in what is spoken or written, and it is most directly intimated in the verbs related to being, especially the third-person singular "is." Heidegger asks himself what appears to be largely a rhetorical question as to whether this word "is" is an alien (*Fremdling*) among language terms or if it is rather "the word of all words, wherein all terms first can be terms"—"oder ist es das Wort aller Worte, worin alle Wörter erst Wörter sein können?" (121). The "is" can be thought of as a stranger among language signs because it is a sign apparently closest to what Heidegger calls the "word 'of' being," at least in the sense in which it draws attention to being by highlighting what cannot be talked about and yet may be said nonetheless alongside all that is talked about. As a sign, the "is" becomes indeed the privileged, if not unique, word for being in Heidegger's thought, as he devotes considerable attention to it in various texts and at various points in his work. Even though a sign can be unique in this sense, word in the idiomatic sense it acquires in Heidegger cannot be "unique," as I explain in chapter 1. The sign may hold the rank of something unique, but the word gives to be in a manner that is singular because it is one-time: *einzig* and *einmalig* at the same time. The uniqueness of the sign "is" must therefore be inflected, each time singularly, in order to discern in it the resonance of "the word 'of' being." That this is indeed the case follows from Heidegger's subsequent explanation that the word grants beings the possibility to be described and assigned a sign (*Bezeichnen*) in the sense of being signified (*Bedeuten*). The two verbs *Bezeichnen* and *Bedeuten* combine signification with reference or designation, so that they come to describe the overall operation of the sign that has been rendered possible by the word.

This oscillation between signs and words is of crucial importance for philosophy, since in Heidegger's account it irrevocably changes the very manner of thinking. When we approach Heidegger's texts through the prism of their attention to silence, and more specifically to how silence and stillness inflect the way in which thinking moves in language, what emerges is a new poietic thinking, where what is to be thought is never only expressed by signs and meaning or secured in propositions but comes to be oriented by links, folds, and bearings among word stems, prefixes, or even single letters. Of course, thought still largely proceeds in signs and propositions, and will always remain metaphysical in this regard. What changes is the fact that thinking finds its openings not so much in new definitions or concepts as in the way such concepts come to resonate poietically, that is, are guided by each time newly emergent possibilities of rewording. Such thinking attempts to calibrate itself to "the silent force of the possible," which echoes through the particulars of the event and opens them to the future. Rather than gaining new knowledge or a controlling grasp over the situation, this thinking aspires to stay alert to the way the event guides it with "the silent force of the possible." Its flexibility responds to and emulates the unforeseeable charge of the event. As the event comes to word, it discharges itself into signs and meaning, while holding what comes to be articulated in this way within the silent envelope of the word, that is, within the playing field of the force of the possible. Poietic thinking thinks more in terms of what might be called, echoing Samuel Beckett while using Heidegger's own terms, the "stirring still" of the word. It is, therefore, not just a critique but a poietic dismantling and transformation of the metaphysical framework of experience that rests on signs and meaning to the detriment of the force of the possible.

The Unprethinkable of the Word

What molds Heidegger's thinking is attentiveness to how words (*Worte*), already resting in word-signs (*Wörter*), nonetheless actuate something unprethinkable (*Unvordenkliche*) in them, expanding signs and meaning by enveloping them in the fluctuating charge of the possible. Never limited to "dictionary words" and their signification, poietic thinking expands beyond the propositional mold of language and truth in order to inflect thought through the prism of the one-time occurrence of the event.

Heidegger borrows the word *Unvordenkliche* from Schelling and uses it several times in *Zum Wesen der Sprache und Zur Frage nach der Kunst,* without ever sufficiently developing the specific resonance of this term with respect to the distinction he draws between word and sign. In the section titled "Word—the Truth of Language," he simply writes, "Das Unvordenkliche, Erschreckende, Überholende, Zwingende im Wort" (*GA* 74, 104)—"The unprethinkable, the terrifying, the outstripping, the compelling in the word."

These four adjectives are thus suggested as the vectors of the clearing, of the truth of the world and language resonating in its force of possibility. The unprethinkable in the momentum of the word is what outstrips, presumably signs and signification, and with them, also what can be said or written as the articulated or sounded word. And because of this outstripping or over-hauling of "dictionary words," the word startles, or even terrifies, and in the same gesture also compels. Yet why would the word be startling or terrify-ing at all? Perhaps in just this sense that the imparting of the word from the event—*das Ereignis wortet*—and its dispatching into signs, remains always unpredictable and unprethinkable because of the way the event holds what becomes present open to the future, and brings this historializing force into language. The way of words toward their articulation is not pre-thinkable in the sense that the uniquely and always one-time imparted word envelops and inflects the apparent constancy of signs and the repetitiveness of signi-fication, opening them into the possibilities that emerge precisely through the historializing momentum "of" being, as *seynsgeschichtlich,* or being-historical. As Heidegger explains, this imparting, which clears in its wake the room for signs and meaning, has each time its proper while (*Weile*) as well as span or width (*Weite*), which requires renewed alertness and poietic precision of thinking. The sign and its signification can never account for, cannot fore-think, as it were, the always-moving word, quietly charged with the possible. It is, therefore, the job of thought to hold signs, concepts, and meaning through which it operates open to the event's "force field" of the possible. Opening up the genuinely new, the word is, in its very unfolding and thus essentially, unprethinkable, which evokes fear, outstrips and each time singularly overhauls signification, and does so in a compelling way, Heidegger implies.

The compelling that Heidegger mentions here in relation to the outstrip-ping and the startling should not be associated hastily with power or violence. As he explains in the never-delivered lecture course on Anaximander, likely written in 1942 and published in 2010, at issue is a specific sense of "compel-ling without the use of violence or coercion" (*ein Zwingen ohne Gewalt- und Zwangsmassnahme*) (*GA* 78, 133). Heidegger explains this notion of compel-ling by invoking the manner in which an example can be compelling without force, compulsion, or violence, simply by its sheer way of being. This distinct way of compelling is specifically not thought of with regard to power but in the sense indicated by the Latin word Heidegger employs: *ne-cedere,* that is, as not ceasing, stopping, or terminating. *Ne-cedere* in this context refers to the singular way in which being does not cease to let (beings) be, as it not only does not let up animating the play of time-space but has it unfold without cease or remission. As Heidegger puts it, "Im Zwingen des also Zwingenden waltet ein Lassen, und zwar von der seltenen Art des Nicht-Ablassens"—"In the compelling of what compels in this way, there prevails a letting, and indeed in a rare manner of not-letting-up."[14] "Letting" here unfolds through the singular momentum of not letting up (*das Unablassende im Lassen, GA 78*, 134), where this intrinsic *Unablassen* (*ne-cedere*) is a pure compelling without power or violence. It does not force anything but only specifically lets something stay for a while (*weilen lassen*), holding open the space-time proper and fitting to things' way of being, which allows them to exist in their characteristic staying a while. As Heidegger further explains, "Das reine Zwingen als solches Lassen beansprucht das Anwesen, um es zu lassen" (*GA 78*, 134)—"The pure compelling as such a letting lays claim to presencing in order to let it be." In addition to the complicated meaning of *lassen* that Heidegger continues to evolve over several decades, this sentence hinges on the verb *beanspruchen:* to ask, call for, claim, demand, be in need of, involve, necessitate, postulate, reclaim, require, take up, or want. In the above context, this complex verb brings into play the notions of need and want in order to indicate that letting needs the presencing as it places a claim or even a demand with regard to it. Yet what this claim means is that it is specifically the letting named here that takes up the presence at stake, thus necessitating and claiming it at the same time. Such letting happens in response to what comes into presence but as such a response it reclaims what it responds to, namely the presencing of things, and does so in a particular way that needs, even necessitates, this presencing, and involves itself with it, without, however, forcing, manipulating, or taking charge of it. Letting is, therefore, inscribed into an exceedingly difficult and complex response (*Antwort*) and responsibility (*Verantwortung*), and thus acts as part of how language imparts its pre-word (*Vorwort*) into signs.

This notion of letting (allowing) is certainly not equivalent to indifference; *au contraire*, it entails becoming involved and engaged. The compelling, unceasing letting indicated by the "there is," facilitates and makes possible (*Vermögen*), as Heidegger remarks in "Letter on Humanism," by enabling something to be as it is. "Thought in a more original way such favoring (*Mögen*) means to bestow essence as a gift [*Wesen schenken*]. Such favoring is the proper essence of enabling [*Vermögen*], which not only can achieve this or that but also can let something essentially unfold in its provenance, that is, let it be. It is on the 'strength' of such enabling by favoring that something is properly able to be. This enabling is what is properly 'possible' (*das Mögliche*), whose essence resides in favoring" (*BW*, 220).[15] Letting is compelling specifically and paradoxically as such a *Ver-mögen*, which unceasingly enables by rendering it possible (*möglich*) for something to be what it is. This enabling shows favoring and care, as it ceaselessly embraces in the elemental sense, that is, allowing and rendering possible as an element allows, say, breathing, flying, hearing, or seeing. This idiomatic sense of compelling as not ceasing (*Unablassen*) is how the clearing opens, "compelling" the movement of language to speech and writing. "To embrace a 'thing' or a 'person' in its essence means to love it, to favor it" (*BW*, 220). Highlighting the etymological links between *Mögen, Vermögen,* and *das Mögliche,* Heidegger explains letting (*Lassen*) as a kind of unceasing elemental enabling, which renders possible not simply because it is capable of it but does so instead out of favoring, as though caring for a being to be what it is in the span of possibilities open to it.

The idiomatic resonance of "letting" in Heidegger is crucial to understanding his critique of machination, power, and violence, as well as the possibility of a "rescuing" turn in the essence of technology. As enabling, *Lassen* is not just any kind of "making possible," which means that it is not just a revision of the idea of possibility. Beyond *potentia* and *existentia, Lassen* refers to rendering possible in the elemental sense described above, which remains compelling precisely in its unceasing futural momentum, in its specific way of "favoring" that brings about and holds open the time-space for potentiality and actuality. As Heidegger explains in *Four Seminars,* the giving that he emphasizes in his explanation of the event in "Time and Being" through the phrase *es gibt* (there is, it gives) needs to be understood precisely as this way of letting: "Perhaps one should sooner say, 'There is being' (*Es gibt Sein*), in the sense of 'it *lets* being' (*Es lässt Sein*)" (*FS,* 59). The English verb "to enable" used to translate the verb *Vermögen* contains the adjective "able" as its root, pointing toward the outcome of the act of enabling, to the fact that something or someone becomes "able" or is granted a certain possibility to be. Yet Heidegger joins enabling (*Vermögen*) not simply to the possible (*möglich*) but also to the favoring (*Mögen*), as that which does not let up in "rendering able." This favoring does not cause or lead to the enabling, which in turn would bring about a possibility; rather, as *Ver-mögen,* the favoring literally enables. This possibility, what has been enabled, is never simply the result of an act of enabling but instead is the essence as the occurrence (*Wesen*), as the very way in which letting unceasingly unfolds into letting be. Favoring, enabling, and the possible are not, therefore, three separate states or acts but three instances or vectors of the same momentum, of the same elemental and essential occurrence that Heidegger designates by the name "letting" (*Lassen*). Furthermore, as Heidegger explains, his notion of letting should not be mistaken for indifference or inactivity because it clearly involves "engagement" and concern, suggested by terms like liking or favoring.

This idiomatic understanding of the term *letting* is crucial to the movement of the word in Heidegger. In the way it lets be, the word becomes compelling specifically as setting the tenor, the *Stimmung,* according to which relations come to be formed and configured. Without being reducible to any affect, letting makes room—in the sense of opening the proper element—for all affects and moods. What outstrips language, what each time singularly overtakes signification, is precisely the clearing that being and its "word" open up, especially the unprethinkable amplitude of the possible. Describing the link between "word" and "being"—"*Unvordenkliches (Wort—Seyn)*" (*GA* 74, 108)—the term *unprethinkable* indicates the event's force to not cease in opening up the possible, which cannot be contained in the linear progression of time or in any signification, whether past or future. The unprethinkable is not a possibility, unrealized in the past, suddenly brought to life in the present, or one now still foreclosed but that could be actualized in the future. Rather, the unprethinkable refers to the event's unceasing momentum of letting be, to its continual clearing, whose way of disposing relations and beings remains "unprethinkable." The event's signature word is precisely unsayable in its singularity and unprethinkable in its one-time occurrence: "Language as the saying guards the event, it guards the un-sayable and the unprethinkable"—"Die Sprache als Sage wahrt das Ereignis, sie wahrt das Un-sägliche und Unvordenkliche" (*GA* 74, 112). The German *wahrt* in this quotation is used in a way that indicates that the guarding and securing at stake—the literal translation of *wahren*—have to do not with preserving or conserving without change but with having the saying keep or stay true (*wahr*) to the event, to the "truth" of its unprethinkable, and therefore never sayable, occurrence.

The pairing of the unprethinkable and the unsayable spells out the unceasingly "new," one-time and singular, letting be unfolding from the event. The unprethinkable remains unprethinkable because it unfolds each time only for a while, as Heidegger writes about it, for instance, in his description of the relation between thing and world in "The Thing": "The thing stays the fourfold. The thing things world. Each thing stays the fourfold into an each time just for a while onefold of the world" (*PLT,* 178, modified)—Das Ding verweilt das Geviert. Das Ding dingt Welt. Jedes Ding verweilt das Geviert in ein je Weiliges von Einfalt der Welt."[16] The last sentence employs inventively the verb *verweilen:* to abide, linger, sojourn, stay, which Heidegger uses as transitive in order to point out that the thing "stays" the world for a while, and thus holds or maintains it: the thing lets the world be a world for each time a singular and nonrepeatable while. Modifying the sense of "while" as a verb in English, one could say that the thing lets the world "while," that is, abide or linger awhile. To underscore the temporal singularity with which this "whiling" happens, Heidegger splits the German adjective *jeweilig* (respective; related to the adverb *jeweils:* in each case, at times) and invents a new substantive, *ein je Weiliges,* which indicates that the world happens as each time a singular, unprethinkable, "while." The one-time occurrence is poignantly indicated by the substantive Heidegger derives from *jeweilig: je Weiliges,* a "once whiling." It emphasizes the verbal happening, the "while" span of the clearing, the nonrepeatable "once" of its opening. The verbal inventions point to the fact that the while here is always each time, and that it is not to be miscategorized in terms of the singularity ascribed to beings or even to temporal moments, which come to be taken as beings of sorts. The one-time of the while is not a singular that can be differentiated from other instances, and repeated as it were in their differences, for opened in its own nihilative momentum, it never "is" in the manner permitting such ascription. The each time "singular" while at issue here is un(pre)thinkable in terms of the singularity of beings. Because the clearing and its world is *je Weiliges* in this manner, something each time only a while, it is also unprethinkable and in this sense unsayable (*unsäglich*). This unprethinkable extension of the "while" is what language strives to say—to let it linger along with signs—even though it remains unsayable in its each-time emergent singularity.

In *GA* 74, Heidegger discusses the clearing as both the while and the span, literally, the width (*Weite*) of the event, as he writes about "dwelling in the lingering span of the event"—"das Wohnen in der weilenden Weite des Ereignisses" (43). This "lingering span" is not mere uniformity of space and time, just as little as it is simple extension or movement.[17] In a characteristic gesture, Heidegger writes about the mirroring "whiling span" and the "spanning while," associating the lingering span with the rift in its depth and the spanning while with what he calls the height of the serene or the clear. (47) The serene (*Heitere*) inscribes the lightening, illuminating aspect of the clearing (*Lichtung*), and can be seen as the temporal momentum of the event. The rift's (*Riss*) span or width, which also bespeaks its depth, would then be the spatial momentum of the event's occurrence as language. The short text in which these remarks appear, titled "The Word," is perhaps the most puzzling of the several portions of *GA* 74, in part because it introduces terminology that adds to and complicates the terms known from other texts in which Heidegger discusses language, event, and the clearing. To my knowledge, however, "The Word" is the only text in which Heidegger expressly introduces sexual difference into his discussion of language, as he links the memory (*Gedächtnis*) of the lingering span, and thus of the spatial, with "woman," and the remembrance of the spanning while, with "man," so that these two aspects constitute the human essence (*Menschenwesen*) in its feminine and masculine articulations (*GA* 74, 48). While these designations are obviously and disappointingly conventional, an interesting aspect of Heidegger's formulation is that both the masculine and the feminine are never "pure" or "separate," but keep modifying each other: the while (masculine) always happens in the feminine key, so to speak, as a spanning while (*weitende Weile*), while the feminine spatiality unfolds as a *weilende Weite*, a "lingering span," modified with the masculine inflection of temporality. Though undeveloped, this reciprocal assignation of temporality and spatiality, masculinity and femininity, as the vectors of the way that the word makes into signs, indicate perhaps the site and the moment in Heidegger's account of language where the question of sexual difference could be drawn out and elaborated.

The notion of the unprethinkable in Heidegger is also crucially important for thinking yet more complexly about the notion of what is "proper" in the word according to Heidegger. "The *words*—properly, which means belonging to the event—appropriatively assigned from it"—"Die Worte— eigentlich, das heisst ins Ereignis gehörend—aus ihm zu-geeignet" (*GA* 74, 104). *Eigen*, or rather *eigen* as the verb describing the event in the momentum of its clearing, does not indicate simply possessing a proper, true essence or being endowed with constancy, with enduring properness and properties—all these assignations become possible on the level of beings. Inscribed into the hyphenated *er-eignen*, the proper does not lie in constancy or presence but rather in the compelling way in which the while and the span of the word outstrips (*überholen*) any standing presence, constancy, or essence. The "proper" of the word happens each time singularly and only one time, in the way in which being (in its sense of *Seyn*) has no other, as Heidegger remarks. As such it marks with its unprethinkable momentum any sense of presence and constancy (*Anwesenheit* and *Beständigkeit*), so important and 'proper' to the Western way of thinking. "The event-like essence of the word brings the clearing, into which what is eventuated (beings) arises in such manner that these beings are now for the first time delivered over into what is their own and the departed [*das Abschiedliche*] is announced over against the word. Language is the answer to the word"—"Das ereignishafte Wesen des Wortes bringt die Lichtung, in die das Ereignete (Seiende) ersteht dergestalt, dass dieses jetzt erst in sein Eigenes übereignet wird und das Abschiedliche gegenüber dem Wort ankündigt. Die Sprache ist die Antwort auf das Wort" (*GA* 74, 71). The word's disruptive entrance into language conceived as a sign system announces a twofold occurrence: the unfolded proper of beings and the departive momentum of the word withholding itself from signs. This two-fold disruption can be described as impartive and departive at the same time, where the withholding indicates precisely the "properly" unprethinkable of the event, which the word registers. The crucial point is that the "proper" is twofold, both imparted and de-parted in the same gesture, which means that it should never to be confused with the appropriated or misappropriated presence or essence. Gauging the proper requires maintaining its fold, that is, its singular and one-time outstripping of its own givenness or presence, its instance and repetition.

To underscore this point about the word and its "transpropriation" of beings, Heidegger at one point distinguishes between "the inceptual word" of being and "the transpropriated word" of language: "The word of beyng— the inceptual word / The word of language the *word* delivered into its own, which has to find itself in the jointure of terms"—"Das Wort des Seyns— das anfängliche Wort. / Das Wort der Sprache das übereignete *Wort, das* in das Gefüge der Wörter sich finden muss"(*GA* 74, 71). In this context, the word of being is described as distinct from the words of a language, since the word of being is inceptual, initializing the movement of language, while the word as it finds itself as a term in a language is no longer inceptual but transpropriated into word-signs: it becomes a "dictionary" word. Language is, therefore, not expression (*Ausdruck*) but response and responsibility (*Verantwortung*): an answer that enacts language's response in terms of what the word has trans-propriated into signs. This is why the word is not encapsulated or replicated by a language, by its dictionary words, but rather needs to be heard or scripted in its idiomatic departure from signs, perhaps in the shadows that the event's clearing or lightening (*Lichtung*) leaves in language. As inceptual the word opens the clearing, gives its free and proper reign, its "while" and "width," opening up and lighting the relays and relations within it. It is to this silent inceptual word that what Heidegger calls "the word of language," that is, the differential economy of signs, is transpropriated.

A few words are needed here about the sense of inceptuality that Heidegger associates with the event as word.[18] Heidegger employs the term *An-fang*, translated usually as "beginning" or sometimes as "inception," and differentiates it, often emphatically, from *Beginn:* a start or a mere beginning. *An-fang,* frequently hyphenated by Heidegger, does not indicate a temporal moment in which something starts or commences, the instant of genesis or beginning, but instead an opening into an initial, inceptual projective outline or capture, from the verb *fangen:* to capture, catch, seize; that is, a proleptic extension that gives the momentum to what is coming and thus catches it within the tonality set at and by the beginning (*An-fang*). When Heidegger writes about the origin of philosophy in ancient Greece and refers to it as "the first beginning," he does not mean simply the historical point of origin, a moment in the past in which the Occident "began," but the manner in which Greece is caught up in our thinking, continues to set the tone for it, and thus keeps catching up with it, as it were. The first beginning of thinking in ancient Greece has thus appropriated "Western" thought to its peculiar tonality of presence, idea, substance, and so on, which still resonate today through the key structuring terms of Western thought: representation, subject/object, essence, substance, presence/absence, and so forth. In this sense, Greece, though inescapably Latinized, keeps "beginning" over and over again; or, to put it differently, our thinking, no matter how changed, developed, evolved, or modern and distant from the first beginning, finds itself repeatedly claimed by its tonality. Hence Heidegger's investment in the possibility of the other beginning has to do crucially with a different tonality for thinking, and a transformed relation to language, which would breach the inceptual arrogation of the Greek beginning and possibly allow thinking to begin otherwise.

This notion of beginning, usually discussed in the context of the overcoming of metaphysics and the other beginning, gains its proper stature in Heidegger's thought only when it is seen with regard to the transformative role it plays in changing our relation to language, and, more specifically, in bringing out the play between words and signs. The metaphysical beginning has appropriated us in a relation to language seen as communication and information, information open to and even inviting manipulation or experimentation, which, however, does not transform the metaphysical tone in which we have come to experience language. To say that the event is the inceptual word is to suggest the initial and initializing outline of a saying, which the word brings into signs. "Die Sage ist selbst die Anfängnis des Anfangs. Sage bringt stimmend ins Wort (nicht Wörter) und erschweigt den Anfang"—"The saying is itself the inceptuality of the beginning. The saying brings the beginning dispositionally into words (not terms) and also silences the beginning" (GA 71, 297; E, 258, modified). The word is "inceptive" or "inceptual" precisely in the sense that it tonalizes or disposes (stimmt) language (by keeping reticent in words taken as signs the saying of the beginning): it gives the disposition to signs, grammar, signification, social and communicative functions, literary and philosophical uses, and so on. If the word in Heidegger's idiomatic sense is legible at all it is so only as the pitch, that is, as the silent saying, which it has imparted to signs, to human languages. And if the event is indeed the inceptual word, then what this means is that the event prompts and perhaps makes possible a transformation in our relation to language, the transformation beyond the tenor and tendencies of the first, metaphysical, beginning.

What is most crucial to bringing about this transformation is the displacement of the emphasis from the signs and meaning in order to, as Heidegger puts it: "Follow the hint of the word in the saying. / Avoid the pointing of the wordless terms."—"Folge im Sagen den Winken des Wortes. / Meide das Deuten der wortlosen Wörter" (*GA* 74, 53). To make his point, Heidegger goes as far as to modify the plural *Wörter,* word taken as signs or terms, with the adjective "wordless," in order to indicate how language, by focusing on the way in which signs point to and mean (*Deuten*), tends to evacuate the word's emergent, poietic momentum. When this momentum is obscured and forgotten, language presents itself as ripe for analysis based on the notion of the sign, that is, for an explanation in terms of meaning and, eventually, for the reduction of language to informational content. Heidegger's call to "avoid" the tendency of language signs or dictionary words (*Wörter*) to function as "wordless" and instead become attentive to the word's hints leads him to try and indicate, especially through several remarks dispersed in *GA* 74, the need and the possibility of a nonmetaphysical approach to the sign (*Zeichen*). Interestingly and importantly, however this approach differs in significant ways from Derrida's later deconstruction of the sign. Derrida brings to the fore and works through the differential instability of the signifier and the signified, and thus proceeds as it were from within the sign, in order to show how the constitutive difference between the signifier and the signified is already an effect of the trace working as *différance,* which means that it remains intrinsically, that is, differentially, unstable and repeatedly open to play. "It is not the question of a constituted difference here, but rather, before all determination of the content, of the *pure* movement which produces difference. *The (pure) trace is differance.*" And later, "*The trace is the differance* which opens appearance [*l'apparaître*] and signification."[19] Both the relation between the signifier and the signified as well as the sign's relation to its object are explained as parts of the spacing and temporalization of the différance understood as the originary production of difference. Heidegger's approach can be seen, by contrast, as bypassing this specific issue of the internal composition of the sign and its differential relation to other signs within *langue,* that is, within the language code or system, conceived by Derrida as part of the broader notion of writing, or arche-writing. The signifying and referential functions of the sign, one operating through the prism of the signifier/signified, the other relating the sign arbitrarily to what it designates and represents in the "external" reality, appear to be inscribed by Heidegger, though not discussed as such, into the doubling of *Deuten* in German, as both pointing (reference) and signifying (*Bedeuten*).

A separate study would be necessary in order to map more carefully the relation of Derrida's deconstruction of the sign to Heidegger's thought of language, especially to measure the extent to which Derrida's revision of the sign can and/or cannot be thought of in tandem with Heidegger's re-inscription of signification into the showing saying. As much is indicated by Bernasconi's analysis of "The Way to Language," in which he repeatedly points out the need to avoid forgetting the transformation of language at work in Heidegger's texts and the mistaken reinscription into them of "the metaphysical dualism of inside and outside. But the discussions of *Ereignis* and *a-letheia* which arise out of the transformation of the language of the his-tory of philosophy into the language of the history of Being have precisely the effect of rendering otiose the application of the two strategies to a discussion of what Heidegger understands by 'another beginning.' With the notions of 'another beginning' and 'another writing' Heidegger and Derrida have at-tempted to think the sense in which there is today both a changing of ground and a dissolution of the notion of ground."[20] While my analysis focuses on developing Heidegger's position, key issues to consider in such a compara-tive analysis, especially given Heidegger's critique of the notions of making and production, would be Derrida's notion of différance as the productive, spatiotemporal momentum of the unfolding of differences and Heidegger's idiomatic enveloping and transforming of difference through the event un-derstood as the play of nearness and remoteness. Furthermore, Derrida bases his understanding of writing and grammatology on the deconstruction of the notion of the sign and the reformulation of the role the sign plays in thinking and in the production of meaning: "From the moment that there is meaning, there are nothing but signs. We *think only in signs*."[21] Heidegger, on the other hand, focuses on the fold between words (*Worte*) and words taken as signs (*Wörter* or *Wörterzeichen*), exploring how poetic thinking thinks not only in signs but also, and primarily, in words. He opens thus the problematic of the inscription of signs in the poietic momentum of "the word 'of' beyng" (*Seyn*).

The Sign as Shown from the Word

Heidegger's explanation of the sign from the perspective of the originative showing (*Zeigen*) or showing saying in *On the Way to Language* is well-known. Disclosing their forgotten index of the "phenomenal" showing, Heidegger ex-plains signs in his published lectures and essays as deriving from the showing taken as pointing, which means that, since *Deuten* derives from *Zeigen,* both meaning and designation (*Bedeutung*) are "secondary" to the way language moves in showing. More precisely, they arise at the point of language's arrival into signs and thus can only point to the hints of the clearing that has instan-tiated and brought into motion the play of signification. In *Zum Wesen der*

Sprache und Zur Frage nach der Kunst, Heidegger offers numerous remarks on signs that try to wrestle them away from their metaphysical determination as *phone semantike* and to re-sonate their event-like momentum of the showing. The metaphysical delimitation of the sign holds to the determination of signs as things, that is, as sign-things (*Zeichendinge,* GA 74, 79). In this approach, "the sign is a sign for . . . and signifies. The essence of the showing remains undetermined, or else is constituted as re-presenting, indicating, pro-ducing for representation and comprehension"—"Das Zeichen ist Zeichen für . . . und bezeichnet. Das Wesen des Zeigens bleibt unbestimmt, oder aber es wird nur gefasst als Vor-stellen, Vor-zeichnen, Bei-bringen für das Vorstellen und Auffassen" (79). As a result, the sign is conceived as pointing to something and representing it to consciousness or the soul. Or else the sign is understood in terms of designation, where *Bezeichnen* is seen as *notare, insignare,* and *designare* (GA 74, 80).

To these metaphysical modes of conceptualizing the sign as *sema,* Heidegger counterposes the nonmetaphysical notion of the showing as originary and event-like, whose disclosive momentum can be explained neither as signifying nor as designation: "Das ereignishafte ursprüngliche Zeigen 'bezeichnet' nichts" (81)—"The event-like originary showing does not mean [or indicate] anything." In other words, the event-like showing is not determined as *Deuten* in its double sense of signifying and designating. As long as the sign is thought of in terms of signification or designation or both, and not in relation to the word and the event, the essential momentum of the sign, that is, its unfolding momentum (*Wesensmoment*), remains understood onesidedly, so that this one side does not simply continue to be privileged but is taken expressly as the only one that exists. Consequently, "the aletheically sheltering essence of the sign is not recognized"—"das alethetisch bergende Wesen des Zeichens [ist] nicht erkannt" (81). To attend to its forgotten aletheic origin, the sign needs to be recast in terms of the aletheic showing, which in turn should be thought of even more inceptually and with regard to the event: "Das Zeigen *alethetisch* und dieses noch anfänglicher als *entbergendes Bergen*—ereignishaft" (GA 74, 85)—"The showing *aletheically* and this even more inceptually as *unsheltering sheltering*—event-like." The showing (as saying, *Sage*) charts the way of language, within whose wake designation and signification come into play. This is why "*designation [Bezeichnen]* is something other than the inceptual showing, as is also signification [*Bedeuten*]"—"Das *Bezeichnen* etwas anderes als das anfängliche Zeigen, insgleichen das *Bedeuten*" (GA 74, 81). The showing, that is, the clearing in its spatiotemporal expanse, is subsumable to neither signification (meaning) nor reference, because it brings to word instead the disposition of relations (*Stimmung*) arising within the clearing. Displacing them into the showing, Heidegger points out that signs (*Zeichen*) must be thought of "in the inceptual sense of the event"— "Die Zeichen im anfänglichen Sinne des Ereignisses" (*GA* 74, 86).

In Heidegger the sign is not rethought through the differential play of the signifier and the signified or its function within the language system but instead recast as event-like, that is, as arising from the originative aletheic sheltering, both unconcealing and concealing, in the sense in which the true is only possible as the untrue. At the center of this radical reformulation of the sign is the critical reassessment of the ontological difference: when understood in terms of signification and designation (*Bedeuten* and *Bezeichnen*), the sign is predetermined in terms of beings and relations among them. Rethought from the event, the sign exhibits the pull that being exercises over language: "The event-like sign as the draw of beyng—not of beings"—"Das ereignishafte Zeichen als Zug des *Seyns*—nicht des Seienden" (81). Since signification and designation operate properly in relation to beings, they presuppose an understanding of being on which the notion of beings and their valence in various relations rely. Signification and designation, and therefore the sign in its metaphysical valence as well, all depend on the articulation or more often misarticulation of being through beings, that is, as beingness. Sign and signification, together with the differential play of the signifier and the signified function thanks to the metaphysical hypostatization of being into beingness (*Seiendheit*), which fails to recognize the ontological difference to begin with and thus blocks the possibility of raising the question of being.

Heidegger acknowledges in his remarks in *GA* 74 that his elaboration of the sign in *Being and Time* remains insufficient and hobbled by the notion of the sign as a being or thing. Consequently, *Being and Time* fails to elucidate the showing at work in the aletheic dimension of the sign: "Das Zeigen des Zeichendinges (Zeigzeugs) ist auch in "Sein und Zeit" kaum erläutert. Dieses besondere Zeigen hat sein Wesen im ereignishaften Zeigen, das in der Wahrheit des Seyns sich verbirgt" (*GA* 74, 84)—"The showing of the sign-thing (a showing tool) is hardly explained even in *Being and Time*. This peculiar showing has its essence in the event-like showing, which conceals itself in the truth of beyng." In other words, *Being and Time* does not link the sign to the event and thus misses the crucial, originary momentum of the sign as arising from the event-like showing. To address this problem in his previous and partial, or one-sided, though unfortunately often better known, approach to the sign, Heidegger declares that what is needed is not a new theory of the sign or signification but the thinking of signs as the footbridges or crossbars of the event. When the sign is thought of in its "masked event-like unfolding" (*das verhüllte ereignishafte Wesen der Zeichen*), then "these signs are the paths"—"Diese Zeichen sind die Stege" (*GA* 74, 82). We likely must wait for the publication of volume 72 of the *Gesamtausgabe,* titled *Stege des Ereignisses,* to see a more sustained development of this notion of the footpaths or bridges within the event and perhaps to get a better sense of how Heidegger links this idiomatic notion to the rethought idea of the sign. What Heidegger explains in volume 74 is that the sign thought via the showing exhibits the critical pull of being (*Seyn*), which means that the sign is not confined to the sphere of beings, where the notion of beingness continues to be the obstacle on the way to the *Seynsfrage* and to the event-like understanding of language.

To break the hold of metaphysics on the sign, Heidegger proposes to see the sign as event-like or event-related (*ereignishaft*) and to understand its momentum of showing "being-historically," rather than in terms of signification, designation, description, or representation. In some undeveloped remarks, Heidegger insists that, when thought of this way, the sign appears "*earth*-like" (Erd-*haftes*), yet this earth-like character is only "hinted at" (*er-wunken*) in the sign and never posited as an object (*GA* 74, 82). In metaphysics, "the sign appears native to differentiation and signification of the sensible and the nonsensible. Yet to think this way is to misunderstand the aletheic-event-like essence of the showing, and this misunderstanding finds its support in the sensible-intuitive character of the sign understood initially as a sign-thing"—"das Zeichen scheint in der Unterscheidung und Bezeichnung von Sinnlichem und Nichtsinnlichem beheimatet zu sein. Aber das zu meinen, ist eine Verkennung des alethetisch-ereignishaften Wesens des Zeigens, welche Verkennung im sinnlich-anschaulichen Charakter des zunächst gefassten Zeichendinges seine Stütze findet" (*GA* 74, 96).

Pointing to the distinction between the earth-like and the sensible, Heidegger seems to want to disrupt the obliteration of the being-historical unfolding of the sign and its traditional trapping into the sensible-nonsensible binary. The earth-like remains the indeterminable in the event-like sign, and this indetermination tends to close off the event of signs (*das Ereignis der Zeichen, GA* 74, 82), especially when it is explained in terms of the sensible and equated with the knowable actual. For the event of the sign is neither sensible nor intelligible strictly speaking, but instead opens up and initiates this very relation, thus allowing the sign to signify and designate. As Heidegger writes, "'the signs' are not existing objects that are used in the service of representing, producing and arranging / The signs eventuate—conduct, bring, tune"—"'Die Zeichen' sind nicht vorkommende Gegenstände, die verwendet werden im Dienst des Vorstellens, Herstellens und Einrichtens. / Die Zeichen er-eignen—geleiten, bringen, stimmen" (*GA* 74,

83). The objective-metaphysical explanation of signs as things (*Zeichendinge*) renders signs impossible to understand, as it covers over the aletheic showing instantiated by signs. Since "the originative word is the event-like showing" (*Das ursprüngliche Wort ist ereignishaftes Zeigen, GA* 74, 85), the sign understood as a thing or an object forecloses the possibility of experiencing the momentum proper to the word. The sign taken as an object is defined in terms of the play of the signifier and the signified, and is confined to how it represents, produces and organizes language through its functions of signifying and designating. The idea of the sign for Heidegger operates within the notion of beings understood as objects and thus reconfirms the forgetting of being.

By contrast, when rethought in this originative momentum, "the sign is guarded and kept within the essence of the word. / The word—the lightening soundless voice of beyng": "Das Zeichen, ursprünglich gedacht, ist im Wesen des Wortes verwahrt. / Das Wort—die lichtende lautlose Stimme des Seyns" (*GA* 74, 87). Counter to its semiological understanding, Heidegger radically redescribes the sign, inscribing it into the essential occurrence of the word. Here the sign occurs prior to signification, parallel with the word, and only in the last stage, so to speak, emerges as a sign-thing and thus as part of the sign system in the linguistic sense. Heidegger goes as far as to grant to the sign what he calls the parting or departed essence, writing about "Das abschiedliche Wesen des Zeichens" (*GA* 74, 88). This means that in its arrival as a sign-object, the sign also departs, that is, it is never completely captured by the play of signification or confined to its functions within language understood as a system of signs. As Heidegger puts it emphatically: "Das ereignishafte Zeichen 'bezeichnet' nie, das Zeigen der anfänglichen Zeichen 'präsentiert' nichts und 'repräsentiert' nicht; noch weniger ist es eine Chiffre, die nur sind, wo der Unterschied des Rationalen und Irrationalen ungemindert das Warheitswesen beherrscht" (*GA* 74, 89)—"The event-like sign never 'signifies,' the showing of the inceptual sign 'presents' nothing and does not 'represent'; even less is it a cipher, which only exist where the difference between the rational and the irrational dominates the essence of truth unmitigatedly."

This inscription of the sign within the event-like envelope of the word constitutes the pivot of the transformation of the relation to language. This transformation depends on the shift in the "meaning" of being from presence to departing, from *Anwesenheit* to *Abschied* (*GA* 74, 92). When being is experienced and thought of as presence or even as presencing, that is, as coming to presence, then the sign appears as "the metaphysical signum—presenting from the *presencing* into beings"—"das metaphysische signum—von der *Anwesenheit* her in das Seiende dar-stellend" (*GA* 74, 90). When being unconceals as the *Abschied,* that is, as the withholding and nihilation animating the event's clearing, then the sign can be allowed to emerge "as a *hint* and a glimpse into the abyss" and its non-ground: "als *Wink* in den Ab-grund" (*GA* 74, 90). This is the moment in which Heidegger re-links, over the history of metaphysics and its first beginning, the sign to the turn of the event: "Die Kehre—*das anfängliche Zeichen selbst*"—"The turn—*the inceptual sign itself*"(*GA* 74, 90). *Signum* relies on the notion of presence, bringing it about, as Derrida shows, in its unstable and never completely decidable play with absence. This link to presence and presencing is what indebts the sign—even though its value is an effect of differential play—to a being-like essence, thus holding the explanations of the sign hostage to the necessary forgetting of being as *Seyn*. By contrast, the *Abschied* or the departure reopens the being-historical resonance of the sign, holding it in proximity to the event and its word. The turn of the event opens the hyphen holding together the event's initial word (its An*wort*) with regard to the word of the answer (*Antwort*). This event-like sign "turns," and it turns the sign itself upside down, against its metaphysical delimitations. Before signifying or designating, the sign turns—or the event's turning makes a sign—giving the hint and imparting it to language. Yet this hint is imparted only as departive, as allowing the play of signification precisely by taking leave from it. "Every being, as soon as it is propriated and illuminated by being, is in a showing that is in the event"— "Jedes Seiende ist, sobald es im Sein als geeignet gelichtet ist, im Zeigen in das Ereignis" (*GA* 74, 89).

Thought event-like, the word lets be, spends itself in this giving, and never registers as a being; in other words, it can be neither present nor absent, because it is the opening up of presencing and thus also absencing. It is in this nonmetaphysical sense that the word "occurs" or "eventuates" the human being: "*Das Wort ereignet den Menschen*" (*GA* 74, 99). It does not represent (*Vorstellen*), produce (*Herstellen*) or organize (*Einrichten*) the human in its essence. What is decisive here is that the human being as it is eventuated and appropriated by the word is neither natural nor prelinguistic, and thus cannot be re-presented in language, nor, by contrast, is language simply the site of the construing or producing of the human. Neither constructed/performed nor immediate, the human comes to be by way of the word and its complex emergence. The conceptions relying on the notions of construction or those that, by contrast, invoke immediate experience, equally cover over the word under signs construed as *signum* and, forgetting *Seyn,* hold the human and the sign confined within the purview of beingness.

Perhaps a fitting conclusion to these remarks on the sign is a series of questions about word and sign that Heidegger raises in *GA* 74: "Are words

[*Worte*] signs? [*Zeichen*] / Are terms [*Wörter*] signs? / What is a sign? / How do we perceive the word? / Just the same we are not yet in possession of the origin of the essence either of the word or of the sign" (91). The German plays again between the two spellings of the plural "words," sounding and written nearly identically, and yet never simply different or separate. Signs are interlaced with words, sometimes almost to the point of merging, in order precisely to indicate their fold or default into terms, the way that *Worte* make into *Wörter*. The key here is that this way of the word may still be able to resonate in the dictionary words, if these words are thought of nonmetaphysically, that is, not by way of *phone semantike*, which grounds language in the human being, assigning priority to speech, writing, and signification. At issue is not a new definition or theory of the sign but the attempt to evolve a style of thinking that would be attentive to this nearness of *Worte* and *Wörter*, keeping them near without assimilating or separating them. Yet to be able to experience language signs in this nonmetaphysical manner, thinking must face what is possibly the most difficult challenge Heidegger spotlights, namely the inflection of difference through nearness.

This inflection can be espied precisely in the proximity between *Worte* and *Wörter*, whose nearness is also their apparently unbridgeable remoteness, since the sign conceived as *signum* remains far removed from the event's word. And yet Heidegger suggests that the sign in its fold as both *signum* and "the word 'of' being" is precisely the footbridge, the spoke, that holds the event in its each time distinct yet precise turning. The fold of nearness/ remoteness is how Heidegger proposes to inflect the ontological difference when he comes to the conclusion that, although necessary, the articulation of the question of being becomes blocked precisely through difference, as difference cannot really inscribe the nondifferential relation of *Seyn* to beings. This change, still too often overlooked in critical responses to Heidegger, is already made clear in 1936–38 in *Contributions to Philosophy,* where Heidegger critiques his initial posing of the question of being in terms of the ontological difference, because difference always involves beings and thus cannot avoid collapsing being (*Sein*) into beingness (*Seiende*):

> For, as necessary as the distinction is and even if it must be thought in terms of the tradition in order to create a very first horizon for the question of beyng [*Seyn*], it is just as fatal—since it indeed arises precisely from an inquiry into beings as such (beingness [*Seiendheit*]), and that path never leads immediately to the question of beyng. . . .
>
> Therefore, the task is not to surpass beings (transcendence) but, instead, to leap over this distinction and consequently over *transcendence* and to question inceptually out of beyng and truth. (*CP,* 197)

This passage decisively sets apart the task of inceptual, poetic thinking not just from phenomenology and transcendental thought but even from Heidegger's initial reformulation of the question of being in terms of the ontological difference. Here the ontological difference becomes recognized as a hindrance to the question of being, and not as an unproblematic access to it. What is required is a turn from the ontological difference to the event, which would leap over this distinction: *"first,* to bring this distinction to an initial clarity, and *then* to leap over that very distinction" (*CP,* 197). This revision renders "The concept of the 'ontological difference' merely preparatory, transitional" (*CP,* 203) and, as Heidegger adds, *verhängnisvoll:* fateful and disastrous, necessary and yet veiling and obscuring when it presents the question of being as the difference between being and beings, or as a difference to begin with.

Ontological difference becomes problematic for Heidegger because beings are neither different nor separable from "being"; rather, they are given to be by and from being as event, and are always and only experienced together with being. This means that beings are so near being (*Seyn*) that in fact their nondifferential closeness forces being's repeated miscognition as beingness (*Seiendheit*). And precisely because of this miscognition through the ontological difference, beings are also, paradoxically, exceedingly remote from *Seyn.* At the same time, this means that being is "unique" and alone, without the need for difference: "The simplicity of beyng [*Seyn*] is marked by *uniqueness.* This simplicity does not at all need to be set in relief and does not need differences, not even the difference from beings. For this difference is required only if being itself is branded a kind of being and thus is not at all preserved as the unique but is instead generalized into the most general" (*CP,* 371). This failure of the ontological difference to register the fold of nearness/ remoteness at play in the relation between being (*Seyn*), no longer considered metaphysically, and beings leaves a trace and thus affects the operations of difference as such. Since difference is unable to hold in view the *Einfalt* as the one-in-fold, forcing its separation into a onefold (unity, identity) and a fold (difference), Heidegger concludes that the ontological difference "is something transitional in the transition from the end of metaphysics to the other beginning" (*CP,* 369).

Nearness, or the Nondifferential of the Sign

Heidegger himself does not provide an explicit explanation of how the word's momentum contrasts with the differential economy of the sign. One way to approach this difficult question would be to draw into proximity the German notions of *Differenz* and *Unterschied*. It is worth noting that when Heidegger launches his inquiry into the question of being, he does so by writing about the ontological difference (*ontologische Differenz*), and when he decides to call the ontological difference into question and even put it aside, he turns to the Germanic term *Unterschied*, intimating the possibility of two distinct ways of thinking the initial unfolding into difference. Similarly, writing on the relation and the diffential play between identity and difference, he uses the term *Differenz*. In its distinction from *Differenz*, *Unterschied* can perhaps be understood as forming a fold in how one understands difference, that is, as constituting the difficult twofold of nearness and differentiation. Though mostly seen and functioning as difference, that is, in the same valence as *Differenz*, *Unterschied* also guards a nondifferential and non-identitarian momentum, which is brought out in terms such as the *Ab-grund* (the abyssal non-ground) and the *Ab-schied* (de-parture), that is, in the play of the prefix *ab-* that indicates parting, taking leave, and moving away.

This idiomatic critique of difference indicated in Heidegger's texts offers the possibility of evolving an account both distinct from and more "radical" than the one proposed by French post-structuralism and recent Continental thought. What I mean by "more radical" in this context is that Heidegger moves away from thinking difference on the model that would perhaps resemble the work of "différance" (destructured *Differenz*, with its Greek and Latin resonances) and places decidedly more emphasis on transforming the sense of the scission and of the between underscored by the German *Unterschied* toward a new oscillation of nearness and remoteness indicated by the term *Abschied*. Switching the focus among the prefixes from "*unter-*" to "*ab-*" opens a hitherto unexplored perspective on difference, in which difference is thought from being's withdrawal and its abyssal non-ground (*Abgrund*) with its characteristic retreat and refusal (*Ab-sagen*). The rethinking of difference (*Unterschied*) as de-parture (*Ab-schied*) indicates a sense of spacing that is nondifferential, and a distinct, nihilating and nonrecuperable pull marking being's withdrawal. The momentum of the *Abschied* is one of bidding farewell and taking leave, which puts the primary emphasis on non-return and non-repetition, that is, on the one-time occurrence, or on what I propose to call "the singular of nihilation." The parting here—before it can register as difference—is about this one-time occurrence (*Einmaligkeit*) of being, about its nonrepeatable "momentariness," brought about by the pull of nothingness, indicative of being's characteristic momentum of unfolding through a withdrawal. The singularization this nihilating pull instills as the momentary and unprethinkable, yet essential, occurrence of the event outstrips and folds the terms of difference. It changes the valence of singularity here, as Heidegger's *Einmalighkeit* can no longer be thought in difference from or in opposition to universality or generality. This is also the case because the back draft of the event, its way of refusing itself so that there can be beings, is nonetheless nondifferential with regard to beings: the event is never different from beings without for all that becoming ever identifiable with them. It is in the "time-space" cleared open by the withdrawal indicated in the German prefix "*ab-*" that any manifestation and signification of difference becomes possible to begin with, including the signification of the other.

What Derrida discusses, for instance in the essay "Différance," and what he ultimately inscribes in the overall production of différance, is the ontological difference (*Differenz*) as the difference between being and beings. Yet this difference, as Heidegger observes in a series of texts beginning with *Contributions to Philosophy,* is really the difference between beings and their beingness (*Seiendheit*), which fails to register and misnames the idiomatic relation of "beyng" (*Seyn*) to beings. The idiomatics of *Seyn* lies in its pull or draw (*Zug*) of withdrawal (*Entzug*) and departure (*Abschied*). Thus the way in which being (*Seyn*) gives to be by departing from what is given, that is, through its *Abschied,* is not a difference and does not arise strictly speaking from différance. Derrida would likely argue that any distinction or relation is referable to différance and thus constitutes a form of difference and must hence be thought of in differential terms. Heidegger, on the other hand, holds that to think the giving of beings from being (*Seyn*) as (ontological) difference, even as the most important, original, or minimal difference, neglects precisely the departive and nonrepeatable hint or intimation of *Seyn.* It thus inevitably metamorphoses being into beingness, so that being then equals beingness (*Sein = Seiendheit*) and the ontological difference functions as merely another difference between beings: on the one hand a being, and on the other hand its beingness conceived as something that "is" and hence "is" as a "being." Ontological difference still thinks of being as presencing (*Anwesenheit*); in fact, differential thinking cannot help but keep reverting to being as presence, thus continuing to forget that being as *Seyn* is the *Abschied.* Examining critically his initial formulation of the question of being, Heidegger eventually realizes that at issue in the *Seynsfrage* is in fact not difference but the giving by withdrawal, so to speak, in the wake of which, or more precisely in whose clearing, differentiation—including the ontological difference itself—comes into play. The back draft of the event becomes the projection of the ground for the ontological difference: "Such projection brings this questioning [of being] altogether outside of that difference between beings and being. This questioning therefore now even writes being as 'beyng," which is supposed to indicate that being is here no longer thought metaphysically" (*CP*, 344).

At first Heidegger expresses his own departure from the priority of (ontological) difference by distinguishing *Unter-Schied* from *Differenz*: while *Differenz* refers to differential relations and thinking in terms of identity and difference, *Unter-Schied* focuses on the scission and the parting. He discovers that this parting, especially the clearing brought out by being's withdrawal, as well as the relation of this characteristic departure to beings, must be thought of as other than difference and identity. For this purpose, Heidegger introduces the idiom of nearness (*Nähe*) and its reciprocal folding with remoteness (*Ferne*). Nearness happens as being's withdrawing draw, as its continuing pull on beings once being has always already retreated from them, and the implosion of its withdrawal continues to hold open the clearing. This retreat is available only as a hint, where the hint indicates the always singular giving to be that occurs through the withdrawal's clearing. This hint is singular in the sense of occurring only one time (*eimalig*).

The crucial question here is whether the oscillation between nearness and remoteness can be folded into the différance and perhaps be seen as another effect of différance itself. Heidegger would disagree, I think, as nearness for him is the momentum of giving within the event, from which difference unfolds to begin with. Highlighting *Unter-Schied* and juxtaposing it against *Differenz* brings attention to the root *Schied*, that is, to the scission and the parting that initialize differing. In *Über den Anfang*, Heidegger coins the term *Schiednis*, which could perhaps be seen as a forerunner to "différance." *Schiednis* could be approximately rendered into English as *parted-ness*, referring to the instance of the originative fissuring or riving, from whose initial impulse differentiation receives its impetus, turning into the engine of differentiation, so to speak.[22] The initial hyphenation of the *Unter-Schied* highlights the *Schied* (scission) and allows it to be demarcated and eventually turned into the *Schiednis* to underscore the active, generating momentum of the *Schied-nis* over against the notion of a "settled" or decided difference, *Schied*. *Schiednis* thus designates the unfolding and spacing out of difference, testifying to the fact that Heidegger's primary interest lies less in difference than in what makes difference and relation possible in the first place.

This is confirmed by Heidegger's shift to thinking eventually of the *Unter-Schied* by way of the *Abschied*, of departure, and not *Differenz*, or difference. This point is crucial to understanding Heidegger's own critique of the ontological difference and to resituating difference and differential thought within the fold of nearness/remoteness. This shift is signaled, as is usual in Heidegger, less through explicit statements or descriptions and more through the turn from one prefix to another, in this specific case from *unter-* to *ab-*. *Unter-* indicates the cut and the scission that open and hold together mutually differentiating and differentiated elements, and can thus be linked to English prefixes such as *inter-* or *infra-*, which would signal that the German *unter-* indicates the spacing and temporalization proper to difference. By contrast, the prefix *ab-* conveys the movement away and apart, freeing and loosening away, as in departure. Again in *Über den Anfang*, Heidegger makes clear the stakes of this departure when he puts as the title of one section the remark that "the overcoming of metaphysics is the abandoning of difference *(departure)"—*"Die Überwindung der Metaphysik ist das Verlassen der Unterscheidung *(Abschied)"* (*GA* 70, 77). Through this abandonment (*Verlassen*), difference becomes dis-grounded or released from grounding (*entgründet*), whereby the possibility and the necessity of grounding, that is, of grounding by reference to a being or to beingness are both withdrawn. As Heidegger explains, "the abandoning [letting aside, *Verlassen*] is no longer agreeing to the priority of beings and to any secondariness whatsoever, secondariness of being as beingness, however this be formulated in its various metaphysico-historical permutations"—"Das Verlassen ist das Sichnichtmehr-einlassen auf den Vorrang des Seienden und die wie immer geartete Nachträglichkeit des Seins als der Seiendheit in ihren mannigfachen metaphysikgeschichtlichen Abwandlungen" (*GA* 70, 78). At issue is, on the one hand, recognizing the way in which difference is always disposed and tuned by the unfolding of being (*GA* 70, 79), and, on the other, understanding being's necessary and continued falling into (*Ein-fall*) beings and beingness. This means that the thought of difference within metaphysics as well as the attempt to ground metaphysics in difference continue within the tonality (*Stimmung*) imparted in the first beginning, which has difference unfold in terms of the underlying collapse of being into beingness. This is why the transformation of the relation to language, which finally recognizes the role that *Stimmung* plays in (differential) thinking, is indispensable to this rethinking of difference. What marks all differences and the working of difference itself, that is, of the *Schiednis,* is the overlooked and forgotten hint of being's "collapse" as beingness into (in)difference from beings. In other words, difference as we have come to know it unfolds from the collapse of being's distinctness from beings, which constitutes the inceptual, metaphysical disposition of thought. The forsaking (*Verlassen*) of difference means that "difference is not erased. It is, however, essentially transformed"—"Der Unterschied wird nicht ausgelöscht. Aber er wandelt sich wesentlich" (*GA* 70, 80).

More concretely, this change means that the *Unterschied* and thus differentiation come to be thought of from the *Abschied* and not from the Greek sense of *diapherein*. In *Das Ereignis*, Heidegger twice remarks that what needs to be resolved and decided with regard to difference (*Unterschied*) is precisely the saying of how thought can be twisted free of difference and directed toward the notion of the departure. "Die Verwindung des Unterschieds in den Abschied"—"The twisting free of the difference into the departure" (*GA* 71, 126/*E*, 107). "Der Austrag ist die Sage der Verwindung des Unterschieds in den Abschied"—"The discharge is the saying of the twisting free of the difference into the departure" (*GA* 71, 256; *E*, 221, modified). *Austrag* can mean settlement, decision, discharge, or resolution, yet the emphasis in Heidegger falls on the process of carrying or drawing out this decision, which leads me to opt for translating the term in this context as "discharge." For what matters is how thought and difference are discharged in the process of this transformation, whereby the discharged thinking comes out of, yet also pulls away from, metaphysics. As Heidegger explains, this notion of de-parture (*Ab-schied*) implies nothing negative, because it is precisely as the *Abschied* that the event begins, in the sense of the *Anfang*. What is more, "language originates from the departure. / Language answers the beginning. / The cor-responding is double."—"Die Sprache entstammt dem Abschied. / Die Sprache antwortet dem Anfang. / Die Ent-sprechung ist zwiefach" (*GA* 70, 25). The *Abschied* in the specific sense elaborated by Heidegger does not denote ending or ceasing but rather the "last" (*Letzte*) of the inception, that is, its retreat into itself that inaugurates the inceptuality of what begins. "The 'ultimate' of the beginning is only the inceptuality of what is 'first,' that is, of the sheltering"—"Das 'Letzte' des Anfangs ist nur die Anfänglichkeit seines Ersten, d. h. der Verbergung" (*GA* 70, 26). It is this inceptual de-parting that opens language and, as Heidegger remarks in the later essay "Language," allows dif-ference (*Unter-schied*) to emerge. Thus difference is to be thought of inceptually from the de-partive opening and movement along the pathways of language. Approached in this manner, difference is always enveloped and inflected by the singular nihilation in being, which marks its nearness to beings precisely by remaining remote. This transformed difference would be not "only" deconstructed difference but difference altered through the departive withdrawal's inceptual nearness, nearness yet and still unthinkable as difference. Heidegger's reflection on language, specifically on the fold of words and dictionary words (signs) that enacts this crucial play of nearness/remoteness, holds thus the key to his critique of difference and to the transformation requisite for the possibility of the other beginning.

This transformation is presented graphically by Heidegger in *Über den Anfang:*

> Das Sein ist der Unterschied.
>   – Unterschied
>   Schiednis
>   Er-eignis
>   Anfang
>   Untergang
>   – Abschied
>   Der Abschied des "ist." (*GA* 70, 35)

"Being is difference. /– difference / partedness / e-vent / inception / decline /– departure / The departure of 'is.'" This graphing of the transformation begins with the notion of being as difference and proceeds by transforming *Unterschied* into *Schiednis*. It is only with *Schiednis* that the *Er-eignis* or the event makes its appearance as the pivot that takes us away from difference, moving through inception and decline to the *Abschied,* or to the character-istic way in which the "is" takes its leave from beings. *Untergang* seems to mean here not downfall or ruin but instead going under as going into the between (*unter*) of difference in order to come to the originative momentum of the de-parting. This graph provides also the illustration of the "turning" of the event, which has always already arrived into difference but, through the attentiveness of thinking, can be seen to have already (re)turned from the *Abschied* through the *Schiednis* to the *Unterschied,* or to difference. This is what Heidegger may mean by the circularity of the event, by its pivoting from the *Abschied* simultaneously, in the same movement, *to* and *away* from differ-ence. In this way, the departure (*Abschied*) appears overwritten by difference while at the same time "underwriting" difference, though it does so in a very peculiar manner, namely through the hint of its taking leave, its withdrawal or parting. It is by such de-parting that the *Abschied* parts and imparts (in the sense of *Schiednis*) difference (*Unterschied*), each time singularly and one time. The *Abschied* imparts the parting—as the movement of differentia-tion—while departing from the difference it allows to arise. As Heidegger clearly states it, "The essence of difference is not differing, but the essence of differing is difference as departure"—"Das Wesen des Unterschiedes ist nicht die Unterscheidung, sondern das Wesen der Unterscheidung ist der Unter-schied als Abschied" (*GA* 70, 73). Thinking of Heidegger's recasting of *Wesen* as essential unfolding or occurrence, we see that what influences difference, that is, what disposes and pervades it through and through, in the sense of *Durchstimmung,* is the *Abschied.* To underscore this point, Heidegger places a similar graph to the one discussed above a page later in *Über den Anfang,* again literally having the *Abschied* underwrite it, with the graph pointing specifically to the differing, *Unterscheidung* (see *GA* 70, 36).

The most difficult and continuously to be recalled aspect of Heidegger's recasting of the *Ab-schied* comes out through its relation to the *Ab-grund,* or the abyss of non-ground. Just as the *Ab-grund* is not the negation of ground but rather a freeing and a loosening away from grounding altogether, the *Ab-schied* is to be read less literally as departure or leave-taking than as a freeing from the *Schied* and thus from—and in the same gesture also for—scission and differing. Freeing does not mean, as Heidegger makes clear, obliterating or erasing difference in order to assert unity or homogeneity but rather a turning and a twisting of difference itself, which permits leaving it aside (*Verlassen*). What I read as the boldest moment in Heidegger's thought is indeed marked by the prefix *ab-* and its loosening of the grip of difference (and identity, unity, totality, etc.) on thought. Even in the translation, especially when de-parting is hyphenated, the term brings into the open the specific resonance neither of simply parting nor of canceling this parting, both held between the English prefix *de-* that signifies leave taking and, in the same gesture, the undoing of this very partition. Without the double momentum of that prefix and its peculiar inflection of difference, the event does not register as the *Er-eignis.* It is important again to underscore here the significance of the way Heidegger *writes* the transformation he tries to prepare in thinking through prefixes and the introduction of abundant hyphenation. This ubiquitous hyphenation comes to signify a paradoxical reversal whereby the normally more important root part of the word cedes priority to prefixes in a way that, I would argue, comes to write in Heidegger's texts the critical departure from beings (root, meaning, essence) and signals the redirecting of thought to the withdrawal of being. The fact that this writing is intrinsically topographic is confirmed by Heidegger's statement: "Das Da-sein als die Ortschaft des Anfangs und der Abschied"(*GA* 70, 99)—"The there-being as the localization of the beginning and the departure."

When constellated together, the distinctions between *Differenz, Unterschied,* and *Schiednis* in Heidegger's work spell out the possibility of a critique of difference, one that, by contrast with Derrida's deconstruction of metaphysics and Heidegger's own initial *Destruktion* of the question of being and the subject, evinces a nonmetaphysical view of difference, that is, difference rethought with a specific regard to nearness: nearness overwritten by difference, yet nonetheless speaking through it, hinting in the way in which the word hints as though from within the sign, from its "dictionary" form and usage. This entwined momentum of difference unfolding within yet overshadowing and forgetting nearness is reflected in the play of the hint and the trace Heidegger develops in *Mindfulness*. If the economy of difference works through traces, than the de-parting characteristic of being in its nonmetaphysical resonance leaves, by contrast, only a hint. Writing about *Seyn*, Heidegger declares: "What raises no claim, is trace-less (*Spur-lose*) and powerless (*Macht-lose*), is hardly credible to the representation that knows only beings. And when such representation concedes that 'the claim-,' 'the trace-,' and "the power-less' *is*, representation must assess it right away as what is feeble and nothing and thus lacks what distinguishes beings as the actual (the effective)" (*M*, 178). Disengaging being (*Seyn*) from power, Heidegger concludes that only beings can leave a trace (*Spur*), while being remains trace-free. Seen from this perspective, the differential thought of the trace appears to remain anchored in the thought of beings and, consequently, in the miscognition of being as beingness. By contrast, *Seyn* for Heidegger is power-free, released and unencumbered by power, because, as he remarks on several occasions, being's event has no need of power (it is *machtunbedürftig*). In other words, being means trace-less and power-free letting be. Crucially for our deliberations here, this trace-less letting be remains unthinkable and unrecognized without attention to the continuous fold of *Worte* in *Wörter*, that is, without the transformation of our relation to language. This transformation is necessary since "letting be" appears to lack "actuality," to be "feeble," because the fact that it does not need power is miscognized as lack of power. This is why this trace-less essential occurrence of being finally seems to be "nothing," understood negatively as the absence of any beings and thus as a void or a nullity. Yet Heidegger's formulation in *Mindfulness* reverses these connotations, taking them away from binary and oppositional thought so that the apparently power-less means not the absence of power but freedom from power (the suffix -*los*, indicating here release in the sense that becomes crucial to the notion of *Gelassenheit*: releasement). Similarly the trace-lessness is not ineffectiveness or inexistence, so weak and powerless that it cannot even leave a trace, but instead the nobility (*Würde*) and gentleness (*Milde*) of letting be that forsakes (*Verlassen*) "marking" or "tracing."

Though Heidegger does not go in this direction, these remarks suggest that traces are always effects of existent beings and of power, in the sense that they underwrite the production and effectuation of what becomes different. Traces are traces of (other) beings, while being's departing is never a being and therefore "nothingness" (*Nichtigkeit*), which in its momentum of nihilation (*Nichtung*) leaves only a hint, much fainter and less legible than a trace. "But beyng [*Seyn*] never leaves a trace in beings. Beyng is the trace-less; is never to be found among beings as a being" (*M*, 178). If the trace is a trace of a being, then the hint is not a hint "of" anything but rather a hint "into" nothingness. As Heidegger describes it, "It would be a hint into the refusal that as such gifts itself seldom to man so that his ownmost reaches out into the belongingness to beyng and finds therein the supreme necessities . . ." (*M*, 193). It is precisely because being unfolds as trace-less and power-less—as free from power and its traces—that makes possible its unique allotment, each time singular and one-time (*M*, 176).

If differentiation proceeds by leaving traces, difficult as they sometimes are to detect and read, nearness in its fold into remoteness characteristic of the *Abschied* allows merely a hint, even more fragile than a trace because never arising from being marked by a being. To try to explain this hint left by the freeing withdrawal of being—freeing in the sense of opening up into the clearing—Heidegger deploys in numerous contexts, beginning with *Contributions to Philosophy* and *Mindfulness,* the play of nearness and remoteness. As he indicates in *Mindfulness,* "nearness and remoteness are not measures, and above all, not measures for the spatio-temporal determinations of distances, but the essential occurrences [*Wesungen*] of beyng itself and its clearing. This clearing lends an openness to the familiar 'space' and the usual 'time' . . ." (*M*, 97, modified). Once grasped as pertaining to distance or to temporal spacing, nearness and remoteness become leveled into numerical and quantitative differences and their singular momentum disappears. Heidegger explains that both nearness and remoteness are to be thought of with regard to the *Abgrund,* that is, with a view to displacing the need or necessity of grounding. As he puts it, "Nearness is the abyss of remoteness, and remoteness is the abyss of nearness. Both are the same: the abyss of the clearing of beyng." And later on the same page, "Nearness and remoteness belong to the clearing of beyng as event" (*M*, 97, modified). These remarks make evident that nearness/remoteness become Heidegger's terms for sketching the unfolding of the clearing from the event precipitated by the event's characteristic departure; they are, in fact, the way the clearing becomes instantiated through the event's back draft. They are the "same," which in Heidegger's idiom means that they are neither identical nor different but instead folded into each other in the manner of the *Einfalt:* of the simplicity of the one-in-fold. As we know from Heidegger, the simple is, however, what is most difficult to think, since it requires thinking both from and through the turn of the event, its imparting to and departing from difference in the same turn of the phrase, as it were. The simple calls for thinking nearness/remoteness on the one hand as already translated or faulted into spacing and temporalization, into the "distantial" (*Abstandhafte*) implied by any and all differentiation, and, on the other, it requires turning the distantial back toward the abyssal non-ground of the event. If not turned again toward the abyssal non-ground, nearness and remoteness remain caught in the distantial, which allows for calculability and machination. "In their one/infold [*Einfalt*] that holds unto the abyss [*Abgrund*], nearness and remoteness are the 'resonating in-between' of all countering and the limits—held unto the abyss—of all blending that is needed by calculation and machination" (*M*, 98). These remarks suggest that Heidegger crucially thinks of the in-between in a double sense: on the one hand, by way of difference and its spatiotemporal distancing and parting, where the between is thought of from the traversal of a distance implied in the Greek *diapherein;* and, on the other, through the infold of nearness and remoteness as non-distantial, whereby both unfold from the departure, even while their play continues to proliferate the differential parting. The differential in-between parts and parses out, opening a distance. Here the distance, the *Abstand,* is (en)countered by the *Abschied,* where in one case the momentum of nearness/remoteness becomes differed into a distance and in the second it remains in their distance-less *Einfalt.* In a way, nearness/remoteness can be thought of as this refusal of the distantial (*Abstandhafte*) and thus as a withdrawal from the differential and with it from the identitarian, which both come into the picture at the same time.

In this context, Heidegger's claim that "Nearness and remoteness are the preserve [*Bewahrung*] of the refusal as the highest gifting" (*M*, 98) can make sense. The highest donation is precisely the refusal characteristic of the non-distantial infold of nearness and remoteness, its withholding itself form the distantial economy of differentiation and its spatial and temporal instances, which it nonetheless makes possible. What Heidegger here calls, rather bombastically, the highest bestowal or beneficence concerns the momentum of nihilation that each time singularly and one-time, hence unprethinkably, gives to be. What is thus imparted or given away (*Verschenkung,* translated in *Mindfulness* as *gifting*) is the possibility of the new, the possibilization implied when Heidegger refers to being as "the quiet force of the possible." It is the nearness of this quiet force in its very refusal to (be)come as a being, which grants the existence of what is. Nearness means specifically the way in which beings could not be without (having been given by) being. This nearness is closer than any minimal distance or difference, because it is not in any way separate or separable from beings; it is, in fact, non-distantial and non-differential without being either identical to or identifiable with beings. Because being is not "distantial" (*Abstandhafte*) in relation to beings, it can be neither different nor identical to them. But this is why it is also the most remote from beings, in the sense that being, as Heidegger reminds the reader and himself on numerous occasions, cannot be envisioned with regard to beings, just as it keeps its distance from the logic of identity and difference.

Being is remote from beings precisely by virtue of being the nearest to them, much nearer than any other and different beings can ever be. *No being can be as near to another being as being (*Seyn*) comes to it in letting this being be.* And yet this also means that being (*Seyn*) remains *farthest from what it lets be,* because it cannot ever be approached as a being. This is the way in which nearness and remoteness are each other's *Abgrund,* neither different nor not different, remoteness lost in the nearest nearness, nearness opening the farthest remoteness, without ever opening a distance or becoming different. Yet what this non-distantial, neither differential nor identitarian de-parting gives, is precisely the ability to differentiate, to experience beings and their relations, their spatiotemporal configurations and its changes.

As "The Essence of Language" makes evident, this sense of nearness is also how Heidegger proposes to understand the saying in its way into signs: "der Einblick ... inwiefern die Nähe und die Sage als das Wesende der Sprache das Selbe sind"—"an insight as to what extent the nearness and the saying, as what essentially occurs in language, are the same" (*GA* 12, 202–203; *OWL,* 107, modified). The saying in its arrival into signs marks the "way-making," as which language occurs each time only one-time. The way of language is the en-countering of the world as the fourfold, which comes to be described as the eventuation of nearness: "Die Be-wëgung des Gegen-einander-über im Welt-Geviert ereignet Nähe, *ist* die Nähe als die Nahnis"—"The way-making of the face-to-face with one another in the world-fourfold eventuates nearness, *is* the nearness as nighness" (*GA* 12, 202; *OWL,* 106, modified). Nearness is the way of language in which the elements of the world, its fourfold, face each other, without being either a unity or an assemblage of four separate items. Nearness occurs as the way in which these elements say themselves precisely as folds in the fourfold, as existing through each other. But it is also nearness in the sense in which, as these four are given, that which lets them be does so precisely by withholding itself, while keeping near—and nearly "identical" to them—in its departed remoteness. Nearness constitutes the way in which "the event comes to word," the way in which its turn forms the nonmetaphysical unfolding of the sign, irreducible to the sign-as-thing and the play of signification. As nearness, language is the saying through which the world's fourfold emerges, and in this sense it constitutes the relation of all relations. This relationality of all relations is not difference (*Unterschied*) but nearness, which in its *Abschied,* remains remote from—by virtue of being nearest to it—what it allows to come into the open. "The saying gathers everything as the way-making of the world-fourfold into the nearness of their face-to-face and indeed does so soundlessly, as quietly as time times, space spaces, as quietly as the play of time-space plays"—"Die Sage versammelt als das Be-wëgende des Weltgeviertes alles in die Nähe des Gegen-einander-über und zwar lautlos, so still wie die Zeit zeitigt, der Raum räumt, so still, wie der Zeit-Spiel-Raum spielt" (*OWL*, 108, modified; *GA* 12, 203). The word's way into signs is not a differential movement per se, though it unfolds words-as-signs (*Wörter*) in their differential play. The word "nears" the world, it says the world in *being* the nearness of its fourfold. In other words, nearness marks the remoteness of the "is" from any and all beings, while providing the momentum for holding in relation all that comes to be by way of the play of the world. Nearness is the actuation of the word, which in its de-parting from the sign "is" lets signs make sense.

Heidegger's approach to the sign is neither structuralist nor post-structuralist, offering instead a unique account of the poietic force of language. As he suggests, except for a brief and quickly occluded moment in ancient Greece, such an understanding of the sign has never been developed in the course of Western thought. This is why the sign as Heidegger envisions it remains to be experienced precisely in its event-like, poietic force of emergence—but this possibility hinges on the transformation of our relation to language, especially to the silent marking of the event-like word within the play of linguistic signs. Because of the distinct way in which Heidegger rethinks the sign by folding it back into the word, this account is important beyond the question of language. And it is so especially because the relation between words and signs—the nearness of *Worte* and *Wörter*—figures Heidegger's most important and radical critique of difference. Since "nearness" charts the way in which Heidegger rethinks difference, and with it, the entire question of being, the transformation in our relation to language assumes the pivotal role in Heidegger's thought after *Contributions to Philosophy*. The unprethinkable manner in which "the event comes to word," having its words unfold into signs and meaning, points toward a thinking that proceeds by way of an intrinsic openness to what it cannot predict or fore-think, like the possible vectors of transformation within the essence of technology, which Heidegger indicates by claiming that the essence of technology is double-headed like the god Janus, pointing in both directions at once. To understand technology and perhaps disclose the potential for a turn within it, it is not enough to diagnose its provenance or to critique its operations, but it is necessary to turn it away from machination and planning toward what cannot be fore-thought, and, what is more, to make the unforethinkable the "measure" for thought instead of its obsession with planning, control, and machination. If thought can be attentive to it, the way in which words for Heidegger are both concealed and sheltered in signs may hold open, each time anew, the possibility not only of a critical distance but also of a transformative shift in experience. Since language is the relation of all relations, a transformation in our relation to it would entail a critical change in how the relatedness configured as world happens, affecting our role and actions within it. This is no longer simply a linguistic turn or a critique of metaphysics but, if the event indeed occurs by coming to word, this could be a turn—via the turn of the Janus-head of the essence of technology—of the world, through which human beings can become, from the first and for the first time, attentive to being as event. Changing their relation to language, humans can perhaps come to think and to be differently, no longer entirely pre-formed or bound by metaphysical precepts about language, experience, and thought.

THREE

Poetry and the Poietic

The Poietic Momentum of Language

It is common knowledge that Heidegger's growing interest in Hölderlin's poetry in the 1930s became one of the factors strongly contributing, together with reflections on Nietzsche and the critique of power, to the significant change in Heidegger's understanding of the *Seynsfrage* and with it also of language, poetry, and art. Heidegger's approach to poetry and art is quite idiomatic, as "The Origin of the Work of Art" makes amply evident, since he is not concerned with classification, historical developments, or theories of art but instead specifically with what can be called the poietic momentum of language and art. This poietic force is to be thought idiomatically as *Dichtung,* which does not refer specifically to verse, poetry, or literature, but instead indicates the inventive momentum of artworks. Although *Dichtung* is a term commonly used to refer to poetry or more broadly to literature in general, Heidegger at the same time limits its scope to the poietic and disengages it from simply designating literary production, so that he comes to understand it in terms of *dictare, dicere,* and *deiknumi* as a specific manner of manifestation through saying and as saying.[1] This is why *Dichtung* can characterize any type of art, and not only language arts or poetic composition, just as it can also come to the fore in thought or in philosophical writing. In this idiomatic use, *Dichtung* refers to the poietic register of language, which comes to be disclosed in a special, transformed relation to language. For Heidegger this register is indeed most poignant and evident in poetic works but pertains as well to painting, architecture, or music. Though this sense of the poietic becomes more visible in the later writings, it is at issue in the call for transforming our relation to language articulated for the first time in *Contributions to*

Philosophy and becomes therefore associated with the critical turn Heidegger introduces into the question of being in the 1930s. *Dichtung* is linked directly to the notion of the saying (*Sage*) and thus to the broader notion of language as the "way-making," where language is not limited to the "narrower" sense of human speech and writing, which would circumscribe the poietic simply to language works or texts, whether literary or philosophical. Because language occurs as the saying (words) on its way to signs, and because the word is not originally a sign and thus not part of language as a code, words—*Worte* in their distinction from *Wörter*—can resonate poietically also in artworks that have nothing explicitly to do with language or linguistic signs, for instance, in architecture or music.

Heidegger himself writes expressly about the poietic, *poietisch,* only on a couple of occasions, perhaps most significantly in "The Question Concerning Technology." The term in its German spelling, *poietisch,* obviously reworks the Greek notion of *poiesis,* estranging it away from its customary sense of making or producing and establishing its primary link to *Dichtung* taken as the poietic momentum of language. Indeed, the term *poietic* should be understood with regard to the significance of *dichterisch* (poetic), used much more frequently by Heidegger in his texts about poetry and in particular with reference to the notion of poetic dwelling developed from Hölderlin's writings. This sense of the poietic in fact comes to serve as the lens for a stringent critique of production (*herstellen*), making (*machen*), and power (*Macht*), and their gathered force that Heidegger encodes into the term *Ge-stell,* enframing or com-positing, understood as the technological revealing that comes to hold sway in modernity. As the essence of technology shaping modern existence, the *Gestell* becomes the foil for Heidegger's attempt to think the poietic specifically as that dimension of being and of language which remains free, released from power. This dimension can reveal itself in a modality distinct from what Heidegger describes as the technic revealing, or the *Gestell* as the "essence" (*Wesen*) of technology. Rather than being simply linked to art or poetry, the poietic—delineating here the scope of the resonance Heidegger imparts to a cluster of terms such as *Dichtung, das Dichterische, poietisch*—becomes critical to the notion of the *Seynsfrage,* as it comes to map the turn intrinsic to the event and the way the event comes to word.

It is with respect to the notion of the poietic that I venture most significantly beyond the scope of Heidegger's work. Heidegger develops many of his comments on poetry primarily through his engagement with Hölderlin, which means that his own language and thinking remain most often implicated, if not invested, in Hölderlin's Romantic rhetoric. This is reflected crucially in Heidegger's discussion of the fourfold, the relation between mortals and immortals, and the problematic of gods and the "last god." The encounter with Hölderlin and its broad influence on Heidegger's subsequent thought also seems to shape Heidegger's interest in predominantly neo-romantic poets, Rilke, Trakl, and George, perhaps with the exception of a short text on Rimbaud or Heidegger's reported admiration for the more experimental poetry of Celan. Though thematically limited largely to the German literary and artistic context, Heidegger's remarks on the poietic in art and language, especially because of his own inventiveness and radical use of German, far outstrip in their implications his own statements about poetry or the parameters of Hölderlin's rhetoric, formative to many of Heidegger's essays on poetry. I have examined these issues, including Heidegger's debt to Hölderlin or the significance of his notion of the poietic for modern poetry, art, and aesthetics, in my previous books and essays.[2] In this study I elaborate instead the role that the poietic plays in Heidegger's *own* writing, in his style of thinking, especially how it motivates his use of German with regard to his declared attempt to transform our relation to language. To this effect and given the large existing literature on the topics mentioned above, especially Heidegger's relation to Hölderlin, I forego here discussion of Heidegger's readings of artworks and commentaries on poetry. I would like to address only one specific issue that has the most significant impact on developing the notion of the poietic beyond Heidegger's thought, namely its relation to what Heidegger calls the end of metaphysics and to its direct correlative—the end of art.

Heidegger makes his quite radical comments about the end of art in two works from the late 1930s and early 1940s, following his "The Origin of the Work of Art": *Metaphysik und Nihilismus* (*GA 67*) and *Über den Anfang* (*GA 70*). In *GA 70*, he goes so far as to expressly define the saying as inceptual *Dichtung*: "Diese Sage aber sagt nichts aus über Seiendes, sondern sagt das Sein, ist *sagenhaft*, d. h. "Dichtung" in dem anfänglichen Sinne, der nur aus dem Sein selbst als dem Ereignis sich bestimmen lässt" (51)—"This saying does not state something about beings but instead says being, it is *sayable*, that is, 'poetry' in the inceptual sense, which lets itself be determined only from being as the event." Writing about Hölderlin and *Dichtung* in the same volume, Heidegger remarks that what must be thought of in the context of the critique of metaphysics is perhaps the "last essence of *Dichtung*," which is linked to the radical possibility of overcoming art: "Vielleicht das letzte Wesen der Dichtung. / Vielleicht die Überwindung aller 'Kunst'" (*GA 70*, 167)—"Perhaps the ultimate essence of poetry. / Perhaps the overcoming of all art." Here the poietic comes into relief in its decisive momentum that could perhaps allow for the overcoming of all "art," that is, for leaving behind all metaphysical accounts of art, whether aesthetic, poetic, sociocultural, techno-productionist, or other. The notion of art is inextricably linked with the metaphysical underpinnings of experience and culture. This is why in *Metaphysik und Nihilismus*, Heidegger declares bluntly that the end of art coincides with the end of metaphysics: "With metaphysics ends also art."[3] As is evident from Heidegger's writings from the second half of 1930s, for him the end of metaphysics is marked at that time by the culmination of the modern operations of techno-power in the calculative and manipulative modes of relations characteristic of our techno-scientific society. It is signaled by the widespread inability even to notice the thoroughness with which modernity is pervaded by the machination, regulation, and management of all facets of life and experience.

Contrasting his approach with Max Weber's diagnosis of modernity, Heidegger insists on the thorough enchantment of modern society by its own manipulative power and what it makes possible, namely, the rapidly increasing ability to order and regulate life in all of its aspects and down to its minutest details:

> We are used to calling the era of "civilization" the one that has *dispelled* all bewitchery, and this dispelling seems more probably—indeed uniquely— connected to complete unquestionableness. Yet it is just the reverse. We merely need to know where the bewitchery comes from, namely, from the unbridled dominance of machination. When machination attains ultimate dominance, when it pervades everything, then there are no more circumstances whereby the bewitchery can be sensed explicitly and resisted. The hex cast by technology and by its constantly self-surpassing progress is only *one* sign of this bewitchery that directs everything toward calculation, utility, breeding, manageability, and regulation. (*CP*, 98)

The availability of reality as resource, as manipulable and disposable information and data in our computer age, is gathered by Heidegger under the rubric of *die Technik*—literally, technology, but better rendered into English as *technicity* or *technics* in order to avoid mistaking it for the customary sense of technology, its products or processes. What interests Heidegger is not technology per se but its essence, that is, the technicity characteristic of modern relations, whose power consists in the ability to posit (*stellen*) what exists in a way that marks it intrinsically as available: whether for production (*herstellen*), representing (*vorstellen*), or ordering (*bestellen*). Production, representation, and consumption constitute some of the manifestations of the way Heidegger sees technicity, that is, the essence of technology, as operating as the *Gestell*, that is, as the enframing, emplacing, and pervading modern reality. The term *enframing* points to how technicity puts into place the contemporary world in such a way that what actually exists becomes entirely coextensive with its availability as a standing reserve of resources, ready to be at the disposal and eventually disposed of. The enframing itself, however, "is nothing technological, nothing on the order of a machine. It is the way in which the actual reveals itself as standing-reserve"(*BW*, 328–329). Not to be identified with inventions, processes, or products, technicity should also not be confused with the overwhelming proliferation of technological products and the omnipresence of machines, which become increasingly disposable and at the same time indispensable to the everyday functioning of the modern world. It should also not be mistaken for the general descriptive category for the diversity of technological products and processes saturating developed society. In Heidegger's idiomatic account, technicity or the "essence of technology" describes the way modern relations and experiences are decisively prestructured and revealed into a standing reserve (*Bestand*) of resources. This means that anything that exists comes to be revealed, first of all and above all, as existing always at hand, which means that it is constituted in its essence as available and disposable. The problem for Heidegger does not lie with technology and technological products but instead with technicity as the dominant mode of revealing and only because, as he notes, "it drives out every other possibility of revealing. Above all, enframing conceals that revealing which, in the sense of *poiēsis*, lets what presences come forth into appearance" (*BW*, 332).

What is important for my discussion of language here is the valence that the terms *Dichtung* and the *poietic* acquire with regard to the specific sense of the end of art Heidegger alludes to. In a remark related to the one already cited about the concomitant end of metaphysics and art, Heidegger adds: "Poetry [*Dichtung*]—no longer as art; with the end of metaphysics, the end of 'art'—techne"—"*Dichtung*—nicht mehr als Kunst; mit dem Ende der Metaphysik das Ende der 'Kunst'—τέχνη" (*GA* 67, 108). This comment makes clear that *Dichtung* at its most radical signification in Heidegger's thought is neither poetry nor literature as we tend to think about them, including the pivotal work of Hölderlin. Instead, *Dichtung* refers to what may come to be understood as the poietic "essence" of "art" after metaphysics, were it to come into being. In "The Origin of the Work of Art," poetry (*Dichtung*) is differentiated from verse or poetic literary genre and is recast to indicate the dimension that makes art art: "*All art*, as the letting happen of the advent of the truth of beings, is as such, *in essence, poetry*" (*BW*, 197). "Poetry" defines here the event-like occurrence of the artwork, which can assume distinct forms in different arts. As such, "Poetry, however, is not an aimless imagining of whimsicalities and not a flight of mere notions and fancies into the realm of the unreal. What poetry, as clearing projection, unfolds of unconceal-ment and projects ahead into the rift-design of the figure, is the open region which poetry lets happen . . ." (*BW*, 197). In this essay, Heidegger is already beginning to think about the poietic and *Dichtung* in terms of a topology of language, even if he does not yet call it by this name. Unfolding the "open region," that is, the *Lichtung* or the clearing, the poietic dimension of art, puts our everyday world into question, displacing the usual ways in which we represent, know, do, or evaluate, as Heidegger remarks. It can decisively transform not only our relation to language but also our manner of being in the world. Heidegger idiomatically recasts the term *Dichtung* to describe this specific poietic capacity, and does so expressly in order to distinguish it from the cultural or literary senses of poetry and even from literature con-ceived more broadly. In this specific poietic sense, all art is "language," that is, the event coming to word, opening up the clearing as the way of language. The poietic indicates, therefore, a different "language" of relating to being—through words and not just signs—relating that is at stake and at work in various arts. One of the crucial claims of "The Origin of the Work of Art" is that only when we can see past aesthetics, that is, past the metaphysical idea of art as an aesthetic object and/or a cultural product, it may become pos-sible—Heidegger writes *vielleicht*, "perhaps," in *Über den Anfang*—to discern this poietic momentum of art as opening up a distinct modality of relations, perhaps transformative with regard to the technicity constitutive of the mod-ern being in the world. Heidegger's *Metaphysik und Nihilismus* announces that this different "poietics" can emerge only when art in its metaphysical incarnations comes to an end. What this means is that the end of art comes to imply the possibility of a new sense of the poietic, with the emphasis dis-placed from representation and aesthetics to the question of the possible, of the "unprethinkable" and the emergent.

This notion of the poietic understood as a mode of revealing is then juxtaposed in "The Question Concerning Technology" with technicity, that is, with the revealing of being as availability. Technics and poietics constitute the two ways of revealing the actual in modernity: revealed in its poietic momentum, the actual is not simply "seen" as different from the ordinary but comes to be otherwise than when it is disclosed technically. To put it briefly, in the poietic mode, the actual is not constituted as available, that is, as the "standing-reserve" of resources ready to be ordered, manipulated, or produced through the multiple operations of power pervading modern technological society. Instead, the actual is disclosed poietically as essentially futural, open to possibilities and transformations, never fully present or at our disposal, and thus never truly reducible to what becomes available of it as resource. As ". . . Poetically Man Dwells . . ." and "The Thing," among Heidegger's late essays show, when revealed poietically, the actual is not the technologically and informationally 'transparent' "standing-reserve" of resources, but a complex and shifting relatedness that needs to be taken care of and kept open as the fourfold through which humans would continuously reexamine and rethink their place in the world.[4]

This idiomatic distinction between the technic and the poietic becomes of critical importance to Heidegger's comments about art, language, and poetry, with the possibility of the existence of artworks after the metaphysical "end of art" hinging on that distinction. In *Metaphysik und Nihilismus,* Heidegger suggests that art as an outgrowth of metaphysics turns into *techne* and thus turns out to be part and parcel of the enframing. Since what comes to prominence at the end of metaphysics is *techne,* the end of art marks the emergence into view of the essentially technical nature of metaphysically conceived art. In it, *poiesis* becomes tantamount to production or creation and thus comes to constitute a variation of *techne,* which is underscored today by the growing influence of technology on contemporary art, including Web-based artworks or telematic art projects, in short, the rise of the so-called information arts. Trying to see if art could preserve a distinct domain, Heidegger ventures a remark in *Metaphysik und Nihilismus* that suggests that *Dichtung,* the poietic, which can come after art should be *kunstlos* or art-free.[5] No longer seen metaphysically and aesthetically, that is, as essentially technical, art becomes refigured into a poietic event. The end of art—that is, the fulfillment of art's metaphysical idea as an aesthetic object of artistic creation—attests to art's essentially technicist nature, namely to its consonance with and participation in the technological revealing. Still, this Heideggerian "end of art" does not mean that art can be simply left behind or rejected but rather that another, poietic, dimension of the artwork could perhaps come into view and alter our experience of what "art" is and does.

Clearly, the end of art does not mean the cessation of art's historical inscription within the modern institution of art or the larger operations of culture and capital. The end of metaphysics does not simply strip these layers—aesthetic, cultural, institutional, commercial—from the work of art but, conversely, makes them starkly visible in their complex and interlaced functioning. The point here is that this complicated modern enframing of art does not explain or exhaust art's work and should not be mistaken for how art essentially occurs. What these short and undeveloped remarks hint at is that at the end of metaphysics the multilayered makeup of the modern work of art becomes better visible in its specific technicity, that is, it becomes recognizable as contributing—often despite itself—to the technical revealing and power-oriented machination of being. If indeed the Greek beginning of Western culture indicates that art is always already part of *techne,* elaborated and repeated in its essential features through aesthetic conceptualizations of artworks without ever being decisively differentiated from other technical modalities of making, then art does in fact need to "end" in order for its poietic force to emerge at the end of metaphysics. Yet for that to happen, art needs to cease to be "art," because the very notion of art pivots in modernity on the technicist determinations of art's nature as creation, that is, as a form of artistic production. Such an end of art could "perhaps"—Heidegger insistently uses *vielleicht* in this context—open for us the future of a changed, distinctly poetic work, where "artworks" would be seen as the event's coming to word, that is, as the clearing of the world's fourfold, which emerges and is held open in the manner of *Dichtung.*

This specific, nonmetaphysically circumscribed notion of the poietic needs to be thought through the prism of Heidegger's transformative understanding of language, especially in terms of the fold between words and signs described in chapter 2. The discernment of the poietic depends thus on thought's ability to become attentive to the distinction between the saying as showing and the saying as signs. For these reasons, the poietic is intrinsically fragile, easily obscured, masked, or even erased by the ebullience of signification, the plethora of meanings and images, the certainty and assertiveness of propositions, or the recounting ability of narratives. That Heidegger was aware of the tenuousness of what I am calling here the poietic (momentum of language) is easily seen in his repeated insistence on the notions of attentiveness, sheltering, guarding, keeping watch, and the like, which he deploys throughout his works with regard to language, thing, or world. The ease with which the poietic entrance of words into signs becomes obscured and turned into a fault, cutting off and erasing the way-making of language by circumscribing attention to language signs and highlighting meaning, is indicated explicitly in *Zum Wesen der Sprache und Zur Frage nach der Kunst* through the notion of *Versprechen,* which suggests that the poietic is barely discernible as something promised and thus needs not only to be carefully discerned but also evolved from its merely promissory note. This is the case because this promise spells out in the same gesture, in the same sign, *Versprechen,* its own repeated mis-speaking (*Ver-sprechen*).

Commenting on the ease with which language, implicitly in its register of signs, can squander, distort, use up, and lay to waste (*verschleudert, vernutzt und verzerrt und verwüstet*) the truth of being (*Seyn*), Heidegger claims that language can guard its event-like occurrence only by following the contours of how the event comes to word: "Die Sprache wahrt das Ereignis—weil sie dem Wort entspringt und beim Wort bleibt. Die Sprache ist das *Versprechen* des Ereignisses an den ereigneten Menschen. In der Sprache und als Sprache verspricht das Wort des Seyns die Wahrheit (Versprechen)" (*GA* 74, 112)—"Language holds true the event—because it arises from the word and remains by the word. Language is the *promise* of the event to the appropriated human being. In language and as language, the word of being promises the truth (promise)." The event happens only as a promise that must not only be recognized and answered but also carried out and decided by human beings. Any possibility of attending to the truth of being, as Heidegger makes clear in the quotation above, hinges on this promise and the ability to remain attentive to the fact that truth comes to pass only as un-truth. This promise is also a task, calling for a commensurate response that would carry out the de-ciding indicated by the hyphen in the un-truth, but do so without, however, providing the false reassurance that the hyphen could at some point disappear or be effaced, so that truth could eventually be secured as separate from and uncontaminated by the untrue. The promise of truth is also its mis-speaking into signs, its mis-saying into statements. What is crucial for understanding the poietic working of Heidegger's thought is that the expression that the saying (*Sage*) finds in the statements (*Aussage*) has the trajectory of the promise: its words promise to say the truth by virtue of their admittedly adequate and sure formulation into expressions and statements, while this necessary twisting in fact retains words and truth merely as a promise, or perhaps if we script it distinctly in English, as a pro-miss. By scripting *promise* as *pro-miss*, one retains in writing, while rendering it unheard in the spoken word, the duplicity and the implied misspeaking of the German *Versprechen*. For the promise to be a promise, it must retain its promissory note, as it were, both in its script and as an audible note, that is, in its tenor (*Stimmung*). This promise is in fact the fundamental, futural *Stimmung* of language, which means that in order to remain a promise, in order to keep promising, it must be held open as a promise, never to be fulfilled, because being completed, it would disappear as promise. The promise needs to mis-speak (*Ver-sprechen*), to push speaking to its edge and turn it, in order to keep its promise.

The way Heidegger repeatedly uses the hyphen to write this promise as *Ver-sprechen* illustrates the extent to which the movement of Heidegger's own language carries out the transformation of thinking, here altered precisely through the change in the understanding of the notion of truth. The true can only be thought through the hyphen, as it were, always in transition, because only in this way the characteristic folding of words into signs and the attendant difficulties with keeping the promise of the event as language can be held open literally in the hyphen. The promise does not promise any *thing,* neither the highest being nor the totality of beings; in fact it promises no beings at all, for the promise is of and from being (*Seyn*). "Ver-sprechen ereignishaft—die *übereignende Zueignung* des Wortes in die Sprache, *das Wort in die Sprache ausgeben.* So wird—aber so allein ist auch Sprache das Ver-sprochene, meist aber nicht beachtete" (*GA* 74, 113–114)—"Promise in terms of the event—the *delivering* of the word *into its own* in language, *to issue the word into language.* In this way, but only in this way, language is likewise what is promised, even though mostly not heeded." The promise here is not a promise *of* something but rather the anticipation of the promise *as* pro-miss. It is the issuing of the promise, its *Versprechen,* that is at stake here; not what it promises but the very way this promise happens as the faulting of the word into the sign. The promise does not promise to deliver or grant us something but rather promises to hold us attentive to and give us the possibility to be mindful of the event-like issue of the promise itself. The promise promis(s)es, that is, anticipates, its own occurrence as promise; and this is precisely how language and the event, and thus being, promise. It is only by missing, in advance as it were, its promise to enter language and signify that being (*Seyn*) as promise holds true to itself.

The promise promis(s)es precisely by the withdrawal and the withholding of being, thus clearing in its back draft the opening for beings and relations. As "The Essence of Language" puts it, "Language must in its way avow to us itself—its essence. Language unfolds as this avowal"—"Die Sprache muss auf ihre Weise sich selber—ihr Wesen uns zusprechen. Die Sprache west als dieser Zuspruch" (*OWL,* 76, modified; *GA* 12, 170). Here Heidegger uses the verb *zusprechen*—to award or to avow, literally to speak oneself to. To experience language as event, to heed language's promise to us, thinking needs to be attentive especially to the way in which language promis(s)es. Thought needs to traverse each time its way with language, by being in language and as language, listening to it, that is, thought needs to extend itself in parallel to the pro-mise (*Ver-sprechen*) in order "think" precisely (in) the hyphen as the proper way of language in its (mis)saying. To keep up with the event, thinking needs to transform its relation to language and to learn how to think not only by way of concepts or ideas but poietically, by way of the hyphen, as it were. What matters more than the ideas *about* the poietic or *about* poetic thinking discussed by Heidegger, is the emergent poietic momentum of thought that his writings "promise" in ways described above. To discern this movement and thus to understand what poetic thinking means, it is necessary—beyond the discussion of Heidegger's writings on poetry—to open thought to Heidegger's alternative account of the sign and thus to recognize the elemental role played in thinking by the word's transition into sign. Elemental means here granting the element for language, signs, and meaning.

If what language promis(s)es, that is, avows and bespeaks precisely in missing it in advance (as its pro-miss), literally in the word's advance into signs, is the poietic *Wesen* of language—the essence as the way in which language unfolds—then the promise Heidegger writes about in *GA* 74 is the one he also scripts as the famous formula in "The Essence of Language": "Das Wesen der Sprache: Die Sprache des Wesens" (*GA* 12, 170)—"The being of language: the language of being." Here the event's turn is scripted *as* and *through* the colon. What language promises is specifically its word as the turn of the event, that is, as the event unfolding as the language of being: language speaking about being, with regard to, or as expressive of it: "In der Sprache und ihren Wörtern, im Sagen, ist dem Menschen das *Wort gegeben,* ist ihm *ver-sprochen* das Seyn" (*GA* 74, 113)—"In language and its terms, in the saying, the *word is given* and language is *promised* to the human being." The event unfolds as the "word 'of' being" and brings this word into signs: from the being of language as "the word 'of' being," that is, as *Worte,* it becomes the language *about* being—speaking in *Wörter*—and consequently it turns into statements about beingness and beings. The promise of language is its promise to say something "of" being (*Seyn*) in word-signs, even though what the signs say is not "of" beyng (*Seyn*) but always *about* beings, where being (dis)appears only as beingness.

This missaying of being as beingness is not a lack in language but rather its proper fault or fold, its *Einfalt.* On several occasions, Heidegger admonishes the reader not to judge from his remarks that either language or human understanding is somehow at fault when the promise turns into a pro-miss. *Ver-sprechen* is not an error or a deficiency of language but the hint of its movement, which cannot be expressed in word-signs (*Wörter*), because it does not have meaning that could be expressed in assertions or statements *about* the nature of language. The difficulty of language's promise is that "what" it promises is not really a "what"—an essence or *quidditas*—but the movement and the turns of the promise itself. This is the case because the promise is linked to the unsaid and the unprethinkable, as Heidegger indicates in *GA* 74 (112). In fact, given these parameters, this is perhaps how the notion of the poietic should too be thought, namely by interlacing the notions of *poiesis,* the unsaid, and the unprethinkable. What the poietic in Heidegger takes over from the Greek sense of *poiesis* is the force of bringing about or into the open, an emergence, that cannot be explained, however, through the idea of creation or production. As Heidegger remarks, "*the word brings us to something* but does *not* create it"—"*Das Wort bringt uns auf etwas*—schafft es aber *nicht* her" (*GA 74*, 108). And again a few pages later: "Das *Wort* ist ein *Bringen einziger Art. / Ereignend bringt es noch das Unvermutete im Vermuten, das schon angemutet ist*" (*GA 74*, 112)—"The *word* is a singular kind of *bringing*. / Eventuating, it brings the unexpected into the *expecting*, which has already been supposed." The singularity of this poietic bringing lies precisely in its unprethinkability, which remains *as* unprethinkable even when it is brought out into the open. The word holds its promise by bringing in a particular way that discloses the unsaid as what specifically remains properly unsayable (*Unsägliche*) and renders the each-time singular and one-time occurrence unprethinkable. Until this poietic bringing is recognized and allowed to transform our relation *to* language, the promise will only be seen as a pro-miss: as the mis-saying of language rather than as its saying in withdrawal.

Heidegger's comments on *Versprechen* in *GA 74* make this quite clear. "Das 'Wort' *halten* und das 'Wort'—*brechen* . . . , das Wort darauf geben, das Wort—das *gegebene Versprechen*" (*GA 74*, 113)—"To *hold* the 'word' and—to *break*—the 'word' . . . , and therefore to give the word, the *word*—the *given promise*." The promise is the simultaneous giving and breaking, giving *as* breaking, of the word, holding the word precisely in its having been broken. This promise is nothing other than the minimal enactment performed as the *es gibt*: as "there is" or "it gives." And it is this giving and coming to be that needs to be kept in language, that is, attended to in signs and what they render meaningful: "*Ver-sprechen*—kommen lassen und dieses *wahren, das Wahren des Kommens* . . ." (*GA 74*, 113)—"*Promising*—letting come and *guarding* it, the guarding of the coming. . . ." What is guarded as the promise of language is the coming, that is, the beginning, the fact that each moment "there is." This "coming" remains irreducible to propositional statements and has to be brought instead to bear on the very way in which thinking moves, providing it with a new tonality. This promising, in its proper one-time occurrence, is enigmatic and reserved: "Versprechen (eigentlich) ist rätselhaft, wahrt die Erfüllung, spart sie. / *Das Sparende im Versprechen*" (*GA 74*, 113)—"The promise (properly) is enigmatic, guards the fulfillment, spares it. / *The sparing in the promise*." Heidegger puts the emphasis here on the sparing and holding open, which play the key role in the promise: the promise as event turns on this sparing that renders the clearing open through the withdrawal or the departure (*Abschied*), the back draft of the event. The fulfillment of the promise is "not something that comes after the promise or is added to it, but the fulfilling be-gins / in the promising: "'Erfüllung'—nicht angestückt und nachträglich, sondern im Versprechen / be-ginnt das Er-füllen" (*GA 74*, 113). The fulfillment is the coming and the transformation (*Das Kommen und die Wandlung*) taking place as the proper movement of *Ver-sprechen*, as indicated by the hyphen. As Heidegger puts it, the promise is *Versprechen* in the sense of *Verheissen:* promising and auguring as literally *ver-heissen,* calling forth and naming in the same gesture, perhaps calling forth into names, inscribing in names and thus mis-saying in these names. It is the only way in which language can be "*let belong to being*"—"*Seyn gehören lassen*" (*GA* 74, 113).

Heidegger's remarks on the promise describe the difficult manner in which being can be named. The promise carries names and lets them belong to being, yet at the price of breaking the promise of signifying being or giving it meaning. The hyphen bespeaks, or more properly, scripts, this turn intrinsic to the promise, on which the possibility of language rides. Hyphenating the prefix, Heidegger indicates how the event comes to word as what spares, reserves, or holds back, that is, as *das Sparende.* This "sparing" comes to outline the new style of thinking in the aftermath of philosophy and metaphysics, which Heidegger calls *Besinnung,* a kind of thoughtful and rigorous contemplation, which leaves aside the primacy of assertions, propositional truths, or philosophical systems. The style Heidegger is interested in would be informed and shaped by words (*Worte*) and not regulated exclusively by signs or language terms (*Wörter*). This thinking would proceed by listening to silences intrinsic to its own event-like (*ereignishaft*) coming to speech and writing: "The issue is then neither to describe nor to explain, neither to promulgate nor to teach. Here the speaking is not something over and against what is to be said but is this latter itself as the essential occurrence of beyng [*Seyn*]" (*CP,* 6).

Silent Thought

This mode of thinking, without philosophical precedent in the Western tradition, needs to be developed because the event's language, in order to come to word-signs, to speech and writing, restrains its own poietic force: the event retracts, keeping itself unsaid, unprethinkable, and silent amidst the proliferation of phenomena. The force of the event is only hinted at, as though all that appears are only hints scattered by the event's back draft. Reticence or holding silent (*Stille halten*) becomes necessary as an adept way of thinking and writing, in order to shift writing away from being primarily an activity of enunciation and turn it into a form of a response (*Antwort*), attentive to the inceptual word. As Heidegger remarks in *Contributions to Philosophy,* this is a "style" of thinking necessary for attentiveness to being as event: "*Restraint* / is the style of inceptual thinking only because it must become the style of future humanity grounded in Da-sein, i.e., only because it bears this grounding and is its pervasive disposition" (*CP,* 28). This restraint underscores bringing to word and articulation but in such a way that what comes to be said holds in silence the singular and one-time character of the saying, its *Einzigkeit* and *Einmaligkeit,* that mark the event and, nihilated by the very movement of the saying, remain irreducible to the singularity of meaning as a form of being. As he later adds, "When this restraint reaches *words,* what is said is always the event [*Ereignis*]. . . . The saying that bears silence is what grounds [*Das Sagen als Erschweigen gründet*]" (*CP,* 64; *GA* 65, 80). The mode of thinking that Heidegger begins to evolve from that time onward is expected to correspond and respond (*ent-sprechen*) to how language brings itself, in its way-making, to the "sounded word," as "The Way to Language" expresses it. This style is thus fitting for encountering and countering—among the meanings of *entsprechen* are to meet and to accord with—what unfolds in the origin of language itself. "Bearing silence arises out of the essentially occurring origin of language itself"—"Die Erschweigung entspringt aus dem wesenden Ursprung der Sprache selbst" (*CP,* 63; *GA* 65, 79).

Since language holds itself in reserve, in order to encounter language and experience its movement, thought needs to fit itself to or accord with this reticence, to bespeak it by holding silent precisely the departure (*Abschied*) as the characteristic promise of language. Heidegger makes this point about the withdrawal and restraint "essential" to the unfolding of language in "The Way to Language": "The way to speech unfolds essentially in language itself. The way to language in the sense of speech is language as the saying. What is peculiar to language thus conceals itself on the way, the way by which the saying lets those who listen to it get to language" (*BW,* 413). Signification as we know it becomes possible in the aftermath of the peculiar manner in which language opens into words by withdrawing itself from them: saying makes signification possible by withholding itself from being said in and as signs. This restraint and the reticence it calls for in thinking is not a deficiency or a lack in language, something missing that could be recuperated by a more "precise" manner of speaking or redeemed by the certainty of propositional statements, but instead delineates the proper way that language happens, that is, through a withholding intrinsic to the manner in which language "allows to be said":

> If language everywhere withholds its being [*Wesen*] in this sense, then such withholding is the very being of language. Thus language not only holds back when we speak it in the accustomed ways, but this its holding back is determined by the fact that language holds back its own origin and so denies its being to our usual notions. . . . Accordingly, the being of language puts itself into language nonetheless, in its own most appropriate manner. (*OWL,* 81, modified)

This withdrawal marks the poietic momentum of language, whose unprethinkability can be traced in its singularity and one-time occurrence, though only by way of a listening and restrained response. This specific listening response, its reticent holding in silence (*Erschweigung*), where what is said nonetheless bears silence in it, comes to set the tone, the *Stimmung,* in which poetic thinking operates.

What must be given due in conceiving of language after Heidegger is precisely this pervasive disposition necessary for new thinking: neither a cosmetic, "stylistic" change nor only production of new concepts—as, for instance, Deleuze and Guattari define philosophy—but a transformation of thought from the ground up, that is, from its non-ground (*Abgrund)* held open by the poietic momentum of language. If we take Heidegger's words—whether the event, the enframing, the poetic, or the saying—as simply new concepts, or new ways of defining the subject matter in question, for instance, as a new kind of phenomenology, then no change in thinking, certainly not on the scale or in the manner Heidegger envisions, can happen. For more important than the terms themselves is the disposition they give to thinking, changing precisely the way thought proceeds: not from idea to idea, or statement to statement, but instead listening to how language moves thinking, alert to unprethinkable openings possibly granted by language in their abyssal nihilation, ready to follow its words beyond what the signs indicate or mean. The style is not a matter of preference but of need: not for new statements or definitions but for thought to become able to make and stay its way, understanding that its momentum lies not in words but in ways or paths it traverses. If at issue is being and not beings, (mis)conceived as present things, thought can no longer grant emphasis to concepts, which hope to capture and define beings. Instead, thought must make its way by following the contours of the event, trying to render as its path the very outline of "being" that the one-time occurrence charts each time singularly.

If one were to single out one word that best reflects how radically Heidegger tries to change thinking from its preoccupation with concepts and statements, it would have to be the German term *die Stille:* silence that is also stillness. If philosophy proceeds with the help of concepts, statements, and arguments, poetic thinking takes its cue from "silence," which requires a different measure and rigor than philosophical or scientific thought, a rigor that, as Lyotard remarks, eschews "grasping intelligence."[6] Letting go of grasping intelligence, to paraphrase Lyotard, poetic thinking contours its path according to the shifting and unprethinkable occurrence of the event and its essential non-ground. To be exact, it contours the silence and stillness that mark the outline of the event's back draft, in which wake the scene comes to be dominated by beings, phenomena, and incidents. To see how Heidegger plays poetic thinking and grasping or conceptual thought off of each other, one needs to follow the complex relations he draws among key terms having to do with silence/stillness and sound, terms such as *Stille* (stillness, quiet, peace, silence, calm); *Schweigen* (silence, to keep quiet or silent) and its various incarnations in language; *Laut* (sound) and related words, *Schall, Klang, Hall;* and finally *Stimme* (voice), whose resonance comes from *Stimmen* (to dispose, tune or tone). Tracking and mapping these relations would require a more developed study in itself, especially since the later writings draw attention to the importance of *die Stille* already signaled in *Being and Time,* even though it is only marked there in the phrase "the silent force of the possible" without much elaboration. The silent force of the possible (*die stille Kraft des Möglichen*) returns in "Letter on Humanism," troping specifically the quiet and silent—that is, departive and un-remarkable—way in which, in its giving, being keeps rendering possible: *es gibt.* The term occupies a much more important place in Heidegger's vocabulary once he turns toward the notion of the event and begins to foreground the poietic ways in which "the event comes to word." Consequently, he comes to use the word *Stille* with regard not just to the event but also Dasein, *Seyn,* the word, the origin of language, or the clearing. In other words, stillness/silence becomes the originative tonality or disposition of being in its event-like issue into speech and writing.

Explaining the distinctness of words (*Worte*) from terms (*Wörter*), Heidegger indicates that "The word is the hinting silence"—"Das Wort ist die winkende Stille" (*GA* 74, 62). This silence is then described as the essential occurrence of the word as "voice" that disposes what comes to be: "Beständnis der Stille—die Wesung des Wortes als stimmende 'Stimme'" (*GA* 74, 100)—"Insistence of silence—the essential occurrence of the word as the tuning 'voice'." Undermining the grasping power of the concept, Heidegger declares this silent stillness as constituting the first word: "*Die Stille* / als Lichtung des Da—das *erste Wort*" (*GA* 74, 132)—"*The stillness* / as the clearing of the there—the *first word*." The stillness with which and into which the clearing opens the there, the site of Da-sein as relation to being, is the foreword at the moment of its very onset. It is precisely this stillness of the word's onset that must be held reticent yet unforgotten, as Heidegger makes clear writing about the "*Erschweigung der Stille*" (*GA* 74, 132), which can be translated as "bearing the silence of the stillness" or keeping reticent in stillness. This approach requires a thinking that, instead of proclaiming statements or producing new concepts, listens, befits and thus pays attention to the inceptive stillness of the word in order to hold it in its properly resonant silence: "*Die Stille halten*—sich fügendes, einspringendes, d.h. *achtendes [Hören]*"

(*GA* 74, 133)—"*To keep silent*—yielding, stepping in, that is, an *attentive* [listening]." Even though language constantly moves, opening new paths, silence indicates here the poietic dimension, a stillness that inheres in all the shifts and movements of signification. This silence or stillness is the word's fold in which any and all signs are held, given room for their functions.

Neither irrational nor mystical, the stillness Heidegger has in mind comes from the characteristic departure (*Abschied*), through which being recedes—into its clearing (*Lichtung*). This receding is a kind of an implosion or a recession—the event's back draft—that composes itself into the clearing into whose expanse beings appear. Writing about this refusal (*Verweigerung*), Heidegger is emphatic that "refusal does not say that beyng is withdrawn, or would be merely unknowable or, metaphysically speaking, ir-rational: Verweigerung besagt nicht, dass das Seyn entzogen oder auch nur unerkennbar, metaphysisch gesprochen 'ir-rational' sei" (*GA* 74, 149). On the contrary, being as the clearing through the refusal can be experienced in a manner distinct from explanations or mystical intuition, both of which remain entrapped in the notion of representing something present, only taken to be hidden for the moment or simply requiring a more penetrating insight.[7]

The difficulty Heidegger presents us with is that this *Stille*, stillness or silence, is not of the order of presence: it is not communicable as something that could be potentially present or presented, and which either requires a special, "mystical," intuition or else remains inaccessible to rational inquiry and as such can be deemed irrational and dismissed as insignificant to thinking. Instead, at issue is a poietic, or to be exact, *the* poietic, stillness that marks the unprethinkable, each-time singular and one-time entry of "the word 'of' being" into signs. Because this poietic silence par excellence contours the word's movement into signs, what remains of it within signs and signification is barely a hint. This quiet stillness has to do with the fact that language can never be delimited as a system of signs, because it has already been "in motion," occurring as event, even when it is only experienced in its ordinary or customary, narrowed down articulations as speech or writing. And since the event occasions language, as it comes to be language—"Das Ereignis wortet"—even if language seems to either appear from the event or add itself to it, what is "proper" to language is the hint of its singular and one-time arrival into signs, precisely of its nonrepeatable event. Because the stillness through which the word imparts itself to and in the same gesture departs from the sign is singular and one-time—it is the stillness of being that has no other, after all—it exists only as a hint that cannot be signified, explained, or kept "meaningful" but must be thought of in the peculiar tonality of reticence, capable of singularizing and "one-timing," as it were, the event. For these reasons, the experience with language cannot be adequately described through linguistic conceptualizations of language or addressed in its event-like occurrence by thought that relies primarily on concepts, assertions, and propositions. Stillness/silence (*Stille*) cannot be stated, described or given meaning as a proposition, but requires instead a corresponding experience of thought, which, encountering (*entsprechen*) this silence, can hold its contours in words and thus have the words co-respond to it. Heidegger insists that in order to understand language we need to recognize a dimension in experience that does not explain itself through the binary of the rational and the irrational. Although this dimension does enter language and thus the field of expression, it does so always only in the manner of hints, hesitation (*Zögerung*), and refusal.

To intimate this complex response in language as corresponding to the outline of the stillness in which language moves, Heidegger offers one of his most puzzling phrases, *das Geläut der Stille,* the peal of stillness, or perhaps the ringing of silence. We all know the experience of the "ringing silence," a heightened mode of attentiveness and listening in which what comes to reverberate and be heard, without being a sound strictly speaking, is precisely the stillness as silence, and sometimes its peculiar echoing in the ears. This is what Heidegger seems to have in mind when he describes the word as the hint of such stillness, which means that the word is never sound or script to begin with, never the signifier, and even less the signified or meaning. The stillness exigent of the word's occurrence is not explainable through the terminology developed around the notion of the *signum,* but requires a transformed relation to language: to signs, meaning, speech, and writing, but primarily to silence. Crucial here is that this silence is not opposed to sound: it is never a simple absence of sound. As such, it needs to be held distinct from being speechless or voiceless: silence in Heidegger is to be approached from *Stille* (stillness) and not as *Verstummen,* or muteness, whether understood as the absence of sound or the inability to make sound.

In *Zum Wesen der Sprache und Zur Frage nach der Kunst,* in the section titled "Das Erschweigen der Stille" (section 149), Heidegger introduces important distinctions between *Verschweigen, Schweigen,* and *Erschweigen,* where the third verb, *Erschweigen,* uses the prefix er- to intensify and evoke the specific sense of holding in reticence or bearing silence, distinct from keeping silent or secret. In order to profile his idiomatic use of *Erschweigen,* Heidegger provides descriptive definitions of all three terms. *Verschweigen* means "to keep secret," and Heidegger explains it as "not saying something that could be said, that is, not communicating"—"etwas Sagbares nicht sagen, das heisst nicht mitteilen" (*GA* 74, 152). The second verb, *Schweigen,* means "to be silent," which Heidegger explains as *"wanting* to say something ineffable but not being able to (keeping silent out of inability); leaving something unsayable in its unsayability (keeping silent out of ability)"—"ein Unsagbares sagen *wollen,* aber nicht können (Schweigen aus Unvermögen); ein Unsägliches in seiner Unsagbarkeit lassen (Schweigen aus Vermögen)." The first two verbs, *Verschweigen* and *Schweigen,* indicate silence about something existing or present, whether as sayable, unsayable, or unsaid, and describe the unnamed object's relation to the human capacity or incapacity to bring it to expression. The third verb, *Erschweigen,* refers to what Heidegger calls *das Ungesagte,* the unsaid, which is not, however, understood with regard to the capability to say it or its lack. This unsaid is not a matter of either keeping something silent or being unable to say it properly but refers instead to what is pre-said, co-said, and after-said with what happens to be said (*Gesagte*). "[D]as Ungesagte—weil wesenhaft in allem Sagen Vor- und Mit- und Nachgesagte in seinem Grund, den Grund seiner Ungesagtheit zurückverwahren und allem Sagen verwahren, um es gründig zu erhalten"—"the unsaid—because in the ground of all saying it is pre-said, co-said, and after-said, going back to the preserve of the ground of its unsaidness and preserving all saying, in order to keep it grounded." Being unsaid as the ground of what can be said constitutes indeed "the abyssal non-ground, into which beyng itself unfolds" (*der Ab-grund, als der das Seyn selbst west,* GA 74, 152). Here the unsaid of the saying has nothing to do with something unsayable, ineffable, unnameable, or unspeakable, which all presuppose the existence of "something" to be said, while indicating that it either cannot be said or is kept intentionally unsaid or secret.

What Heidegger designates by *Erschweigung,* reticence that holds silence, is, therefore, what is poietically not of the order of saying in the sense that it is not something either to be said or not to be said. *Erschweigung* points instead to the clearing where the saying finds itself already moving, to the way-making of the saying, which the saying only hints at without ever saying or expressing it. In other words, the reticence Heidegger writes about is not a matter of saying or not saying but, alternatively, of being attentive to this saying in a way which would allow the hint of what envelops and holds all saying in its proper stillness. As Heidegger remarks, "Das Er-schweigen entspringt nicht aus der Mangelhaftigkeit der Rede, sondern aus der Zugehörigkeit zur Stille und für sie" (*GA* 74, 152)—"The reticence stems not from the deficiency of discourse but from belonging to the stillness and for its sake." Belonging to the stillness means being alert to the word "of" being, for "The word is inceptually the reticent voice of stillness"—"Das Wort ist anfänglich die erschwiegene Stimme der Stille" (*GA* 74, 152). The word *of* being discussed in detail in chapter 2 is nothing other than this stillness, which occurs as the disposition or tuning pervading beings and relations (*Stimmen*) and thus also as the "voice" (*Stimme*) that can be imparted into signs, made visible and audible through them. Although the silence/stillness appears to be broken when language reaches expression, when naming and representation take over, the stillness remains in fact unbroken—kept silent and quiet—when language pays attention to it as what specifically co-says itself with signs as their non-signifiable way-making. When Heidegger identifies the stillness/silence as "the over-flow of the abyssal non-ground" (*Stille: der Über-fluss des Ab-grundes*, GA 74, 153), he indicates that this abyss is not something that is missing from the said or otherwise lacking in language, but instead what arrives properly as pre-, co-, and after-said in the saying. The quiet or stillness Heidegger has in mind is one that, speaking as language always does, nonetheless holds what comes to be said over the abyss of nothingness, shelters—albeit only as reticent—its singular one-time occurrence. The temporality of the *Ab-grund* constitutes also the temporality of the origin of language, the fact that no matter what form the saying takes and which of its temporal vectors comes to the foreground, the *Abgrund* co-says itself with all the three temporal dimensions of the saying without being said *in* them, that is, it holds itself as the *Ungesagtheit*, the being-unsaid lacing what comes to be said. The abyss of being is therefore never unsaid in the sense that language somehow fails to say it; it can be ignored, unnoticed, or forgotten but not unsaid in this manner.

If one wants to speak then about Heidegger's "sigetics," it must be with the understanding that it transforms the valence of silence into the originative, poietic stillness of the event's coming to word. Silence in Heidegger's thinking about language is not silence in the sense of absence of sound or speech, just as little as it would be the presence or absence of writing. Crucially, silence is not to be defined from sound, as its potential presence (sound) or absence (muteness), and thus also not in terms of voice (*Stimme*), but instead as *Stimmen,* that is, as disposition or tuning. That this initial or originative disposition happens in or as stillness is not a notion that could be grasped from the perspective of the sensible or its opposite, the supra- or non-sensible. Heidegger's ubiquitous comments on *Stimmen* and *Stimmung* and their relation to stillness (*Stille*) leave no doubt about the fact that silence as stillness in Heidegger's idiomatic use is neither auditory nor perceptual but instead event-like and poietic, referring therefore to the stillness in which the clearing opens each time as nonrepeatable. This is why Heidegger writes about the still or silent word (*stille Wort*) or describes stillness as "tuning opening *displacement* into the clearing of the self-concealing"—"die Stille—

als stimmende eröffnende *Versetzung* in die Lichtung des Sichverbergenden" (*GA* 74, 155). One could adduce many quotations from Heidegger's work to support this point, but common to all of them is the pre-auditory character of the stillness as *Stimmen*, that is, as the disposing of relations rather than as a matter of something to be heard or perceived, whether as ultimately sayable or as ineffable. This is why silence bifurcates in Heidegger into auditory silence, which can perhaps be conceived as muteness, that is, either in the sense of keeping silent or as absence of sound, and nonauditory, poietic stillness, understood as the movement of language that is only hinted at by the play of signification. This bifurcation of silence reproduces the fault of words into signs, indicating that while signs can be mute or muted, kept secret or even deprived of significance, the word, by contrast, can never be rendered mute because it is not "of" sound to begin with. The word can pass unheard or can be drowned out by sound, noise, meaning, it can be even held hostage to muteness, or it can instead be experienced in its singular onset (as An*wort or* Vor*wort*) precisely when it comes to be held in reticence. As still or "silent" in this manner, the word in Heidegger is neither auditory nor scriptural strictly speaking, just as little as it can be something transcendent in relation to sensibility. The word is the clearing brought about by the back draft of the event that lets the sensible and the nonsensible open in the first place.

As Heidegger explains, the understanding of the beginning shelters the knowledge that the word "essences from keeping silent and the essential saying inheres in the stillness of beyng: that beyng 'is'es beyng"—"das Wort aus der Verschweigung west und das wesentliche Sagen inständet in der Stille des Seyns: dass das Seyn istet das Seyn" (*GA* 74, 20). This quotation provides a good illustration of Heidegger's strategies for scripting what does not belong originally either to writing or to speech and yet remains crucial if thought wants to keep attentive to being. Heidegger seems to be aware in these notes that in order to describe this stillness he has to de-scribe it. To do so, he writes, "das Seyn istet das Seyn." Using the older spelling of *Seyn* to distinguish it from the metaphysical notions of *Sein* as beingness, Heidegger turns the third-person singular *ist* into an infinitive of a coined verb, *isten* or *to is* in English. This verb is used to disrupt and inflect the tautological resonance of the implied phrase "being is being" (*Das Seyn ist das Seyn*), from which Heidegger implicitly derives the line he actually writes. Being never "is" being because that would mean that being would appear as beingness or as a being; instead being "'is'es," that is, occasions, actuates, eventuates—itself. Heidegger deliberately leaves the grammatically correct phrase "being is being" as though (un)written, or, in fact, as overwritten, since the phrase "Das Seyn ist das Seyn" remains clearly visible in the actually written "Das Seyn istet das Seyn." The newly minted third-person singular *istet* changes the valence of the verb from a copula to a transitive verb, whose transitiveness scripts precisely the movement of language—the word's fold into signs. Seen as a coined infinitive, "to is" lends "is" the transitive sense of bringing about and eventuation. While the phrase appears tautological, its import is not to define or describe being *as* being but to disrupt the notion that being can be predicated about and to script instead the non-signifiable momentum of the event's coming to word.

This way of writing is important also in relation to Heidegger's discussion of the structure of "as," and thus of the "as such," especially in the early lectures and seminars or in *Being and Time,* where it remains crucial to explaining interpretation and thus also understanding and knowledge. Moreover, it throws light on the difficulty Heidegger notices in his own thinking, namely the notion of "being as such." This difficulty becomes intractable when one tries to define or describe something as what it is, whether speaking about being or beings. It seems that language makes the "as" structure both necessary and inescapable, which would forever constrain Heidegger's thinking to the idiom of "the proper" understood as one's own, self-identical or part of itself, because of its ability to differentiate and repeat. It would also mean the inevitable recurrence of predication as the dominant language structure that tends to render what is said into statements, while converting the verb "to be" into a copula to anchor predication. Playing by the rules of signification, language renders what is being said "as" something described, defined, or referred to, that is, it holds what exists as something that can be gathered and held within predication. What comes into language is always "as" what it is and can thus also be "as such." One way of circumventing or at least easing this difficulty and thus fraying the "as such" is to highlight the issuing of the proper from and as the strife of the *Unter-Schied,* as Heidegger does, or see it as effected from difference, as Derrida proposes, which means that the proper would always be im-proper, differentially marked, and therefore should perhaps be written as (im)proper. Heidegger offers a different way of approaching the proper, one that eventually dispenses with the "as" and the "as such": if the phrase "being is being" still operates within the perspective of the "as such" and tries to break the hold of the "as" through tautological circling, than the formulation "Das Seyn istet das Seyn" no longer follows this precept, that is, it is no longer under-written by the "as" structure and its differential movement. Describing by de-scribing, the phrase occurs "event-like." What is meant or depicted in the phrase cedes its priority to the momentum of language, that is, to the event's poietic occurrence, which takes over, underwriting the meaning of the phrase by co-responding to the event. And by this occurrence I do not mean simply the invention of *istet* or the mode in which it de-scribes the copula *ist*, or even the transition of the initial *das Seyn* into the latter *das Seyn*, but rather the entire "turn" of the phrase. Here the "turn" of the phrase acquires an idiomatic meaning, namely one evocative of the event's turn. When Heidegger remarks that words, in his specific sense distinguished from *Wörter* or dictionary words, poietically "turn" the event and bring it into language, he looks for a way to think and to write this turning without reducing it to its meaning or its effects, and thus without naming it "as" something. The circularity of the phrase "Das Seyn istet das Seyn" is, therefore, not tautological but event-like (*ereignishaft*); it does not operate in the manner of the "as" structure but rather "turns" and "folds," transiting being in order to let be. It is this transiting "of" being that unfolds into the clearing. The phrase then "does" what another of Heidegger's phrases describes: "the event comes to word."

It is absolutely crucial not to mistake the invented verb *isten*, "to is," for what Heidegger understands idiomatically as the word, for instance, for the "silent word" or "the word 'of' being," and so forth. For the verb form *isten* becomes here another sign, a neologism, a devised or one might even say a contrived sign, but a sign nonetheless. The word in Heidegger's poietic sense lies elsewhere, specifically in the inflection from *ist* to *istet*, scripted as the literal addition of *et* to the otherwise conventional verb form *ist*. Or one could say that the word pertains here to the momentum, to the transit or the traversal, indicated by the initiated transitive function of *isten*. The word, as Heidegger explains in *On the Way to Language*, "is not," and is, therefore, not "substantive," not a being, but instead only a poietic hint.

Another way in which one could have English correspond to how Heidegger marks here the fact that being equals stillness is by hyphenating "de-scribe," which in its conventional valence indicates the ability to depict or portray, but when so hyphenated, brings out the simultaneous erasure: de-scribe writes and depicts, but does so only by de-scripting or un-writing. Since *Seyn* "is" not and cannot ever "be," for it is not (to be) a being, not a something to be differentiated from beings, it can be de-scribed through novel ways of writing, such as the inventive in-scribing of *ist* into *istet*. *Seyn* is thus never a word(sign), never a locution or a linguistic construct, but rather the impetus of giving (into) signs. When the phrase "Das Seyn istet das Seyn" gives *Seyn* over into signs, as though giving up on it by turning it into a being, it in fact de-scribes and undoes the idea that *Seyn* can be a substantive. Even if the grammatical construction implies this substantivization, it does so in order to allow us perhaps to experience precisely the transit characteristic of the movement of language.

This detailed unpacking of Heidegger's phrase provides a way for navigating Heidegger's complex vocabulary that is built around the poietic interplay of the terms for *stillness, silence, reticence,* on the one hand, and *sound* and *articulation* (*Verlautbarung*), on the other. It is also meant to be an exercise in how thinking proceeds by taking its cue from turns and inflections of words more than by using the grasping intelligence of concepts. The verbs *to say* and *to speak* (*sagen* and *sprechen*), multiply inflected through a host of prefixes and prepositions, serve as the medium, literally as the transit site, for the entrance of the stillness (*Stille*) into word-signs (*Wörter*). This cultivated vocabulary and its use by Heidegger are fairly consistent over many years and various texts, though they are certainly not iron-clad or inflexible. Yet even when the terms shift and do not completely correspond to their uses in other related texts, the main issue and its attendant difficulty remain the same: how to "say," or to make resonate within signification, that which can be said only as "unsaid" when it is approached from the perspective of expression and articulation. This is why many of the statements that Heidegger makes with regard to this tension between the said and the unsaid remain paradoxical: "Das erste Gesagte ist das *Ungesagte,* d. h. *das Sein. Aus* ihm— der *Lichtung*—wird gesagt, und *es* wird—ungesagt zunächst—gesagt" (*GA* 74, 131)—"The first said is the *unsaid,* that is, *being. From* it—the *clearing*—is said, and *it* is—for the most part unsaid—said." This sentence turns repeatedly from the said to the unsaid, pointing specifically to that which is "said" by remaining unsaid. Obviously, the sentence speaks from the point of view of signs, of language already operating with what becomes said, meant, or referred to. Anterior to what the saying says or tells in this manner, is being (*Sein*), which, still thinking from the perspective of the said, is the "first said" (*das erste Gesagte*). What comes to be "said" first and silently, before signs and therefore before *anything* actually gets said, expressed, or articulated, is, therefore, "the unsaid" (*das* Ungesagte), as Heidegger underscores it here. Since what Heidegger understands by how being "says" itself is in fact the opening up of the clearing, the clearing also comes to be "said" as for the most part unsaid, repeating the same paradox of saying by non-saying. Thus all the attention in the sentence comes to be focused on this oscillation between the said and the unsaid, or between the said *as* the unsaid, pointing to the paradoxical manner of (non)saying that is constitutive to the movement of language. What is especially significant is the fact that this (non)saying is poietic—it brings forth and lets arise—and must be clearly distinguished from "muteness," from the absence of language or of any "saying." Taking a closer look at this manner of (non)saying, one can distinguish between the two senses of "saying": one manner is conventional and has to do with articulation in speech and writing and with meaning; the second one indicates what is poietically pre-, co-, and after-said together with the said, to use Heidegger's formulation.

The difficulty here is that if what is pre-, co-, or after-said is of the valence of saying (*Sagen*), then why does it not come to be actually said? One could follow here Levinas's approach and point to the fact that the moment of saying something, precisely as the instantiation of the saying that has its own momentum, always overflows and exceeds what it signifies: the saying is irreducible to the said. This would be correct with regard to Heidegger, yet with the proviso that the saying is not something "more" in signification, which simply cannot be signified or contained in signs. Heidegger's point is rather that the unsaid is the poietic movement of the saying, which is not of the order of signification or significance, and that therefore it does not and cannot "mean." Heidegger's saying does not interrupt the said in order to point to what "transcends" or overflows it, but zeroes in on the fact that the saying can be brought into word-signs only through the restraint or refusal of its own poietic movement. This poietic momentum can therefore be thought as "non-saying" or as a peculiar manner of silent or still saying, which is not to be mistaken, however, for the negation of saying. As such, this silent saying cannot be talked "about" but must be held reticent for signification to become possible. As Heidegger explains, "'über' die Sprache reden und: das Seyn als den Grund des Wortes erschweigen. Erschweige die Stille des Da-*seins*" (GA 74, 130)—"To speak 'about' language and: to keep silent regarding beyng as the ground of the word. Keep silent regarding the stillness of Da-*sein*." What is held in reticence is being-there; placing the emphasis on *sein* and hyphenating the word as Da-*sein*, Heidegger indicates that at issue is the spatiotemporal play of the event, which outstrips in its "unprethinkable" emergence any description or meaning adduced to it. While one can produce descriptions of this experience, undergoing this experience is what keeps reticent, "non-saying" itself side by side with what can be depicted, signified, or expressed about the experience. In the rush of experiences, in the concatenation of sensible and nonsensible data and stimuli, in the midst of produced or reproduced significations and perceived manifestations, there is the "stillness" of being-there in which all these "phenomena" take place and remain lodged. And while what happens in the there of Da-sein, in the onset it provides for beings and relations, can be talked and written about, the *being*-there can only be held in language as its pre-spatiotemporal non-saying. Heidegger describes this egress of the event into language as *"the stillness holding reticence of the eventuation"—"das die Stille Haltende Erschweigen der Er-eignung"* (GA 74, 131).

What the hyphens here accomplish, transforming words like *Da-sein* or *Er-eginis,* is borne out in "silence," that is, it is neither said nor articulated into signs. The sign *Dasein* is not turned into another or a different sign but, rather, is held open to the poietic momentum of language. What thinking needs to learn here is not simply to grasp Da-sein as a new concept, producing a changed definition of what it means to be a human being, but to transform the experience of thinking by responding and corresponding to what is born out in silence by the hyphen. More important than adducing a new understanding of existence (*Dasein*) is traversing the span of the hyphen and letting thought be measured differently, and perhaps changed, by the silent resonance opened up in the midst of the sign. At stake are not only or simply new concepts but the thinking that holds active and engaged the contours of the silence or the stillness whose proper medium of unfolding is not signification. This silence is not opposed to signs or meaning, and does not amount to their pure absence, but rather points to their poietic envelope, whose resonance must be reopened from within the sign, as it were, and which Heidegger accomplishes most often with the use of the hyphen. While concepts arrest the movement of the saying by grasping it, thus evacuating the poietic momentum of the word, poietic thinking opens thought to the unprethinkable contours of the event, not taken as something that thought needs to recuperate or define anew but as what moves and guides thinking. This is, I believe, what Heidegger means by the "end of philosophy" and the "task of thinking." If philosophy is guided by the creation of new concepts, thus repeatedly trying to grasp experience and rearticulate it, then poetic thinking Heidegger wants to prepare us for takes its measure from bearing in silence what comes to be articulated. The turn here, which Heidegger hopes could free us from metaphysics—without getting rid of it, which is not possible or effective—occurs from the conceptual, grasping measure to the poietic measure of stillness, more difficult to learn and with a rigor of its own. This is why the problem of language becomes pivotal to the whole enterprise of the question of being and the exigent change in thinking. Without transforming our relation to language—from the priority of signs to the measure of the quiet stillness—thinking will not change enough for the question of being to register. If one indeed attends to Heidegger's remarks about the task of thinking, what is ventured there is done precisely by way of molding thought to the silent poietic resonance of words. As I have tried to do here, this thinking evolves literally from the silence, drawing out in writing the resonance of what, while itself bearing language, is only borne unsaid in signs.

The question then is how we can "know" this non-saying, to register or "hear" it (*hören*) at all, as Heidegger puts it, when this "unsaid" is not perceived strictly speaking, since it is neither sensible nor nonsensible. One of the paradoxical ways in which Heidegger tries to register this non-saying in language is by indicating that the word "of" being is both unheard and "over-heard," that its poietic movement is simultaneously too silent and too loud: "Auch ungehört und überhört *ist* das Wort des Seyns, und es gehört zur Wesung des Seyns selbst, ob es und wann es je zur stimmenden Stimme sich ent-schliesst" (*GA 74*, 20)—"Unheard as well as over-heard *is* the word of being, and it belongs to the unfolding of being itself, if and when it each time opens itself as the tuning voice." The italicized "is" makes clear that what lets the word of being register at all is precisely this mode of (non)saying that occurs alongside what becomes said. As most of Heidegger's remarks about this peculiar non- or over-saying, this one also deploys the vocabulary of hearing and voice, though voice is thought and determined by Heidegger not in terms of the phonetic but instead from *Stimmen:* disposition or tuning. The same holds true for the other terms that have to do with hearing, since *hören*, to hear, unfolds inceptually as a mode of belonging: *gehören*. Like the "voice," "hearing" is also not auditory but poietic, since it indicates the fold of belonging to the movement of language. What Heidegger calls "the word 'of' being" designates the between that spaces and locates the human belonging to being, belonging that is already disposed or tuned in particular, historical, ways. The word pertains, in short, to the hyphen in *Da*-sein, specifically to the emphasis that the hyphen shifts onto the verb "to be" in order to foreground the engaged, singular, always one-time unfolding of being-there. The word as the hyphen time-spacing the sign *Da-sein* disposes and lets belong (*Stimmen* and *gehören*) before the sign can "voice" or vocalize, before anything is given to be heard in the first place.

The Quiet Stillness, or the New Sensibility of Language

Separating his approach from the metaphysical understanding of language as *phone semantike* through the prism of the sensible and the intelligible, Heidegger indicates that language is originatively neither sensible nor "nonsensibly spiritual" (*unsinnlich geistige*): "Es gilt ein Anderes—gerade die Lautung, das Spruchhafte, zu wissen, aber eben nicht als 'Ton' und als blosse Versinnlichung, Äusserung, sondern Spruch als Bruch und Erdung *der Stille;* ihr Er-klingen als *Wahrung des Seyns,* ihr Stimmen das Stimmen der Stimmung" (*GA 74*, 131)—"Something other obtains—rather to know the sounding, the dictum, but precisely not as 'tone' and mere making sensuous, expression, but dictum as the fracture [*Bruch*] and the grounding [*Erdung*] of *the stillness;* its sounding as the *safeguarding of beyng,* its voice as the attuning of the attunement." This particular quotation replays once more the scenario known from other texts on language and poetry in Heidegger's work, where he takes the terms of sensible perception in order to twist and inflect them. Heidegger chooses phonetic and auditory terms like *sound, voice, ringing,* and *saying,* apparently because of the metaphysical manner of grounding language and signification in the sound, in *phone,* that is meaningful. As *phone semantike,* language relies on the sensible in its differential movement and strife with the intelligible, which recalls the strife of world and earth in "The Origin of the Work of Art." In this view, language works thanks to the difference of the sensible and the intelligible, where the signifier and the signified function as the originative linguistic difference.

Starting with the phonetic and auditory phenomena, Heidegger proceeds to re-ground them with regard to the event and its poietic disposition (*Stimmung*). This is done by rejecting the notion that words in his idiomatic sense are to be "grasped as a purely nonsensible or 'spiritual' word"—"um das rein unsinnlich 'geistige' Wort zu fassen" (*GA* 74, 131). The words in Heidegger's sense are neither purely spiritual nor mystical or irrational, just as they are also not simply sensible, auditory, or scriptural. Despite his openly critical stance with regard to the metaphysical notion of *phone semantike,* Heidegger nonetheless pursues his exploration of the experience of language in terms redolent of the sensible and the auditory, and primarily of sound. Sound becomes so prominent on the one hand because of the traditional prominence of "meaningful sound" in reflection on language and on the other because the word for language, *Sprache,* is (over)determined by its etymological link to speech. A creative way to understand Heidegger's preoccupation with listening, speaking, and saying could be to see his approach as needing to pass and work through these terms, which define language as the "sensible" medium, in order to disclose the way signs arise from the event as the singular way the event comes each time to word. While this coming to word is, strictly speaking, neither sensible nor nonsensible, its articulation in speech and writing involves a response operating in these very terms. Even if not always consistent or even explicitly presented, this impulse of working through and "beyond" the sensible grounding of language as *phone semantike,* frequently by literally transforming the resonance of these terms, remains unmistakable in Heidegger's thought, even if Heidegger's work leaves it to us to develop this path.[8]

Heidegger reworks *Sprache* (language) through speaking, sign, and saying (*Sprechen, Zeichen,* and *Sagen*) all the way to *Zeigen* (showing), in order to disclose the "word" as the poietic momentum of the event. Similarly, *Verlatubarung* (the term that indicates in Heidegger the "sounding" or articulation into letters and sounds) is inflected through various terms for sound in order to be finally linked to *Laut,* which as Heidegger cautions is not mere sound (*Schall*) and is therefore nothing sensible to begin with, without being, therefore, simply a nonsensible equivalent of sound, that is, its "spiritual" counterpart or even sound-image. Likewise, the ability to hear and the facility of speaking (*sprechen*), together with the correlative notion of language as the sensible/intelligible construct (*Sprache*), all come from belonging (*gehören*) to the movement of the word, which it becomes possible to note through the displacement into Da-sein. This displacement of the human into Da-sein is enacted in Heidegger as a repeated traversal through saying, voice, and sound, which takes us beyond the sensible/intelligible fold into the event's occurrence as its coming to word, that is, into the constitutive belonging and poietic attunement that render language possible for humans in the first place. "The turning essentially occurs in between the call (to the one that belongs) and the belonging (of the one that is called): the turning is a counter-turning. . . . Every language of Da-sein originates here and is thus in essence silence (cf. restraint, event, truth, and language)" (*CP,* 323). In this counter-turning, "*Laut*" acquires a distinct resonance: "*Laut*—nicht von Schrift her als Zeichending, das die Stelle vertritt und an die Stelle tritt für die Bedeutung" (*GA* 74, 108)—"*Sound*—not from script as a sign-thing, which represents the place and comes to stand in the place for signification." In other words, Heidegger departs from conceiving *Laut* in terms of speech or vocalization, as sound related to letters, where both speech and writing have their origin in their relation as *phone semantike* to what they signify or designate—here the German *Bedeutung* brings into view both signification and denotation. Instead, in order to experience the way-making of language, "sound" (*Laut*) needs to be allowed to resound in its proper belonging to being: "*Lauten*—erklingen lassen—einvernehmen, er-eignen in die Zugehörigkeit zum Seyn. Es kommt hier nicht in die Vergegenständlichung und das Rechnen mit Wörterzeichen" (*GA* 74, 108)—"*To sound*—to let resound—to take in, to appropriate into the belonging to beyng. This does not come about in objectification or calculating with word-signs." While *Lauten* means primarily to "sound out," Heidegger uses it to register specifically the movement of "coming to word," since this verb also means "to read" or "to state" in the sense of coming to a particular language form or expression. What Heidegger makes clear is that this coming to word cannot be captured by playing with word-signs (*Wörterzeichen*), because there the inceptual momentum of the word is no longer visible or audible; the relation of belonging in listening (*Zugehörigkeit*) from which language rises to be heard/read has been overwritten by signs.

At several decisive moments in his explanation of the word's relation to the sensible and to sound, Heidegger makes references to the strife of world and earth in order to contextualize his comments on language as *phone semantike*. When he denies that the word could be understood from either the intelligible or the spiritual, he introduces two terms to describe his alternative poietic sense of the word: *Bruch*, fissure or fault; and *Erdung*, earthing, also in the sense of having a footing, perhaps reminiscent of his discussion of the earth as the resting site of the world in "The Origin of the Work of Art." In a section of *GA 74* titled "Das Ereignishaft Anfägnliche 'des Sinnlichen,'" Heidegger indicates that the sensible must be thought as "more" sensible than the metaphysical understanding of the sensible allows for, which means that this sensible would be: "earthier—*more concealing—more inceptual*"; "*erdiger—bergender—anfänglicher*." Similarly, the nonsensible is recast here as "more lightening—unconcealing—*more inceptual*"—"Lichtender—Entbergender—*Anfänglicher*" (*GA 74*, 159). What links these attempts at a nonmetaphysical incarnation of the sensible and the nonsensible is the fact that they are thought more inceptually, that is, from the event rather than from the metaphysical difference between the sensible and the nonsensible. The earthy, Heidegger adds, is "what shelters the open, calls the sky, and only together with those in the circling of the event"—"das Offene bergende, den Himmel Rufende und mit diesem erst im Reigen des Ereignisses" (*GA 74*, 159). With the allusion to the circling of the event, Heidegger indicates that the "sensible" as the earthy is thought of from within the world's fourfold, not simply in difference from the nonsensible but rather as one of the vectors of the unfolding of being. Providing the momentum for the unfolding of the sensible, the earthy participates in the world's occurrence within being's event. In this event, being is "not divine, not human, not non-living and not living"—"nicht göttlich, nicht menschlich, nicht leblos und nicht lebendig" (*GA 74*, 39). The terms of life, humanity, and even divinity cede their priority to being, to its event, which is neither alive nor lifeless, but indicates the recess opened through being's withdrawal, along the back draft of the event, where living and nonliving beings are brought into the open to begin with. When Heidegger refers to *Erdung* or the *erdige*, he does not mean the earth as either a planet or as the material support for life and nonliving beings alike, but appears to point instead to what, within the event, renders possible the experience of the sensible and the nonsensible. The "earthy" provides the "footing" for what exists to be experienced in its sensible and/or intelligible dimensions. It belongs to the poietic momentum of the event as its force of sheltering (*Bergung*), with regard to which the open becomes possible.

The earthy is thus neither simply the sensible nor the material, understood as the basis or the medium for the existence of beings. While Heidegger does not develop this "more than sensible" dimension of the earthy, his re-·marks on the strife of world and earth and on the relation between the binary of the sensible and the nonsensible, on the one hand, and the earthy, on the other, suggest the possibility—one still to be developed—of thinking both materiality and the sensible from the earthy momentum of the event. It does not mean that the earthy or the "earthing" (*Erdung*) somehow precedes the material and the sensible, but rather than our experience of materiality and sensibility is guided, disposed, or given its orientation by the earthy. It is in the specific sense of *Stimmen*—as the originative disposition of sensible and material experience—that what Heidegger designates as the earthy can be understood as anterior to materiality and sensibility. In its capacity for sheltering, the earthy as one of the vectors of the event opens the ways in which one can experience being in terms of materiality and the sensible.

In a similar way, one also can explain the role that *Laut* plays in Heidegger's understanding of language. *Laut* is not a mere sound to begin with, neither *Schall* (sound) nor *Hall* (sound, reverb), but rather the tone, taken as the "ringing" or "pealing" (*Geläut*) of the stillness into which being unfolds. Therefore, *Laut* should be taken initially in relation to *Stimmem*, as what specifically allows one to "read" the disposition or tonality in which experience takes place. The term *Geläut* suggests an echo or a resonance coming off the withdrawal or the departure (*Abschied*) that constitutes the event. Without pushing this metaphorical language too far, the *Geläut* can be thought to come from the inward collapse (of being), the event's back draft, which opens up as the clearing. It is this withdrawal, the "de-partive" clearing, that re-sounds in what Heidegger rather enigmatically calls "the peal of stillness." As being retracts, the "peal" serves as an initial echo-sound or even an echo-location in the specific sense in which one can speak about topology or topographics in Heidegger's later thought. If that is the case, the peal (*Geläut*) is nothing other than the initial "echo map" of the clearing, indicating the vectors of its unfolding, the nonrepeatable rifts and fissures of relations and differences. This poietic—emergent, making its way—topographeme of the clearing and of language in its arrival in word-signs becomes discernible precisely through reticence, which lets thinking move while holding it within the stillness of being: "Erschweigung der Er-eignung (das heisst des Seyns)—Ab-grund (der einholenden Über-kunft)"—"Keeping silent of the event (that is, of beyng)—abyss (retrieving the overflow)" GA 74, 133).[9] This way of keeping silent guards the abyssal non-grounding openness of the *Abgrund*, the fissure or the fault, whereby the stillness comes to be broken by the word (*GA* 74, 102), whose reverberation, outstripping the present, catches up to the coming future.

Perhaps the best way to understand Heidegger's separation of *Laut* from the idea of "mere" sound is to think of *Laut* as the "ontological" outlining of the topography, that is, of the poietic vectors and transversals, of the clearing. This is suggested by a similar twist Heidegger introduces into the term *Schmerz*, or pain, which on several occasions, including his discussion of Trakl as well as his remarks in *Das Ereignis* and in *Zum Wesen der Sprache und Zur Frage nach der Kunst*, he understands poietically as corresponding to the other terms that connote rifts and fissures outlining the movement of language. The difference might be that *Schmerz* comes to function poignantly as one of the fundamental tonalities of the experience of being, not as existential, psychological, or bodily pain but as the signature rift shaping the movement of language: "der *Schmerz*: der Zeit-Raum des *Winkens* . . . Die Sprache als entreissend, aus dem Riss nehmend das Wort fort in das *Lauten*" (*GA* 74, 57)—"*Pain*: the time-space of *hinting*. . . Language as rifting apart, taking the word out of the rift into *sounding*." Here *Lauten* refers to the movement of the word toward signs, when the initially "lautlose Stimme der Stille" (*GA* 74, 150)—perhaps best rendered as the soundless disposition of the stillness—breaks into sound. Trying to explain *Laut* yet another way, Heidegger remarks that it rises from the unfolding stillness and its disposition of relations, from its emergent voice and attunement. The rift in the stillness, the event as the emergent, poietically contoured outline of language: "*The rift* gives the first sound (viewed essentially), *breaks* the stillness, but it precisely breaks the stillness and essences as its break and severance. The sounding as a privation of stillness"—"*Riss* gibt den ersten (wesensmässig gesehen) Laut, *bricht* die Stille, aber bricht eben die Stille und west nur als ein Bruch und *Ab-bruch* dieser. Lautung eine Privation dieser Stille" (*GA* 74, 132). This is the moment in which Heidegger pinpoints the origination of "sound" (*Laut*), which is shown here as the initial sounding of the opening rift. *Laut* encodes the silent design of the rift, the mapping of the event's onset toward words, which "comes off" the event's back draft as the topographic-poietic relief of the clearing. This becomes clearer in the following comment: "The sound is the *reverberation* of the stillness in the in-between of the outcome. The 'vocalization' not essential"—"Der Laut ist der *Widerhall* der Stille im Inzwischen des Austrags. Die 'Äusserung' nicht das Wesentliche" (*GA* 74, 142). In the outcome or the settling of language into signs, "sound" (*Laut*) breaks and separates from the stillness, proceeding to become the sounding (*Lauting*) of language, which turns into the *Verlautbarung*, that is, into the articulation—"resounding"—into speech and writing. Unlike the echoing of the stillness/silence, the spoken or written statements are not as essential to language as the reverberation of the clearing within the movement of the word.

This complex poietic topographic of the clearing finds its reflection in the shifts, displacements, and transversals that Heidegger induces in words and, through them, in thinking. His interest in the poietic momentum of thinking leads him to make many well-known statements about the neighborhood of poetry and thinking (*Dichtung* or *Dichten* and *Denken*), and to claim that *Dichtung* and *Denken* pay attention to and "say" the same, namely being (*Seyn*). This means not that poetry and thinking are identical or equal, but that in their distinct modes of unfolding, both *Dichten* and *Denken*, to the extent that they mind the poietic momentum of language, become able to attend to the "same": to the event in its each-time one-time and singular occurrence. The poietic refers to the characteristic momentum of the word as bringing forth, which gives the first dispositive orientation to what comes into being. This poietic impulse is, therefore, the *Stimmen* that tones and tempers relations and beings in a manner that renders them experience-able. Only as such a disposition, the *Stimmen* becomes "voice," "sound," and human language as *Sprache*. Attending to "the same," thinking makes its ways in the neighborhood of poetry perhaps in the specific sense in which it can transpire as *Besinnung*, that is, as attentive to the "sense," *Sinn*, of being, prior to and inclusive of its sensible and intelligible registers. Thinking can thus backtrack the movement of language as the silent back draft of the event, which opens the span of experience in its initially poietic *Sinn* as it is breaking open into the sensible and the intelligible.

It is in this vein that I see Heidegger's multiple ventures and excursions into the territory of poetry: not simply as attempts at interpreting or reading poetry, but as essays in thinking the "same" that poetry thinks in its distinct manner. While Heidegger writes extensively about poetry and poets, these texts often strike readers as conventional in their approach, because they focus frequently on what certain words or phrases mean and on how to re-think these terms in the context of the question of being. Its conventionality notwithstanding, Heidegger's approach is also quite idiosyncratic and often inventive, especially when he indicates that his interest lies primarily in what remains unthought in the poetry, rather than in what poems either say expressly or convey implicitly. The moments in which Heidegger draws out the unthought from the poems he examines yield interesting and often radically inventive remarks, for instance, about the poietic character of dwelling—that is, about the way poetry brings into the open and constitutes dwelling as dwelling—or about the poetic measure distinct from techno-scientific measurement. Yet Heidegger is even more convincing, and certainly more interesting and innovative, in what he does with and to German in his texts; not only texts on poetry or language but, sometimes even more ingeniously, in the initially unpublished texts from 1930s and 1940s, which count, so far at least, as his most radical writings with regard to their language. The essays on poetry and language known from post–World War II publications inevitably offer propositional discourse and assertions *about* poetry, whether Hölderlin's, Rilke's, or Trakl's. To the extent to which lectures and essays must resort to statements and propositions, these texts continue to erect obstacles to their own attempts to undergo an experience with language or thinking, as Heidegger admits at the end of "Time and Being." This is why it appears more important to follow and develop the paths suggested by Heidegger's thinking in these essays and especially those opened by the idiomatic turns of his own language, whether with respect to grammar or, most inventively, with regard to lexis. If, as Heidegger indicates, *Dichtung* unfolds in the register of the unsaid, the unprethinkable, and the silent, then to be attentive to it one must gauge the resonance of scriptural marks, hyphens, colons, prefixes, and, especially, of how they displace or modify the lexical and grammatical functions of linguistic signs. This is why Heidegger's attentiveness to his own thinking, his deliberate consideration of its twists and openings, and above all his inventive treatment of language and its words, often disclose the poietic momentum of his thinking, more so than his texts on poetry. This is partly the case because of Heidegger's focus on more traditional romantic and neo-romantic poetry—Hölderlin, Rilke, or Trakl—rather than more innovative, avant-garde texts, though Heidegger's interest in Celan's work, or even his short note on Rimbaud, complicates this one-sided picture. In any case, Heidegger's lack of or limited familiarity with more innovative or textually experimental poetic writing in the twentieth century should not foreclose consideration of what these trends in poetry offer for the development of poetic thinking after Heidegger. As I have explored in several essays, the radicalism of Heidegger's treatment of language and its impact on the change he wants to make from philosophy to poetic thinking, can come into much stronger and convincing relief precisely through resonances with innovative poetic practice. To suggest how examination of such poetry can help us bring out the contours of poetic thinking after Heidegger and its potential intersections with innovative poetry, I offer here a discussion of the affinity between Heidegger's interest in silence and restraint in language and a corresponding elaboration of writing's relation to silence by two contemporary US poets, Susan Howe and Myung Mi Kim.

The Poietic, Reticent Practice of the Word

Since it is linked to his critique of power and his idiom of releasement and letting be (*Gelassenheit*), it is possible to say that there is a "feminine" aspect to Heidegger's emphasis on reticence and silence, which may mean here a departure from the letter of Heidegger's work, who does not consider these issues in such terms. Still, this possibility becomes evident when one follows the shifts in the tenor of Heidegger's work, from the "bluster" and apparent self-assuredness of *Being and Time* (though even there Dasein is gender-unmarked, as though its mode of being were resisting the very rhetoric in which it is being described), to the engagé mode of the early 1930s, full of references to power, violence, and so on, to the sharp critique of power, violence, and mastery in the late 1930s, and eventually to the markedly different tone of texts after "Letter on Humanism." There is room here only to remark on it and point to the ways in which Heidegger's late writings try to evolve a style in which the subject (grammatical and human) tends to be called into question and cedes priority to language, especially to its silences and lacunae. If this restraint and reticence is indeed the "feminine" tonality of language, it must be differentiated not only from the "masculine" rhetoric of power and certainty but also, and even more emphatically, given the patriarchal slant of Western thought, from the emasculated or "feminized" powerlessness. This is why the "feminine" here must be seen with regard to the attempt at a new relation to language that would envelop in reticently stringent thinking and in poetic deployment of language the traditional priority invested in meaning, power, or knowledge.

The distinctness and interplay of muteness and silence in Heidegger finds many counterparts in twentieth- and twenty-first-century poetry, yet is particularly salient in Susan Howe's writings. As Howe herself has suggested on several occasions, her work is animated by the project of the recovery of voices rendered mute by the vicissitudes of history and power, and especially of the forgotten voices of women, among which the signature ones are Stella and Cordelia from *The Europe of Trusts*. At issue in Howe's writings, though, is never simply a reclaiming or reinvestment of power, or a redressing of the balance of power by restoring poetic voice to mute characters, stories, and events. This does not mean, however, that such redress is not at all at stake in Howe, but rather that we need to approach it through what is at work and at stake *poetically* in her texts and not foreclose the optics to primarily political terms. For if politics *is* at stake in Howe's work, and it would be hard to maintain that it is not, it is so by way of her poetics, specifically by way in which her writing performs the poetic saying through opening the text to silence. Furthermore, the recovery/reconstruction/restitution of voices underway in Howe's poetry concerns precisely the possibility of evolving a way of writing, and with it a way of thinking that, contrary to the operations of power and its emphatic proclamations, would remain attentive to the underside of words and the power of meaning—or, in short, would transpire as power-free. Reanimation and restitution of voice in Howe, whether to specific persons, texts, situations, or occurrences, does not lie in introducing changes or shifts into the distribution of presence and absence of power, a change of the sign from – to + in front of power. Instead, the articulation and thus the re-cloaking of a given voice, say, of Hope Atherton, within the power of the poetic text, attempts in the same gesture to introduce into the nexus of signification, knowledge, and power, a different modality of saying: a poietic saying that performs specifically the force of possibility in its silent claim, which is neither mute nor lacking power.

This interplay between redressing muteness and performing silence becomes particularly salient in Howe's recent *Souls of the Labadie Tract,* where the title "souls" become in a way reanimated, with their thoughts, affects, and sayings re-voiced and pasted into the poetic text in a manner resembling Jonathan Edwards's fixing of pieces of paper on his clothing while traveling on horseback, which Howe mentions in the *Errand* that opens the book (*SLT,* 9). Unlike Edwards, who tried to bring out naked ideas and extricate them from any ambiguity or confusion, Howe explores the poetic ways in which facts, statements, or ideas, in the sense of *Aussage* in Heidegger, inevitably come as clothed in language. It is this sense of the clothing of what happens in poetic language that guides Howe's texts, as an epigraph from Stevens's "Adagia" reveals: "The poet makes silk dresses out of worms" (*SLT,* 7).

The first sequence of poems in the book, "Souls of the Labadie Tract," can be seen as an exemplar of Howe's reanimating practices described in the "Personal Narrative," including the remark that Howe for the first time encountered the term Labadist during her genealogical research of Wallace Stevens and his wife, Elsie Kachel Stevens (*SLT,* 23). The second long sequence of poems, "118 Westerly Terrace" and the *Errand* prefacing it, explicitly channel Howe's text through a restaging of sorts of Stevens's writing practice: jotting ideas and perceptions on scraps of paper, having them typed by his stenographers, and finally transforming the initial confusion of the typed text into poems (*SLT,* 73). The book ends with Howe's own typically typographical miscellany, "Fragment of the Wedding Dress of Sarah Pierpont Edwards." Opening with a black-and-white photograph of the dress's fragment, this shorter sequence of poems appears as a visual paste-up of miscellaneous notes and fragments, layered, crossed, and warped in ways emphasizing the

trailing off, fragmentation, and erasure, over grammatical structure and semantic completeness. The poems appear to be, that is, manifest themselves
as, more about their visual composition than about lexical meaning. What
is "visible" over and against the meaning of words and sentence fragments
is their layering, overlapping, and crossing (out): the invisible relations and
hinges become poetically visualized on the page. All the poems in the book
but one are centered, habituating the eye to expect the words to occupy the
center of the page and thus visibly expose the blankness that borders it, nearly
symmetrically, on all sides. The last text in the volume is a single, vertical
semi-line, in which a fragmented line of writing has been partially erased
by slightly curved blank paper strips superimposed on its top and bottom.
The line thus has no beginning and no end, and appears partially out of
the opening of blankness only to vanish back into it. One can identify the
breaks between words, but no words can be read, no lexical meaning culled
from the "line." Thus the book's ending could not be more emphatic in its
insistence on drawing our attention precisely to how language emerges out of
silence, unfolds with silence surrounding it, and disappears back into it. The
indiscernible words appear to be released by and out of silence, marked off
against it, and dissolved eventually into it. On the last page of Howe's book,
silence literally appears as the medium in which language exists, as it is the
air in which words can have meaning and in which language can make sense.
In this specific way, silence operates as the ab-sense, as what surrounds, layers, crosses, and keeps sense moving. As ab-sense, silence is the "sense" that
resonates in the German *Be-sinnung,* the sense apart from (as in *Ab-schied*)
and prior to both sense and non-sense, in the manner that recalls the abyssal
non-ground (*Ab-grund*) released from grounding in Heidegger.

This silence at the core of *Souls of the Labadie Tract* is not the muteness
of the voices ("souls") that the text brings "back to life." The voices become
reanimated into a different "textual practice," as it were, one no longer oriented by the presence and power of voice articulated against the powerlessness associated with muteness but instead performed through the layering of
voice and silence. The voices in Howe's texts speak precisely by being attentive
to silence. They do not simply reclaim power by breaking out of muteness
but doing so transform the poetic texts into a miscellany of silence, into the
performance of the force of silence. This is visibly so in the composition of
the sequences of poems: all the poems are short, with short lines, which allow them to occupy the center of the page and give most room to blankness/
silence. By way of attention to words and poetic texts, Howe draws attention
to silence, giving it not simply the priority of space but, more important, the
force of the momentum of the poetic language.

This particular attentiveness to silence can be seen in Howe's re-collaging and re-practicing of Stevens's work. This poetic re-practice has to do especially with the Stevensian attentiveness to the singularity of the experience of the everyday, whose signature expression, as Howe reminds us, can be found in Stevens's poem "The Course of a Particular," which focuses on and delivers what is both ordinary and extraordinary in the familiar at hand (*SLT,* 74). The poetic text becomes a house—"the house of being"?—a poetic dwelling, whose many authors echo in words sheltered by the pages: "In the house the house is all" (*SLT,* 77). Indeed, it seems that Howe is speaking here of something like Heidegger's "house of being," of the poetic language always already clothing reality, the near-at-hand. In fact, every page of the poetic sequences of *Souls* is built as such a house, with the words that, echoing their many authors, come to be enclosed and sheltered by the silent blankness of the surrounding space. Each page is a poetic house, a performance of a poetic dwelling, with the singular experience of the near-at-hand.

This particular composition of the poetic page makes apparent the preeminent role played here by the way in which words, fragments, and sentences become sheltered, or housed, by silence. One could say that in *Souls,* silence *performs* in the specific sense in which it is the house of words and meanings: the ab-sense of language always already making sense. At stake in this performance is a kind of double clothing: of things and experiences into words and of words into silence. The issue is not simply the bringing of what is into words, but doing so in a way that lets what exists come into words and resonate in the course of its particularity, to echo Stevens. What comes to resonate in this clothing into words and silence is precisely being, the *is* in its insistent particularity: "*it*—it in itself insistent *is*" (*SLT,* 97). Beauty here is thought in the way in which Heidegger mentions it in the "Addendum" to "The Origin of the Work of Art" (*BW,* 207), namely as the bringing into being. In parallel to Stevens's poems "A Primitive like an Orb" and "Of Mere Being," Howe underscores the verbal—nominal play of "is" sliding into an "it," becoming something: a thing, an entity, a being, and yet insisting on its "is," on the fact that it "happens," that is, exists as never being reducible to an it. Being is always already (in) beings and yet insists on its silent distinctness: "it in itself insistent *is*."

This insistence of *is* in *it* emphasizes the always one-time and singular—to recall Heidegger—"course of a particular." Poetic practice that performs this insistent *is* must be attentive to silence: not just to the power of words and the muteness, even if sometimes eloquent, of powerlessness but specifically to silence and its clothing of words. It is in the way in which silence clothes and encloses words, like the last page of *Souls,* that the always repeatable words and significations can perhaps maintain the "silent" mark of the nonrepeatable course of the particular, the saying of being. The insistent play of the "is" in every "it"—the verbal resonance inside every nominal utterance—performs the particularity that becomes muffled by linguistic signs. It also reminds us that "we have a / world resting on nothing" (*SLT*, 46): another Stevensian, and also Heideggerian, motif increasingly prominent in Howe's writings. The only way that the course of a particular can perhaps be performed in language is by way of openness and attentiveness to the insistently silent *is* whose spatiotemporal event can transpire as such only when the nothingness (Stevens's "giant of nothingness"?), with its silent force of the possible, can be instantiated in its poietic, that is, originative, momentum. The force of this nothingness is never simply negative, since marking the insistent *is* in every *it*, it also opens up every *it* to the play of possibilities. Yet this force of the possible is insistently silent and can be allowed to play in language precisely through the relation of words to silence; and specifically through the way in which silence comes to be said through and with words. *Is* saying itself silently with *it*, with this *it* being said, signified, and kept by words. *Is* as the word (*Wort*) resonating in every sign (*Wörterzeichen*) for an it.

Howe allows silence the insistence of its *is* often through visual compositions of the poetic page: from erasures, crossings, listing, to centering, overlapping, and emergence/vanishing, as on the last page of *Souls*. Myung Mi Kim's work elicits many comparisons with Howe's, especially when considering how silence and blankness play in their texts with re-voicing and restitution. Without, however, delving here into such comparisons, I want to underscore the point where Kim's poetic practice tends to associate silence with music and perform it often through a musical-like linguistic notation. This is not to say that typographic composition does not play a major role in Kim's poetry but rather to remark that the poetic layout of the page in her works comes to be affiliated, perhaps even shaped by, ways of notating silence.[10] Among the various notational devices deployed through Kim's several volumes of poetry—square, single, and double brackets, colons, commas, vertical slashes, dashes, and so on—perhaps the most interesting ones are the double colons serving as "titles" of poems in *Dura* and the various compositions of slashes in *River Antes*.[11] While the title *Dura* plays on Dura mater (the outer layer of the meninges) and the Dura language still existing in Nepal, it inevitably conjures up association with duration, temporal extension, even Bergsonian *durée*, or, in short, with the rhythm of unfolding time. Not surprisingly, Kim's compositions of the text on the page seem to have a great deal to do precisely with performing duration, rather than with spatial location or distribution. For example, the writing in *Dura* appears deliberately hesitant, cautions, mindful of not making easy connections, resisting what Kim refers to as "conjunction used with abandon" (*D*, 96). Holding off quick transitions, pages of *Dura* prefer to emphasize intervals, hiatus, empty spaces, as in a series of spaced out fragments separated by square brackets, which keep the phrases juxtaposed and at the same time prevent them from conjoining and forming more complete or fuller syntactical structures:

Vision of the form]   [bloody mess of the city
Precisely printing]   [warping
Primary fact]   [migratory (*D*, 96)

At the same time, the square brackets emphasize the hiatus of silence, which, however, does not remain mute but instead in a performative gesture (the literal bracketing open) holds open more possibilities for the phrases to relate or enter into new compositional arrangements.

Another version of such intervals are the elongated spaces between pairs of words or phrases both separated and related by colons: "Proven pulse: barb light" or "Donor: dolor"; or "Braving cut: neck without collar" (*D*, 27). Such longer intervals can be seen in terms of literally allowing more "breathing room" for the line and for language, actuating through blankness the underside of possibilities that accompanies any connection, grammatical or lexical, between words and phrases. These ways of indexing and foregrounding durational silences are framed by practices of having pairs of colons separated by several spaces serve as "titles" or perhaps indications of duration, for most of the poems in *Dura*. As a result, most of the book's pages are crowned by a visual/linguistic notational composition that looks like this:

:   :

One obviously can treat these pairs as purely graphical marks, empty and serving the function of graphically separating poems. At the same time, colons, like the one preceding the illustration of *Dura*'s double colons, can be seen as an emphatic marker, a call to paying greater attention, and as a minimal hiatus allowing for the greater affective and/or explanatory effect of what the colon is meant to introduce. Indeed, another way of thinking about the colons is as markers of introduction. But what the first colon introduces is another colon: an introduction to introduction, perhaps, spiraling into a postmodern version of poetry on poetry. Given the context of *Dura,* it seems more likely that the colons perform visually the relational aspects of words and phrases, of language more broadly. The doubling of colons thus serves to telescope attention onto relation, or, more precisely, onto the relation to relation: (:   :). Pairs of colons form then poetic tracks or channels, spacing and drawing together vectors of relating: the relational force itself. In short, the pairs of colons may indeed form the foundational, or better, the originative gesture of Kim's writing. What this gesture sketches and draws out are simply the indexes of relation, manifesting the fact that silence is never mute; that is, it does not involve the absence of the ability to speak but rather manifests the ab-sense of language as the time-space of possibility.

This time-space performs duration in the sense in which music enacts it and in this context it underscores the musical aspect of poetic language. Not just the musical plays of words, the rhythm and pacing of phrases, or intonational indexes but musical in a more originative sense: as the temporal spacing and composing understood specifically as the performance of the poietic dimension of language. Perhaps not of relations as yet, for these necessitate already the presence of what is involved in the relation, the relata, but of the vectors *for* and *of* relating. Differently said, the colons trace the vectors, otherwise invisible, which animate the time-space *for* words. The colons thus not only relate words or draw our attention to how words can be related, but are therefore preverbal in the sense of indicating the momentum into which words are taken in by being related to other words, by forming phrases, clusters, and sentences. Performing silence as the vectoring of language relations, the colons set the tone, the *Stimmung,* for the text; and they do it quite literally, that is, they set the tonality of the poetic text itself, pre-scribing the ways in which durations of silence house, to recall Howe's *Souls of the Labadie Tract,* meaning, affect, expression, etc. The colons are pre-scriptive not in the normative sense but rather in spatial and temporal terms; they pre-scribe, ante-write the silent vectoring of the poetic page.

In *River Antes,* this temporally and spatially pre-scriptive role is performed by vertical slashes, which, one is tempted to say, dictate the tempo of the second part of the chapbook that consists of five sections of four-page folios, forming a miniseries. Instead of titles or pagination (the entire chapbook dispenses with page numbers), the initial pages of the folios bear a specific notation in the bottom right corner of the pages, which also perform the role of their title page:

$$/$$
$$/. \quad //$$

The absence of pagination may be taken as a sign that the composition is to be read not by (absent) page numbers but in some other way; or at least it invites a nonpaginated, nonsequential reading, underscoring the spatial and temporal duration of the unfolding word compositions. Approached this way, the slashes pre-scribe the tonality for this poetic language, silently indexing the time-space for meaning. If the entire chapbook dispenses with page numbers, the penultimate page of *River Antes* dispenses with words and offers a composition of slashes. What is being signlessly and silently notated here is the outline, the aperture of language, its performative opening, which on the last page of Howe's *Souls* is indicated by the illegible line emerging from and reentering curved spaces of silence. It constitutes then a notation of the event of language, or, more precisely, of the fact that language happens as event, an event irreducible to signification, poetic composition, words, or the silences between them. The penultimate page of *River Antes* is sign-less not in the sense that it lacks signs or remains mute, that is, lacking words or the capability to express what needs to be said. Rather, it is sign-free as in becoming free from the power play of language without simply being reduced to muteness. It shows that the originative tracking of language, its performative pre-scription—before words, before speech and writing—can be *macht-los,* or power-free, in the sense in which Heidegger pushes poietic thinking and poetic language to be released and freed from the power (and the dominance of the sign), and thus to become capable of letting the tonality of the poem accommodate itself to listening open to silence.

This deliberateness of the language listening to itself, to its horizontal and vertical vibrations, to what might be called the duration of its experience, constitutes the poietic momentum of Kim's writing. If poetic writing takes the shape of listening, before "speaking" or as an opening onto speaking/ writing, it is because for Kim it is language that speaks first, and the poet's ear follows it, listening to the possibilities and the constraints shaping the prosody of everyday living. On this point, Kim's poetry can be read in proximity to Heidegger's reflections on listening to the "speaking" of language, for as Heidegger remarks in "Language": "Language speaks. / Man speaks in that he responds to language. This responding is a hearing. It hears [*hört*] because it belongs [*gehört,* belongs by way of listening] to the command [*Geheiss*] of stillness. / It is not a matter here of stating a new view of language. What is important is learning to dwell in the speaking of language. To do so, we need to examine constantly whether and to what extent we are capable of what genuinely belongs to responding [*Entsprechen*]: anticipation in reserve" (*PLT,* 207; *GA* 12, 30). Heidegger's remarks on the priority of listening as indicative of the poietic momentum of language depend here on the way that he himself hears language, here, German, speak. This listening is given its tonality (*Stimmung*) by the way it occurs as belonging to the prosody of being and thus as always already listening to it, provided one pays attention to how such listening takes place.

The writing of poems proceeds from this "poietic" listening. And this listening is poietic precisely because it brings about what is said in the poem, calibrating the liberative potential of writing, to invoke Kim's remark. As one reads the poem or listens to it unfold, one is in fact listening to the way in which writing has already been following (from) the poietic listening, that is, one listens to the notation of this listening "in advance of" writing. Yet this listening happens as "in advance of" writing, that is, as having always already happened, only *in* the writing, that is, in the "now" *occurring* as writing. The priorness of listening (be)comes only within the response, that is, within the poetic writing. Again, this can really be literally read or heard in Heidegger's German, for "response" is *Entsprechen,* a speaking that echoes the speaking of language. Yet the prefix *ent-* indicates that this response/re-speaking already happens through a lapse—it skips a beat, as it were. It responds to the way language happens as language by "corresponding"/co-responding to it, but this correspondence comes with a lapse, a miss characteristic of the promise, the *Versprechen,* of language. The human language is a re-speaking, an after-saying (*nachsagen*), which is already a mis-speaking, which delineates the dispersion onto the page and into signs of the way language comes to language. This originative relation of language is scripted into the human response to language, notated as the hyphen in *Ent-sprechen,* since the hyphen time-spaces the relation between *Sprechen* (the speaking of language itself) and *Entsprechen* (the human speaking after language). The hyphen, even when it remains unwritten, and perhaps then even more so, resonates silently throughout Heidegger's reflection on language, recalling that language occurs as event, that is, as having spoken (silently) in the human speaking (*Ent-sprechen*). The difficulty in bringing this originative relation of language to words is due precisely to the fact that this happening of language—its event—is not spoken or written as such, that it can be only noted and notated silently. As such, it can only be "heard" in what has "always already" been written. That is why statements and assertions are inappropriate for this poietic momentum of language, for, as Heidegger observes, "we must be careful not to force the vibration of the poetic saying into the rigid groove of a univocal statement, and so destroy it" (*OWL,* 64).

Poetry here becomes a writing practice that pre-scribes listening to silence as the guiding momentum of writing. The significance of such poetic and also thinking practice has to do with the vexed issue of power and its relation to language. The differentiation between muteness and silence is an initial index of this problem: how to think the properly poietic capacity of language vis-à-vis power, and if not apart from power, then as its underside, without reducing the "silent force of the possible" to muteness and lack of power. I have suggested that poetic language, at least in the few examples cited here, by way of its attentive perfomance of the "housing" of words in silence, makes it possible to begin tracking a crucial distinction between power (and its verso of powerlessness) and power-free potentiality, proper to the silent vectoring of language and relations. The poietic resonance of language is its reticent event, whose reticence has nothing to do with powerlessness or muteness, that is, with the inability to speak. Rather, it tries to take care to have language speak without allowing what is said to become only the spectacle of power. Of course, power is there and needs to be there, but all depends on the tonality in which the power plays become pre-scripted in poetic language. At issue is not ceding the poietic tonality of writing to the tone of power and its refrain: power—powerlessness, and nothing else. The poietic ability is the originative momentum of silence, power-free, breaking open into possibilities. Its notation is that of the silent force of the possible, of the *is* insistent in all *it,* the course of the particular, each time always already one-time and nonrepeatable. It is this one-time ab-sense of *is,* set off from the signification of an "it," that may resonate power-free.

Poetry, as well as poetic thinking, is then a learning experience of how to dwell in the poietic wake of the silence of language's event, a practice of a listening writing that tries to make manifest the "prosody" and the duration of language's passing into words. As reticent writing, it traces in words the relation in whose wake language arrives as we habitually know and use it, that is, it marks the originative relation of listening and responding. The importance of poetry for Heidegger comes specifically from the fact that, because of the reservedness or restraint characteristic of poetic language, signs in poetic writing can resonate with the poietic force of words. In short, poetry allows words to work as words: "Language and the great stillness, the simple nearness of the essence, and the bright remoteness of beings, when the word is once again effective" (*CP,* 30, modified). When words are allowed to work as words and not just as signs, they manifest what Heidegger calls the "saying" (*Sage*), understood specifically as the "language" of being, that is, as the still word-less letting appear of the world on its way to words. Seen this way, language is not a mere human faculty but belongs to the very movement of the world's event. Letting the world appear, the saying gives beings to be: its words hold beings to their possibilities to be, disclosing the relatedness that keeps the world open as world. "Language, the saying of the world's fourfold, is no longer only that to which we speaking human beings have a relation in the sense of a nexus existing between man and language. Language is, as the saying that moves world on its way, the relation of all relations" (*OWL,* 107, modified).

Placing Heidegger's work in the context of such inventive poetic writing as Howe's or Kim's allows us to develop in more detail the possibilities of poetic thinking after Heidegger. It confirms the notion that not only is Heidegger's avoidance of predication and the copula "is" when writing about saying, words, or the movement of language, deliberate and consistent, but that his choice to mark through a colon how the event comes to word bespeaks a call for a decisive transformation of thinking. Unlike predication, the colon in Heidegger brings into focus the idea that language, as the relation that is also the happening of all relations, imparts both the possibility and the modality of relations by letting beings be. It is in the proximity to Kim's or Howe's poetry that Heidegger's attentiveness to the colon as the marker of the enabling force of possibility and relation finds proper resonance and further indications for developing the poetic register of thinking. The colon marks the saying that, having always already "made way" (*Bewëgung*) *for* signs and *into* signs (*Wörter* or *Wörterzeichen*), still resonates the poietic force of "it gives" (*es gibt*). Delivering a being to its "is," the word is thus always in advance of the sign for this being. But this "in advance of" can be heard only as the proper advance of signs, that is, as the saying that has always already advanced into signs and animates them.

FOUR

Language after Metaphysics

The Transformation of Language:
The Hyphen and the Prefix

To develop in more detail poetic thinking after Heidegger, we must consider the pivotal role assumed in Heidegger's work by hyphens and colons, especially the function of hyphenation in bringing to the fore and amplifying the play of prefixes into a resonant nexus of possibilities for transformative turns of thinking. While traditionally the focus in philosophical thought falls on concepts, explanations, or arguments, I propose to evolve Heidegger's insights by stressing his language inventions, which I regard as providing the most important critical momentum to his poetic recalibration of thinking. While some of the stakes of this transformation and the procedures advanced to carry it out can be glimpsed in Heidegger's lectures and essays published during his lifetime, the most innovative and radical insights are contained, as I have shown in particular in chapters 2 and 3, in the manuscripts and notes published between 1999 and 2010. Many of these texts are composed as fragmentary remarks, often presenting sketches or schematic indications of main standpoints in Heidegger's thinking about language or just directing attention to requisite changes and shifts in the vocabulary, the use of words, or even the modes of writing. Heidegger's manuscripts and notes from *Contributions to Philosophy* onward mostly take the form of individual, numbered sections, some longer, some very short, but overall indicating a decisive departure from the notion of a philosophical analysis or from the model of an analytic, like the one presented in *Being and Time*. Even the published writings, especially *On the Way to Language,* are collections of individual essays, which often tend to be divided into separate sections, as in the case of "The

Way to Language" or "The Essence of Language." Heidegger clearly opts for the segmented and fragmentary mode of presentation, implying that an experience with language he sets out to undergo in "The Essence of Language" renders systematic, analytic, or even continuous forms of consideration untenable in this context, as these modes appear ultimately distortive of the event-like occurrence of language. Although the sections in which Heidegger writes about language adopt a short, sketch-like format, their attention is frequently telescoped further onto individual words or phrases, sometimes even limited to considering scriptural marks or graphically delineated dynamics of relations. As much as gathering and arranging these fragmentary observations into a more sustained schema or a developed outline is tempting and even necessary to a scholarly or philosophical approach, it also contravenes Heidegger's practice, whose designed fragmentariness and graphical predilections must remain in view.

To advance this manner of poetic thinking, it becomes important to take note of and follow the various indications offered by Heidegger's texts about this transformation already underway there, without simply limiting one's explorations to Heidegger's remarks or explanations. Put plainly, it is important to avoid the mistake of overemphasizing the "content" of Heidegger's texts, of what is explicitly said and "meant" in them, to the detriment of the insights opened up—and held out to future thinking as possibilities—specifically through the idiomatic working of his language. What I hope to show in this chapter is that the transformation in our relation to language that is to open the path to twisting thought free of metaphysics is less a matter of Heidegger proffering a definition of this change than it is a matter of his attempt to induce such a transformation *in* and *through* his language. This does not mean that we should pay less attention to what Heidegger writes or clarifies *about* language, for example, his formula in "The Way to Language" or his notion of the neighborhood of poetry and thinking, but rather that we must begin to pay much more attention to the paths and the way-making of Heidegger's own language and texts.

While Heidegger is clearly an inventive, even a forceful writer, as *Being and Time* already makes amply evident, the matter of the transformation in our relation to language outlined by Heidegger cannot be explained simply in terms of performative writing. Transforming our relation to language, and ourselves in the process as well, will not come as a product of invention or performance, certainly not as a result of making up new word-signs (*Wörterzeichen*), but as we know now, it entails instead the dis-placement of signs into the fold of words (*Worte*) in order to disclose their distinctive way-making. Our relation to language, how we hold ourselves to language, how we hold it in regard to us and thus understand ourselves within it, depends on our attitude to what language is and how it unfolds, on whether our relation to language is determined through the notion of language as a sign system or comes to be experienced from the event, as the subtitle of *Contributions to Philosophy* implies.

Distrustful, similarly to Adorno, of novelty for novelty's sake, Heidegger wants to make sure that the transformation of thought would not happen simply on the surface, as it were, but indeed alter our relation to language, and for that to happen, the transformation must issue not just from human invention but from language itself. What makes possible the transformation Heidegger points to in "The Way to Language" is precisely the manner in which human beings belong to language and can become dedicated to or appropriated for language. But why should humans belong to language in the first place, rather than, as metaphysics proposes, count as beings who have or possess language? Why should humans come to be disposed by and to language rather than to dispose over it, turning it into a magnificent tool of manipulation and communication, conveniently available to human power and inventiveness, as modern culture around us testifies? Heidegger's emphasis on listening, on the apparently passive over the active, may seem to derive from his professed need to call into question and critique the prevalence of technical employment of language (as information and calculation) and with it the decisive import of what he calls the technic revealing underpinning modernity. While this derivation is not incorrect, it misses the most important point Heidegger makes about language, the point that he makes precisely *via* language itself. Listening and thus also reticence, as formative of the attitude to language Heidegger brings to the fore, are not simply proposed or imposed by him, nor do they result from his reflection *on* language, but they are instead imparted from language itself, which calls on us to metaphorically open our ears and recognize our belonging to it. This explanation is simply encoded, Heidegger tells us, in German language, where listening (*hören*) unfolds from and comes to play such a prominent role in his thinking by virtue of human belonging (*gehören*) to language. In this context, it would not perhaps be an exaggeration to suggest that all of Heidegger's thinking about language unfolds from this relation and belongs to this moment, which gives Heidegger's German its momentum.

It is not an accident that the listening indexed here—listening not simply as part of belonging but constitutively inscribed in it: *ge-hören*—appears circular. This circularity is not just due to Heidegger's penchant for circular constructions and relations but is proper to the event, to how it comes to word and to how this wording quite literally belongs as listening. The circularity in play here indicates that neither the belonging nor the listening comes first or causes the other. Rather, their inscription in German institutes itself as their relational reciprocity. When the German term is hyphenated, what is brought into the open is precisely the between constituting the relation through the reciprocal folding of listening and belonging. Neither one is "prior" nor more important than the other, while both come to transpire precisely and only in their being folded into each other. Listening can transpire at all because it exists within this belonging, yet the belonging does not come to be, or to "belong," otherwise than through and in this listening, which means that they bring each other into existence.

Even though the hyphen is not literally written in the ordinary German spelling of *gehören,* it is, Heidegger's texts imply, always already encoded by language itself, ready to come into the open if human beings become attentive to it. This key relation, which prescribes the overall approach to language in Heidegger, prompts us to think that the transformation Heidegger writes about is, therefore, a matter neither of *phone* nor of *graphein* strictly speaking. Since this hyphen in the term *gehören* is hinted at rather than written/seen or spoken/heard, it constitutes a kind of a "silent non-writing," which points to the fact that the transformation in question is assignable neither to speech nor to writing, but instead involves the *Stimmung,* the very disposition of language already at work in writing and speaking. Dastur agrees with this point, showing that the listening and hearing in Heidegger are not a matter of phenomenological *phone,* because they are not determined by the notion of the self or self-presence, that is, at issue is not a hearing that hears oneself speak.[1] Hearing in Heidegger refers instead to a listening-belonging that opens up as the very relation that *is* language. Hearing takes place as the movement of language that is already underway, without ever coming to be limited to the self or to presence. The fold of listening and belonging on which language pivots—this is how "die Sprache spricht"—is marked precisely by how the word (*Wort*) resonates within the term Heidegger uses for signs (*Wörterzeichen*). This word is neither scripted nor said, neither graphical nor auditory, as the inaugural relation of language, which constitutes also the relation opening and granting access *to* language, occurs as the clearing "prior" to writing and speaking. Neither this relation nor our access to it can be manufactured; it can only be recognized and allowed to bring us, so to speak, into the fold of language.

The transformation Heidegger writes about in "The Way to Language" is, therefore, not simply performative but instead primarily "attentive," that is, it becomes the matter of attending to how language already "speaks," that is, makes its way into signs and signification. Inventiveness and performativity, which Heidegger's own texts certainly engage in on numerous occasions, are not, however, originative with regard to the transformation at stake: they follow from the attentiveness to language, from what imparts itself and is held in reticence in our belonging to language. Listening and reticence thus provide the envelope for invention and performance through which human beings participate in the transformation but cannot simply induce or produce it. As I show later in this chapter, the priority of this reciprocal belonging/ listening becomes pivotal to Heidegger's critique of power and technicity because it bespeaks the originative relation to language that transpires in the "middle voice" of attentiveness. While never passive, inactive, or indifferent, this relation is also not simply up to human action, performance, or decision.

The transformation in our relation to language cannot be fabricated because it is our belonging to language that disposes (*Stimmen*) and "tones" our relation to it. The English word *tone* brings into play the musical terminology associated with *Stimmen,* setting the key or the pitch, but it also evokes giving or lending shape, as in "achieving the muscle tone," for instance. It is in this double sense that belonging shapes our relation: it can either prompt our listening to language, or, because this language tone is quiet and silent, result in its neglect or forgetting. Our language ability is thus lent us from the way in which we belong to language, are able to recognize the parameters and valences of this relation, and translate them into a transformation in how we think. This is why reading Heidegger requires, in addition to a more conventional grasp of the material, a particular attentiveness to the way in which language sets the tone for his thinking. On occasion, Heidegger explicitly indicates the moments in which his thinking allows itself to be guided by language, when it literally proceeds by listening to words rather than by presenting and analyzing ideas or developing arguments. The word *gehören* is a good example of how Heidegger's approach frequently takes its cue at crucial junctures from words themselves, listening to what they may "say" beyond their signification. Another key term that Heidegger evolves in this way is *das Ereignis,* whose idiomatic "word," that is, the "word 'of' being," emerges when this ordinary term for "event" is hyphenated, its "true" and "false" etymologies brought into the open, and, subsequently, a series of derived and related terms come to be assembled with regard to it: from *Ereignung* to *Aneignung, Zueignung,* and *Übereignung.* Heidegger invents neither *Ereginis* nor *gehören* but adopts instead an attentive and open attitude to them, allowing language to prompt and shape his elaboration of both terms. The invention or performance comes into play here but only and specifically in response to the prompt given by language itself. The invention springs from listening, as it tries to channel what language imparts, rather than producing new phrases or formulations. Here we can see how language opens the possibility of a new relation to it, a relation that Heidegger expressly does not force or manufacture but that he follows and evolves, as it were, out of language itself, and that in turn allows him to bring about a transformed sense of language and thinking.

Listening emerges as most important to how Heidegger's thinking advances because of the unprecedented, transformative role that Heidegger assigns to the hyphen. Heidegger's most significant "insights," that is, the crucial shifts in thinking and in experiencing language, are literally brought into the open by hyphenation. What from the perspective of language conventions looks like excessive hyphenation in his texts comes to leave its indelible mark in language signs. The hyphen holds signs—their conventional functions and signifying power—open to the silent inscription of the word "of" being. Whether the hyphen is actually written or not in particular cases is less important than the fact that Heidegger's practice of foregrounding the hyphen in key instances comes to resonate transversally throughout his language. It affects signs and concepts, making one always ready to take a second look at any and all concepts, in order to expose layers of their meaning and potentialize a critical turn in them. I take poietic thinking to rely primarily on this potentialization, so that what dictates how such thinking advances is precisely the "silent force of the possible" disclosed in words. This is why much more attention needs to be given to the hyphen in Heidegger, especially to the unique momentum it lends to thinking: one less interested in grasping or defining than in emergent possibilities of openings or turns in thought, as if it chanced on an unexpected path. The staggering demands and difficulty of books such as *Contributions to Philosophy, Mindfulness, Die Geschichte des Seyns,* or *The Event,* lie as much, if not more, in the proliferating transformations the hyphen introduces into words and phrases than in the more explicit array of new terms and connections they introduce. The hyphen does not simply change the words or alter their valence but literally holds them in their happening *as* words, in the transition between *Worte* and *Wörter.* Scripted into *Er-eignis, Ent-menschung, Da-sein, Ver-hältnis, An-fang, Ab-grund, Ab-schied,* and so on, the hyphen opens the word-signs as "relations" or instances of the between: engaged, bestirred, happening, and open toward the future. If nothing else, the hyphen radically temporalizes language terms, springing open in them the word-momentum that has delivered the event to signs. Recalling what Heidegger writes about the relation between words and signs, the hyphen can be, perhaps even must be, recognized as the index of the word within the language signs, that is, as indexing the word's already accomplished movement into speech and writing.

The ubiquitous hyphen illustrates how the ability to engage with Heidegger's thought is written by him into his texts and how such an encounter requires not only reading this idiomatic indexing of words but also recognizing its transformative role with regard to thinking. Though it is by far the most frequent exponent of Heidegger's transformation of (the relation to) language, the hyphen is certainly not the only index of this kind. A parallel role in the grammatical register is played on occasion by the colon, which Heidegger deploys at critical points in order to circumvent predication, as if to show that language is capable of "saying" without simply delivering its saying into statements (*Aussage*). The two most important junctures of this sort occur, not surprisingly, with regard to the notion of the word and the outline of the movement of language. In the first case, discussed in chapter 2, Heidegger deliberately declines to attribute predicates to "the word" (*das Wort*), indicating instead through the hyphen how the word: momentum of giving (*Das Wort: das Gebende*). This form of de-predicating the relation through the colon makes emphatic the point that the word is not to be mistaken for a being or a sign with ascribed attributes. In a related remark in "The Essence of Language," Heidegger uses the colon to index the turn from "the being of language" (*das Wesen der Sprache*) to the "language of being" (*die Sprache des Wesens*). The colon marks the very movement of language, its open-ended outline, as it tries to script the singular temporality of the event's coming to word. Because the event—and the word "of" being it delivers—is properly its own back draft, that is, its *Ab-schied,* its "language of being" draws out in its wake the "being of language," that is, the movement of language brought into expression in signs. In both cases, the colon is inserted in place of the copula "is," overwriting it in order to indicate that what the term "is" signifies and predicates can be attached only to what has already been brought into the open by the event's back draft, to what is already "in being." The back draft itself has no sign, no word as such, because it actuates the wording, both accomplishing it and rendering it legible and comprehensible.

The hyphen and the colon, together with brackets and curves graphically spanning and linking words in certain phrases used by Heidegger, are among a host of indexes he uses to inflect conventional philosophical writing. Though the hyphen is already employed to great lengths in *Being and Time,* where it is used primarily to either link component words into overriding and prioritized designations, for example, being-in-the-world, or to highlight the composition of key terms, for example, Da-sein, its use begins to intensify with the texts from the mid-1930s. It comes to play a particularly important role in Heidegger's reconfiguring of Dasein from the human modality of being presented by *Being and Time* into the site or situatedness for the experience of being and language, that is, into Da-*sein*. As becomes evident already in *Contributions to Philosophy*, it is the hyphen in Da-sein, indicating nearness to being and the way in which being's characteristic momentum of nihilation opens the time-space for experience, that Heidegger attempts to think of as the between and the clearing (*Lichtung*) opening onto difference and relation. In a way, the hyphen comes to "define" and delimit both *Da* and *sein*, rather than merely highlighting their connection in the etymology of the term. In his subsequent work, Heidegger calibrates his language in order to keep attention on the opening force of this between and its fourfold dimensionality (world as event) in order to avoid simply collapsing it into the thought of difference or relation. *Mindfulness* shows how the event happens as the "sitedness" or the emplacing of the time-space of experience into its nonrepeatable topology. The each-time unique and singular opening of the clearing cannot be thought of in terms of transcendental conditions or of an a priori but instead needs to be discerned specifically in its uniquely nonrepeatable essential occurrence (*Wesung*). As such, the event does not precede experience; therefore, the task of thinking is to understand experience not by way of its a priori conditions but more accurately through its "site," as Da-sein. This is the case because "to be" is always given by way of the Da, its each-time singular "t/here" opening from and as the event. Being is always already there-being (Da-sein), since there is no "being" apart from, different from, or prior to, the there. This is why being does not condition or make possible, transcendentally or experientially, the Da; rather being happens, that is, opens its "to be" and opens itself to it by way of the Da. Perhaps one could put it this way: it gives (*es gibt*) being as Da-sein.

If the human mode of being, Dasein, was to provide the access to the question of being in *Being and Time*, here the hyphen gets the leading role, as it were, because it holds open the spatiotemporal playing field of the event, silently outlining the topographic of the clearing in which the human being and language come to be experienced through each other. What is at stake here in understanding the hyphen in Da-sein—and rethinking Da-sein specifically through the hyphen—is how the hyphen marks the opening of the access (or the way) *to* being. The only way to experience and think of being without collapsing it into a being is to think how one's being is always already folded in and toward being. The hyphen in Da-sein indicates how this turn "to" of thought to being happens already "in" being, though both prepositions mistakenly assign the vectors of transcendence and immanence to this radical "nearness," as Heidegger prefers to refer to it. If *Being and Time* approaches the hyphen in Da-sein through the ontological difference, then "Time and Being" attempts to rethink this hyphen in terms of nearness, where nearness opens onto and extends, and in this way also reaches—both movements indicated by the German terms *reichen*—the time-space of difference and relatedness. As Heidegger's texts from the 1950s explain, thinking needs to undergo a transformation so that its language could become capable of keeping attention on the nonrepeatable "site" for the event of being, opened by the signature hyphen in Da-sein.

The hyphen's enactment of the originative in-between—of word to sign; saying to meaning; *Stimmung* to *Stimme*—is linked to a nexus of prefixes that from the start play a pivotal role in how Heidegger styles his thinking and writing. To quickly sketch out how Heidegger's approach to language comes to begin transforming thought, one can accentuate several strings of words that he uses to give particular resonance and saliency to his remarks about language: *Wort* (word); *sprechen* (to speak) and *Sprache* (language); *Sage* and *sagen* (saying); *Stimme* (voice) and *Stimmung* (tonality, pitch, disposition); *Laut* and its relation to *Verlautbarung* and other terms for sound (*Schall, Hall, Klang*). Heidegger not only highlights these terms but in fact bases the very movement of his writings on language and poetry on these words and their derivatives, and does so because these terms directly "address" matters of language: word, language, speaking, saying, voice. This cluster of words and their derivatives sketched with regard to language plays in Heidegger's thought in tune with the *Er-eignis* and its related words: *ereignen, eräugen, eigen, zueignen, aneignen, übereignen, enteignen*, and so on. In fact, the various ways in which the event comes to word, resonant in how the sheaf of words with the root *-eignen* is diffused through Heidegger's texts, can be shown to take explicitly the tone (*Stimmung*) of poietic thinking, which means that the event transpires by way of *sagen, sprechen, stimmen*, or, in short, as the relational momentum associated with the word in Heidegger's sense. Briefly, one could say that *Zueignung* (assigning appropriation) echoes in *Zusprechen* (to address, to claim) and *Zusagen* (to promise, to confirm), while *Aneignung* (acquisition, appropriation) resonates together with and in *Ansprechen* (to address, to accost) or *Anstimmen* (to intone), which all come to echo Heidegger's neologism *Anwort*: the word at its onset toward signs.

While there is no exact mapping of these correspondences, word for word or prefix for prefix, or just one way of delineating how the event "gives" onto the cluster of words explicitly moving language (from *stimmen* to *sagen* to *sprechen* and *verlauten*), what is striking is the precise and sustained deployment of the hyphenated prefixes that animate much of Heidegger's writing. This hyphenation, telescoping attention onto prefixes and accentuating the changed valence they lend to stems, makes Heidegger's texts "come alive" in the specific sense in which they keep the folds of relations open, engaged, futural, and charged with possibility. Thus the hyphenation literally writes the very movement of Heidegger's thinking, gives it its momentum and its dominant valence of the possible. This strategic and complex foregrounding of the hyphen means that, over against whatever gets captured by thinking into signs, or what becomes articulated into concepts or propositions, at issue in Heidegger's work is precisely what fails to be captured by propositional statements, as he indicates explicitly at the end of "Time and Being" (*OTB*, 24).

Since the transformation at issue here is expressly the departure from the priority of propositional statements and concepts, inasmuch as Heidegger's texts ineluctably 'write' in propositions, they contravene the very transformation his thought is trying to evince. As if against propositional efficiency, the force of this transformation comes to be located precisely in the very prefix of the term designating the change in question: *Ver-wandlung*. Unlike the Latinate *trans-*, the German *ver-* does not indicate a transition into something new or other, for example, the possibility of a beyond to metaphysics and to metaphysical deployments of language, which still resonates in Heidegger's other term, *Überwindung*, or overcoming. Rather the German prefix induces a twisting and a skewing, a turn or a torsion, which exposes language to its own concealed "verso," thus bringing it into consonance with the twisting (*Verwindung*) of metaphysics. Given Heidegger's insistence on the possibility of such a *Verwindung*, as well as the generally frequent occurrence of this prefix in German, it is not surprising that *ver-* is among the prefixes that come to play a significant role for Heidegger in transforming thinking. The prefix *ver-* plays this role specifically because it opens for thinking an alternative pathway to the thought of transcendence, transgression, or overcoming. The corresponding use of the prefix *ver-* occurs in the term *Verwandlung*, indicating in both terms the emergence of the force of the possible, that is, the possible change requisite for raising the question of being: by bringing metaphysics to completion and thus allowing it to wane away and diminish in power and importance, implied by *Verwindung*; and by intensifying, pushing to the limit the possibility of change, as in *Verwandlung*, where the prefix intensifies the root of the verb, punctuating its ability to turn or twist.

Four other important uses of words with the prefix *ver-* become prominent in Heidegger's discussion of language: *Verhaltenheit* (restraint, reserve), *Verhältnis* (relation), *Versagen* (to deny, to refuse), and *Versprechen* (to promise), with the first two related to the verb *(sich) verhalten*: to behave, comport, conduct oneself as well as to retain, keep, or hold back. The first set of meanings comes to resonate in *Verhältnis*, which serves as Heidegger's term for "relation" with regard to language, namely as another way to indicate the complex play of the clearing as the nexus of relations composing the event-like occurrence of language. Given the resonances between words that Heidegger brings into the open specifically through the use of hyphenated prefixes, *Verhältnis,* or relation, draws attention to the reciprocal turning toward each other constitutive of and continuously at play in relating. This relocated, topographic sense of relatedness in transformation becomes indispensable in understanding the notion of the world in Heidegger, both its relation to language and to the promise of possibility. It also plays off *Verhaltenheit,* which indicates the possibility of twisting the link constitutive of a relation so that this relation becomes as though contracted into a holding back, pointing toward a reserve of silence or otherness. This manner of holding in relation by keeping back or through restraint, by keeping reticent, which refers to the manner in which words resonate in signs, comes to characterize the promise of language as its concurrent pro-miss (*Ver-sprechen*), where the prefix signals at the same time both the provision of the promise and something going awry in the very manner of speaking, so that the speaking, instead of confirming and guaranteeing its veracity, breaks the promise in the very gesture of making it. Similarly, *Versagen* de-scribes, that is, both writes and de-scripts, denying it to signs, the complex way in which the event comes to word only as retracted, drafted back as it were. Though the grammatical function of the prefix *ver-* in this cluster of terms is not identical in each case and is not thematized as such by Heidegger, it does exhibit a certain consistency in his elaboration of these terms: it comes to indicate the crucial momentum of turning and transforming, which characterize the way the clearing and language's way-making movement into signs are instantiated.

In the same vein, this turn—happening through the faulting of *Worte* into *Wörter*—recalls and intensifies the turn (*Kehre*) through which the event itself transpires or issues—its way of giving beings by bringing them to words. We can also bring the verb *Versprechen* into proximity with *Verlassen* (to leave, to desert), with the way in which being, while letting beings be by withdrawing or holding itself back, that is, by never giving itself to be in the manner in which beings come to exist and can be experienced, opens also the possibility of forsaking or abandoning beings, their *Verlassenheit.* What *Verlassenheit* indicates is the moment in which being's refusal (*Verweigerung*) paves the way to experiencing beings in terms of their standing forth, their constancy and presence, that is, as beings "abandoned" by being, forsaken in their apparent constancy by the singularity and uniqueness of its event, so that they come to be (mis)perceived therefore as entities existing in the manner of permanence and solidity. This leaving aside (*Ver-lassen*) is the possibility intrinsic to letting be, where letting goes awry, so to speak, bends out of shape, turning nearly into its own opposite: from giving (letting be) to forsaking. The prefix *ver-* indicates here precisely pushing the letting to the verge—and to its intrinsic possibility—of forsaking and leaving behind. When linked to letting and speaking, the prefix *ver-* signals in Heidegger the danger intrinsic to language, experience, and world in the specific sense in which being's refusal can be misread so as to lead to its disappearance as the emptiest of all concepts, leaving in its wake the primacy of beings and thought's entanglement in the intensifying attempt to master them. Yet in the same turn of the phrase, or of the prefix to be exact, this twist or distortion can also turn into the capability for twisting free and transformation; in a sense, it all depends on the direction of the turning, that is, on the way the event turns and on thought's ability to listen to and respond to this (dis)torsion—occurring in the modality of *Ver-sprechen*—marking the way of language.

Much more could be written about the complicated resonances Heidegger instantiates between prefixes as well as about the movement and twists brought to the fore by their increasing prominence in his texts. The cluster of prefixes of particular importance to Heidegger's work includes, though is not limited to, the following: *er-, an-, ent-, zu-, unter-, über,- ant-, ge-,* and the already discussed *ver-.*[2] Throughout his texts, Heidegger attaches these prefixes to the words that for him script the movement of language: *stimmen, Wort, sagen,* and *sprechen.* He does this because doing so and, at the same time, frequently indicating—by hyphenating the prefixes—the opening possibility of change in the momentum of these relations, allow him to emphasize the directions into which the event unfolds by tuning, saying, wording, speaking, and so on. The prefixes highlighted by Heidegger form a web of their own, marking the moment, the blink of an eye (*Augenblick*), in which the breaking open of the finite relatedness of the world constitutes the there, that is, the clearing, in which beings come to appear. Though "words of being" do not enter signs, for Heidegger they do "say" themselves along with signs, with words having already become signs, as *Basic Concepts* explains.[3] What is "said" in this manner alongside signs is delivered only as pre- or fore-said: as a *Vor-wort.* Its silent resonance does not need to be articulated directly in sounds or letters, for if it is listened to on the right frequency, as it were, its tonality can still be detected in the operations of language. As Heidegger puts it in *The Event,* at issue is a thinking that can sometimes hear in the language signs the word of being.[4]

This hearing that enfolds signs back into words is clearly at stake in the hyper-hyphenation to which Heidegger subjects most of the key German terms he employs, alters, or introduces: *Er-eignis, Da-sein/Da-seyn, Ur-sprung,*

Ge-stell, An-fang, Auf-riss, or, in a slightly different key, the play, the invisible hyphen, as it were, between *Sein* and *Seyn* on which the initially unpublished writings from the decade following the mid-1930s rely. Beyond the generative play of the double etymology of *Ereignis* (*er-eignen* and *er-äugen*) (*GA 71*, 184–185; *E*, 156–157) and debates about which one is more "proper" (*eigen*) to the term in Heidegger's use of it—all crucial and significant in their own right —what is both more interesting and important for developing the poetic thinking after Heidegger is the way in which his writings, using an everyday German word, break it open beyond its signification, beyond its role as a sign, in order to indicate the very momentum of giving that he associates with the word as *das Gebende,* as nothing other than the giving that actuates being. It is precisely this momentum, a vibration beyond the term's possible play(fullness) of signification, that is brought forth and emphasized by the employment of the hyphen in *Er-eignis* and by the simultaneous spotlighting and intensification of the enactive capacity of the prefix *er-*.

The exaggerated hyphenation of prefixes also lends Heidegger's texts an unmistakable spatiotemporal and topographical tenor, displaying signs as "words" always already dislocated and relocated through the way-making of language. What Heidegger induces through the repetitive use of terms with the same roots (*sagen, sprechen, stimmen, eignen,* etc.) and the concomitant assembling of groups of prefixes is an invisible drawing of a map, a topograph of sorts, of language's outline in motion and its shifting relation to the event. As a result, when one sees one of these words charged with a specific prefix, let's say, *ver-sprechen,* or simply encounters it in its root form, *sprechen,* one is always already drawn into the complex layout of these shifting relations and valences among signs and prefixes, not simply with regard to other appearances of *sprechen* as *ansprechen, entsprechen, zusprechen,* but also with regard to the directions or orientations marked by the prefixes themselves. Since the prefixes indicate specific spatiotemporal vectors and movements, the frequency of their appearance, highlighted and emphasized through the hyphens, repeatedly lights up these invisible, yet under-written as it were, transversal connections across Heidegger's sentences and paragraphs. Even if in certain contexts this practice is deliberately exaggerated and can be wearisome, what it does to thinking—though Heidegger does not, to my knowledge, present it in this manner—is specifically to extend and lay over his texts a kind of an invisible array of active, transversal, futurally charged and continuously underway, relations and connections both inside and between words, an array that repeatedly bestirs and remaps the way-making of language into signs. This is why key words in Heidegger not only exist in the usual syntagmatic or paradigmatic relations to other words but come to be inscribed into the transversal networks of under-written connections, often resonant in thinking beyond what finds itself written directly on the page. These inscriptions keep inflecting the meaning and the role of these terms, forcing us to think between texts, concepts, and statements. Sometimes Heidegger does explicitly draw such lines of connection or intersection, clasping together words or phrases with long curved lines or explicitly drawing graphs of complex intersections, which cannot be expressed in propositional statements. But what is perhaps most interesting and inventive in his writing is the animation of the scripted, though not literally written, topographic of the clearing as the event's coming to word.

While what I am sketching here cannot be summarized by way of a description—and seems to be designed purposely so by Heidegger—it can be experienced in reading, specifically by following how the written, hyphenated, or expressly made connections with which Heidegger peppers his essays on language and poetry come to resonate in tandem with this "unwritten" movement of language, as though underwriting or perhaps over-scribing Heidegger's texts. This procedure is particularly salient with regard to the manuscripts published after the appearance in 1989 of *Beiträge zur Philosophie,* which often employ graphic and telegraphic style, which hints at or briefly alludes to the emerging connections, letting the reader pursue or not these freshly opening pathways. Though part of it may be due to the apparently unfinished character of some of these remarks, overall this way of writing clearly allows us to evolve a strategy of introducing multiple vectors and transversal relations between words and prefixes, with the outcome of disrupting the sequential and propositional arrangement of language and bringing to the fore the topographic layout of poetic thinking.

This dislocation with regard to signs and statements is a fitting way for words to mark the in-between that spans their movement to signs through the gesture of opening up the spatiotemporal play of signification. The deliberate manner in which Heidegger assembles and repeatedly deploys collections of prefixes casts across his texts a meshwork of connections, brought invisibly into play each time he composes or invokes such a constellation around his key verbs or else emphasizes, through the insertion of a hyphen, the movement instigated by a particular prefix. What is more, this heightened use of prefixes and hyphenation creates an altered perspective on words themselves, endowing them with a sense of actuation, a kind of linguistic charge, or the impression of "sense in the making." Heidegger's repeated focus on etymology and the root meaning of words is usually only a prelude to his putting a word in motion in order to tear it away from the context of lexically and grammatically stable and prescribed relations, as though making it, or letting it, make its way, each time singularly and one-time, into its functioning as a sign. Rather than the word being a relatively "set" sign, which, already functioning within the language system, is brought into play through the ingenuity of thought and writing, as if repeatedly released to its full signifying potential each time it is used, Heidegger's way with words allows them to appear singularly and one-time: every time arising anew, freshly actuated in the process of being shaped into a sign. This singularity and one-time occurrence discloses the word in its usually forgotten momentum of giving to be (as *das Gebende*), which leads to breaking the word out of its relational confinement to beings and re-linking it with being, even if only for a moment, before it becomes ensconced again in the creative play of signs.

When it is examined through the prism of this originative "between" linking the word and the sign, Heidegger's approach to words evidences constant attempts to open words beyond their operation as linguistic signs. In this context, what could be seen simply as the interpreting or the laying out (*Auslegung*) of the etymological layers gathered in a sign's lexical resonance—whether in relation to Greek and Latin terms or with regard to the complex deployment of German terminology—can, and I would say needs to, be understood as part of the opening of signs to the covered over momentum of giving, that is, to the actuating "between" characteristic of what Heidegger calls the *word*. For instance, when Heidegger discusses the Latin *res* and the Old German *thing* in his essay "The Thing," it is as much to show the philosophical implications of the term *thing,* with its inevitable overlay of conceptualizations and ideas, especially in regard to the pervasiveness of the Cartesian understanding of substance as *res,* as to allow the German *Ding* to acquire the unprecedented and unexpected resonance in parallel with Heidegger's forceful and unsettling claim that we have never allowed things to be things. This etymological and multilingual analysis is geared specifically to bring out in the German term *be-dingen,* which means to condition or to provide a basis, the unheeded role that the thing (*Ding*) plays in carrying and offering us the world. Heidegger thus verbalizes the noun "thing" (*dingen*), though he does not do so forcefully but rather "listening-wise," that is, by allowing German to impart this verbal resonance of "thinging" as a result of his bringing the root of the verb *be-dingen* into the open through hyphenation. When we listen in German to the word that indicates how we are "conditioned," that is, given to be who we are as humans, language allows us a glimpse, heretofore unnoticed or overlooked, into our reliance on the "generosity" of things, which silently, without claim or protest, bear the world in the specific sense in which each thing gathers and holds open, in and through its location or site, the topology of the entire world. Because of this relation, we can experience not simply things but, through them, also the world.

This characteristic breaching of the envelope of the sign finds its signature instance in later Heidegger in the alteration to which he submits *das Gestell,* turning the ordinary term for "rack" or "frame" into a new way of "saying," through the multiple resonances of *stellen,* of the "essence," or the essential occurrence, of technicity: *vorstellen, darstellen, herstellen, bestellen, sicherstellen, verstellen,* and so forth. Once again the hyphen plays the same role here as it does with regard to the event: it estranges the sign and envelops it within the actuating word—from *Wörter* as if back into *Worte*—and emphasizes the gathering at work in the prefix *ge-*. It is quite fitting that the word, since it is not a being like signs, and since as such it does not "exist" as a something and in fact is not an "it" to begin with, would be marked precisely by hyphens: the indices of the in-between, of the spacing-temporalizing play opening into the there of Da-sein. In other words, hyphens in Heidegger enact the originative between of the word's giving (into) sign; they recall the momentum of the always already, which tends to be covered over by the sign's lexical spectrum. The implications for thought of this procedure are critical, one is even tempted to say transformative. This is the case because, in Heidegger, words like *Ge-stell* come to be set up not simply as new concepts. This, in turn, is so because *Gestell* does not acquire a set meaning or a fixed definition, as Heidegger uses it in a manner that deliberately challenges such established ways of thinking. The transformative charge of this word—its force of possibility—resides in the nexus of prefixes drawn into relief by the hyphen, prefixes modulating the meaning of *stellen.* To understand the critical import of a term like *Gestell,* one does not produce a definition or a description of it but instead allows thought to traverse the various paths of the hyphen, so to speak. Thinking thus comes to be inflected in ways resonant with the vectors of movement that the prefixes actuate in the verb *stellen.* Heidegger's texts invite us to think in this manner, that is, by way of a mobile constellation of prefixes, their futural vectors and transversal resonances, so that the critique of the essence of technology does not lead to a new grasp but instead alters the amplitude and the mode of thinking. This changed thinking would no longer be a critique in the usual sense but would instead transpire poietically, prompted to make its turns and advances in correspondence (*Entsprechung*) with the way of language.

It is in this sense that I regard the force of hyphenation in Heidegger as indexing the transformation of our relation to language. Since a new language cannot be invented, hyphens and etymological de-layering bring us into a changed relation to language: from the system of signs and their differential play to words in their originative giving. The *Er-eignis* is above all the event of this transformation, which is hinted at through the circularity of Heidegger's signature phrasings: the world worlds, space spaces, time times, "Die Sprache spricht," and, nota bene, the event eventuates (*Das Ereignis ereignet*). This last phrase says nothing and everything at the same time, naming and unnaming the event in the same gesture of a difficult "naming," which should not be confused here with the notion that the event would be somehow unnameable or "mystically" ineffable. The phrase suggests instead that the event cannot be thought of either in nominal or in verbal terms, and, since the event is not a being, it cannot be "named" or assigned a noun and a signification the way things and entities can. But the event is also not an occurrence or a happening, not simply an "action," and therefore also not a verb. Like many of Heidegger's signature phrases, "Das Ereignis ereignet" ruptures the syntax of predication, holding off the possibility of articulating and grasping the event through the language of statements and in terms of the subject—object relation. This signature phrase of late Heidegger marks the withholding (*Verweigerung*) that opens (onto) time and being. It indicates that what is "proper" (*eigen*) to the event (*Ereignis*) is its *Ent-eignis,* its de-propriation or de-eventuation. The event always occurs with its back turned to any and all beings, as it were, that come to exist thanks to the event's back draft. As Françoise Dastur puts it, "What Heidegger calls *Ereignis* is there-fore as much spatializing as it is temporalizing, but it is so in the manner of the abyss, for its finitude cannot grant it any exteriority nor obtain for it the figure of any 'self.'"[5] The event gives being in not coming itself to be (a thing or a being) and it also gives time in not being itself given (in)to time, and does so each time singularly (*einzig*) and only one-time (*einmalig*). This is in part because the event, not being an "it," does not have an itself. It neither *is* nor *is given* but instead gives to be by force of the back draft of its *Ent-eignis.* This force renders what exists possible by drawing open the time-space for existence. Therefore the "proper" of the event is its most appropriate way of eventuating that happens as a simultaneous de-evatuating (*er-eignen* as *ent-eignen*).

These characteristic Heidegger phrases never stop turning, as it were: turning the noun into the verb and back, making thought move beyond these grammatically set categories. These sayings are deliberately styled to direct thought's attention to how this turn tends to disappear in the process of signification, so that thinking can draw away from its almost exclusive fo-cus on meaning and statement. Kept stretched and oscillating between the nominal and the verbal, thinking is enticed to learn to remain attentive to this tension, even to think by way of it, without collapsing too quickly into the conventional grammatical and semantic categories, which reduces thought's movement to its stated expression in signs. This vertiginous turning echoes back and forth in Heidegger's idiomatic use of *Versprechen,* promising to say the event as event or time as time only to hold them back in the manner of the *Ent-eignis,* showing that the "proper," or, more precisely, the only way the proper comes to be given, is paradoxically each time one-time and singular. The turns of Heidegger's idiomatic phrasings also become accessory to the turn or twist indicated by *Verwindung* and *Verwandlung,* that is, to the transformation of thinking away from the metaphysical thought of the proper as something established, possessed, or attributable in a manner of a feature or a characteristic, on the one hand, and as essence or substance, on the other. Working this turn and highlighting its momentum become the markers of the transformation underway in Heidegger's own language and thought. It is as though Heidegger's ambition was to try and ensure that this unstoppable, though withdrawn and reticent, turning finally came to mark language as the "relation of all relations" over and against the conceptual edifice of metaphysics and its eloquence. It would thus also mark relating and relatedness in their proper turn as *Ver-hältnis.*

These often-elaborate phrasings play, as Heidegger himself tends to remark, a preparatory role in moving thought toward a possible transformation. To that effect, the phrase *Das Ereignis ereignet,* for instance, is not a matter of the conceptual grasp of the event or of understanding the meaning of the proposition, but rather requires a "listening" thought, which could hear in the deliberately quasi-tautological formulation the breakup of the predicative and propositional thought, as well as the turn that brings the word into the sign. In this neither verbal nor nominal valence, the event is neither the condition nor the foundation for time and being, just as "it" is not the agency behind, the "giver" of, time and being. The event "is" not and therefore is not an "it," since the subject *es* in the German phrase *es gibt,* "there is," or literally "it gives," remains empty, a grammatical nonsubject. The event's unique, each-time singular "proper domain" (*Eigentum*) consists in the event happening specifically as the *Ent-eignis,* or "non-event," which is characterized by the nonrepeatable each-time manner of withdrawing the proper. Yet it is not simply the case here that the event has its own "proper" and simply withholds it from thought and signification but rather that the event happens *to be* this specific withholding *from* the proper. Again Heidegger entices us to listen to the way in which the giving proper to the event is paradoxically tantamount to the withholding from the proper, to its "proper" dissipation, that is, to the *Enteignis.* It seems that what he hopes can come to be heard in this (non)event of the proper—or in its singular manner of occurrence as an essential "disappropriation"—is not a contradiction between the simultaneous "presence" and "absence" of the proper but the very opening onto presence and absence.

To hold thinking open to this (non)event, Heidegger's texts focus on the explanation of single words or phrases, on contextualizing meaning through etymologies, on destabilizing the boundaries between parts of speech, etc. It becomes a characteristic of Heidegger's writing for it to be led by words, by what words can offer by way of the unexpected, which is brought into view through a mesh of prefixes, idiomatic expressions, transversal echoing, or etymological derivations, kinships, and affinities. Sentences are guided less by ideas or conceptual content to be expressed or developed than they follow their own poietic momentum: lexical, syntactical, or even diacritical and graphical, thus proceeding by way of hyphens, repetitive inflections, the play of prefixes or even umlauts, as in the term for language's singular way of moving to words: *Be-wëgung.* Characteristic Heideggerian sentences do not purport to explain ideas or offer conceptual grasp or definitions, as they are not simply controlled by signification or expression per se but instead are energized by the poietic openings initiated by listening to language. Seen this way, Heidegger's sentences need to be experienced more in terms of what they instantiate, open up, or activate in thinking, as they try to enact the movement of language by drawing attention to the poietic charge of words breaking through meaning and ideas. Language in Heidegger's writings is thus not simply a medium of expression, representation, or communication, but it tries to contour the breaking open of the originative time-space, which activates ideation and meaning.

Language as Critique of Power

Since language is "the relation of all relations" and the transformation in our relation to language is to bring about a different opening up of the world, the possibilities unlocked by the complicated dynamics of hyphens and prefixes discussed in the preceding section have a direct bearing on Heidegger's critique of power, violence, and sovereignty. This critique needs to be understood in terms of the release induced by this transformed relation to language and by its correlate, a new poetic thinking, prepared and perhaps precipitated by the inventive employment of hyphens and prefixes and by the enhanced awareness of the role of silence they introduce into thinking. The possibilities, especially their transformative momentum bestirred and held charged in the span of the hyphen, keep open the prospects of release from metaphysical operations of power. It is as if the hyphens were introduced into key terms by Heidegger in order either to free their latent potential or to actuate it for the first time, as it were, leading thought to see if these emergent prospects—its vectors mapped out through the nexus of prefixes—could reshape experience in an unprecedented, "unprethinkable" ways.

Heidegger's remarks about transforming our relation to language occur in the context of his repeated critique of the reduction of language to its informational content, so that his emphasis on the poietic momentum of thought comes to be deployed critically against the more and more forceful recasting of language into the technic terms of information. In *GA* 74, Heidegger complains about language being grasped exclusively as the instrument of information, which leads not only to mechanical writing but also to the idea of mechanical translation, as Web translators today make amply evident: "man zum voraus die Sprache als *Instrument der Information und nur* als dieses auffast. *Das Verhältnis des Menschen* zur Sprache ist in einer *unheimlichen Wandlung* begriffen. Der Prozess dieser Wandlung geht in *aller Stille* vor sich" (*GA* 74, 175)—"One construes language in advance as the *instrument of information and only* as this. *The relation of man* to language is in the grasp of an *uncanny transformation*. The process of this transformation goes on in *complete silence*." Similar observations close the more familiar essay "The Way to Language," where the informational grasp of language is inscribed in the context of the enframing (the *Gestell*):

> Speech is challenged to correspond to the ubiquitous orderability [*Bestellbarkeit*] of what is present. / Speech, when posed in this fashion, becomes information. . . . Enframing, the essence of modern technology that holds sway everywhere, ordains for itself a formalized language—that kind of informing by virtue of which man is molded and adjusted into the technical-calculative creature, a process by which step-by-step he surrenders his "natural language." . . . Information theory conceives of the natural as a shortfall in formalization. (*BW*, 420–421)

The informational understanding of language operates between the poles of natural and formalized language, where formalization becomes the most efficient way of grasping the apparently "essential" in language, in order to manipulate it efficiently. So-called natural language marks the ordinary, insufficiently formalized or rigorous use of language that can be rescued from blunders and misunderstanding through the degree and the consistency of formalization.

It is evident that, for Heidegger, philosophy and especially its development of logic, together with their preference for propositional truth, statements and assertions, have played a crucial role in this ongoing formalization of language that finds its culmination today in the achievements of bioinformatics. Against this view, polarizing language between natural expression/

communication and formalized informational science, Heidegger points to the poietic register of language, whose momentum is already covered over and forgotten in "natural language," let alone in information theory:

> what if "natural language," which for information theory remains but a disturbing remnant, drew its nature—that is, the essential unfolding of the essence of language—from the saying? What if the saying, instead of merely disturbing the devastation that is information, had already surpassed information on the basis of an event that is not subject to our ordering? What if the event—when and how, no one knows—were to become a *penetrating gaze (Ein-Blick)*, whose clearing lightning strikes what is and what the being is held to be? What if the event by its entry withdrew every present being that is subject to sheer orderability and brought that being back into its own? (*BW*, 421–422, modified)

Pointing to the clearing and its swift movement into signs, that is, to the instantaneous way in which the event manifest and lets see—Heidegger's handwritten comment links "Er-eginen—Er-äugen, Er-Blicken, Er-Blizten" (*GA* 12, 253)—"To eventuate—to glance, to glimpse, to flash"—the text brings into the open the expanse of the showing saying as the quiet envelope of language, within whose span the poles of the natural and the informational, formalized language become possible. What makes language language and what is singularly peculiar and proper to it (*das Eigentümliche*) is what comes from the event and is, therefore, event-like (*ereignishaft*): "What is peculiar to language depends on the propriative [*ereignisartige*] provenance of the word; that is, on the provenance of human speech from the saying" (*BW*, 422). This is why "The saying [*Sage*] will not allow itself to be captured in any assertion [*Aussage*]. It demands of us to hold the event-like way-making movement in a telling silence [*zu er-schweigen*] within the essence of language, without any talk *about* silence" (*BW*, 424, modified). And if this denial sounds like an assertion itself, replicating the propositional form of the statement that it claims "the saying" avoids, it is the tonality of remarks such as "The saying that rests in the event is, as showing, the most proper mode of the event" (*BW*, 424, modified) that must be listened to attentively. This tonality is not a mode or a modality in the sense of *modus* or kind, for instance, statement, question, or imperative, but, as Heidegger indicates, its *melos* or melody taken in the musical sense. Here we come back to the *Stimmung*, the tonality or disposition that shapes and disposes the movement of language. Such tonality of language does not reside in grammatical forms or conceptual constructions but requires a poetic ear, capable of discerning the momentum of words that, while stringed and circumscribed within the parameters of an assertion, manage to say otherwise.

The "enframing" of language as information is consonant with the dominant mode of the revealing of beings in modernity into their availability as resource for production, manipulation, and exploitation, which facilitates the increasingly global, flexible, and productive flows of power. It is linked in an essential way to the dominant metaphysical tonality of language, which distills language into its supposed informational essence. Being does not happen here as the event in its unprethinkable vectors but instead opens up into an informational code, suggesting that what exists is intrinsically predisposed to being manipulated, that is, predisposed to be at the disposal of power. As a result, being becomes deprived of its "word," reduced to producing informational signs. In fact, it no longer has even signs strictly speaking, since it becomes circumscribed to the sign's information content, whereby signs, despite the multiplicity of languages, all appear to be reducible simply to two marks: to the binary code of informational operations. Today, when being appears to be the most loquacious and oversaturated with meaning it has ever been, disclosing everywhere and everything into potential informational capital and transmitting information with unprecedented speed and on the global scale, it seems to be simultaneously losing its ability to say anything that is not reducible to the predictable stutter of 0 and 1. Here we encounter the Janus face of information: information is the power affecting all, transforming daily experience; information says very little, almost nothing, repeating ones and zeros ever more efficiently.

This critical approach to the essence of technology and its deployments of power comes in the wake of Heidegger's distanciation in the late 1930s from his own discourse of violence and violence-doing (*Gewalttätigkeit*), which he used to explain the Greek understanding of the human through the interpretation of *Antigone* offered in *Introduction to Metaphysics*.[6] The radical shift in Heidegger's thought is explicitly articulated, for instance, in the striking twenty-six points about power from the chapter "The Essence of Power" in *Die Geschichte des Seyns* (*GA* 69, 62–71), which diagnose the operations and flows of power in a manner similar to the later elaborations of power relations by Foucault. Foucault developed his conception of power to a large extent from Heidegger's readings of Nietzsche, and we can analyze now Heidegger's own, much earlier formulation of such a critique, which Heidegger appears to distill from his Nietzsche lectures in the 1930s. Heidegger's main point about power is its intrinsic proclivity to enhance itself, in the manner of spiraling transpowering (*Übermächtigung*). He also shows how power operates intrinsically without aims or goals and needs therefore no wielders or possessors, since it itself carries and determines those who appear to control it. Contrary to the understanding of power as simply domination or violence, power is primarily constructive and productive, as Heidegger remarks, yet even as productive, it exercises itself by compelling, though not necessarily in violent or coercive manner, but frequently through production, empowering, creation, and so on. One of the most significant points, especially important for the consideration of the poietic and its valence of the power-free, is the fact that power tends to monopolize all relations, precluding any alternatives to power (informed) relations and thus forcing everything, even the dynamics of history, into the binary of power and its absence (*Ohnmacht*) (*GA* 69, 66). Thus power effectively disallows any possibility of something that could potentially avoid and question explaining itself as power, since within the operations of power everything must testify either to power's effective presence or its absence. "[P]ower and super-power must always necessarily and *from the ground up* mis-cognize the sway of that which is power-free . . . " (*M*, 168, modified). To illustrate this dominion of power more pointedly, Heidegger explains: "However, because since long ago man, and modern man in particular, calculates everything (and even being) according to power and powerlessness, usefulness and disadvantage, success and uselessness, he is not capable of hearing any word of beyng [*Seyn*] and of thinking its truth without initiating his *calculation*" (*M*, 170). Since various manners of thought and action work by calculating what they try to accomplish or set out to do specifically in terms of the binary of power and powerlessness, they become unable to conceive of anything that could exist without the obligatory reference to power. As a result, such thinking conceives of any and everything as an inevitable effect of power, whether indicative of its presence or its absence.

Likewise, the preponderance of remarks about silence, stillness, and reticence in the late 1930s and early 1940s texts published since 1989 can be directly linked to this far-reaching and intensifying critique of power and violence. Heidegger's extensive and for that time—the late 1930s—quite radical investigation of power, technicity, and machination (*Machenschaft*) makes clear that his later writings on language and poetry, especially on the poietic measure of language and dwelling, must be reconsidered through the prism of this critique of power and its later manifestation, namely the critical engagement with the essence of technology, or the *Gestell*. Furthermore, Heidegger's interest in the possibility of transforming relations away from the doublet of power/powerlessness prompts him to investigate the manner in which stillness and silence enveloping language and the play of signification constitute—albeit quite reticently—such a reservoir of what he calls *das Macht-lose*—"the power-less," or better, "the power-free." Here the suffix *-los* denotes not absence but rather freedom or releasement from power: "The power-less is not the same as what is without power [*Ohnmacht*] which while

it is deprived of power and lacks power nevertheless and simply remains related to power. / The origin of the power-character of beings" (*M,* 166). These
are the reasons why, in *Mindfulness,* Heidegger refers to being (*Seyn*) as the
power-free: "Beyng: the *powerless [das Machtlose]—beyond power and lack of
power*—better, what is outside power and lack of power, and fundamentally
unrelated to such" (*M,* 166). The power-free here forms the underside of the
operations of power: its manifestations into presence as well as the lack or
absence of power, *Ohnmacht.* Tied to the overlay developed in Heidegger's
writing by the network of prefixes, the power-free is instantiated precisely in
the silently resonant vectors and poietic impulses crisscrossing thought and
activating in it the force of the possible. Because the power-free actuates the
very opening onto the play of power, the instances of its presence or absence,
it remains released from or unrelated to power, fundamentally disengaged
from articulations into flows and formations of power.

The idiomatic release and freedom from power—*macht-los* is in some
places paraphrased by Heidegger as *macht-frei,* literally "power-free"—indexes specifically the withdrawal of refusal of being, its *Abschied* or departure, as the quiet word "of" being. The power-free can be conceived from the
Abschied, that is, in its nearness to power, which also marks, in its foregoing or
refusal of power, a radical remoteness from it: "The power-less: what is power,
what is the lack of power? How to understand the *–less?* From out of *refusal*
[*Verweigerung*]" (*M,* 166). This "departure" from power, marks the back-draft
force of the event precisely through the hyphen loosening the suffix *-los*" from
the term "power" (*Macht*). The refusal, as *Contributions to Philosophy* explains, is to be thought of in terms of a relation through restraint (a complex
play implied in Heidegger's term *Verhaltenheit*), an engaged or bestirred yet
reserved relating, which would set the tone for a new, "inceptual" thinking
and for a transformed relation to language, which could allow the event to
resonate in them. The power-free reticent holding in silence (*Erschweigung*)
is precisely what clears the room for and grounds all saying, whether in writing or in speech. It thus envelops power, its abilities and pretensions, in the
peculiar reticence of *das Macht-lose.* Yet the reticence at issue here can be all
too readily overshadowed by the power of words, by their meaning and by
their apparent certainty of knowing. Reticence tends to pale in comparison
with the cognitive eloquence and signifying power of words and can appear
as not too different from the opposite of power, namely, powerlessness, and
muteness. If muteness is equivalent to the inability to act and connotes a
certain lack of power, then silence would be tantamount to indifference, perhaps to a willingness not to act or participate, to a kind of indifference that is
sometimes mistakenly ascribed to Heidegger's *Gelassenheit.* Yet Heidegger's

writings clearly indicate that what is required is neither the power of assertion nor the "mute" powerlessness of inaction but instead a subtle attentiveness to the hint of the event's withdrawal into silence, silence that resonates
as the back draft of the event. For the event, if it takes place, does so only in
reticence, never with fanfares, blasts of power, or rhetorical flourish. These
undermine the event as much as powerlessness and muteness do.

Against these overwhelming odds and counter to some of his own previously employed language, all of Heidegger's major unpublished works from
the late 1930s through the end of World War II undertake the exploration of
precisely such a possibility, that is, the possibility of acting as letting (*Lassen*)
that could be free from power and violence. To be able even to envision such
a possibility, Heidegger launches a thorough examination and critique of
the three terms he progressively identifies with the metaphysical operations
of power: power (*Macht*), violence or coercive force (*Gewalt*), and mastery,
dominion, or sovereignty (*Herrschaft*). This critique comes to pivot on the
notion of *Walten*, to reign, hold sway, or pervade, and its link to *Gewalt*,
violence or coercive force. In a nutshell, Heidegger's texts can be read with
a view to a long and difficult attempt, stretching over many years and texts,
to extract *Walten* from the parameters set through the influence of violence,
coercion, and power (*Gewalt*). If released from *Gewalt*, *Walten* then describes
the kind of reign or sway that characterizes the stillness/silence (*die Stille*) of
being. This influence, attributed to being as *Seyn* as it comes to be played by
Heidegger against the standard modern spelling *Sein*, can be thought as the
unceasing letting be, the ceaseless and unstoppable, certainly not by power
or violence, giving of beings.

While *Macht* becomes the target of Heidegger's critique already in *Contributions to Philosophy*, and *Gewalt* in his subsequent book, *Mindfulness*, it
is only in *Die Geschichte des Seyns*, and even there initially with some hesitation, that Heidegger relinquishes the term *Herrschaft* (power in the sense of
mastery, rule, reign, domination, or sovereignty). In *Mindfulness*, Heidegger
approaches *Herrschaft* through its historical and conceptual link to the Latin
maiestas, conceiving it as majesty and dignity that would have nothing to do
with force or violence. "On occasions we use the word 'power' in the trans-
figurative sense of *maiestas*, which means the same as 'mastery' [*Herrschaft*],
although even this word frequently gets lost in vagueness and approximates
what is of the nature of power in the sense of coercive force [*Gewalt*]" (*M*, 170).
Dramatically contrasted with mastery and dominion, *maiestas* reigns and
holds sway—in the sense of *Walten* loosened from its inscription into *Gewalt*—
from out of its dignity, precisely from its being disengaged from power. As
this remark makes clear, Heidegger vacillates between the various connota-

tions of *Macht, Gewalt,* and *Herrschaft,* sometimes hesitating in his choice of words, testing their possibilities, while trying to maintain their power-free resonances. As a result of this vacillation, Heidegger's texts from the late 1930s are not free from their own ambiguities, fluctuating between various terms in an attempt to evolve a nonmetaphysically pitched idiom of power-free poetic thinking. All these hesitations, difficulties, and language experiments notwithstanding, we can see quite clearly and repeatedly that what is at issue, even in some of Heidegger's tentative remarks and in his continuously evolving positions, is the critique of power and violence as well as the contingent possibility of the notions of "force" and "relation" that could be transformative without being invested with power, domination, or coercion.

When Heidegger ultimately decides to abandon the term *Herrschaft* as inapt and unsuitable for how he wants to think of the quiet force of the possible arising from being, he assigns *Herrschaft* to the domain of power, concluding that it is misleading for the idiom of the power-free: "'Herrschaft' wird so zum völlig ungemässen Wort und deshalb dem Wesensbereich der Macht überwiesen" (*GA* 69, 69)—"Mastery becomes a completely unfitting word and is thus assigned to the essential domain of power." Once Heidegger has recognized the inescapable link between *Herrschaft, Macht,* and *Gewalt* and discarded the attempt to transfigure and retain *Herrschaft* for his critique, he explicitly sets out to find a way of relating that could obtain as free of violence and coercion, or in short, as *gewalt-los.* This idea of violence-free *Walten* recalls the need articulated in *Mindfulness* to think of being (*Seyn*) beyond power and powerlessness, that is, as power-free (*macht-los*). Considered together, these texts draw attention to the transversal resonance of the suffix *-los,* which, attached to power or violence, figures the momentum of release and freedom. The absence of power, or in other words, the powerless in the sense of lacking power or being without it, constitutes part and parcel of power and its operations, and remains essentially related to it: it is the shadow of power, its verso, and its mute companion. The power-less, by contrast, unfolds as unrelated to power, released from it: "And being is thus beyond both power and powerlessness. And yet being is not *something that belongs to the 'beyond' (Jenseitiges)* since being does not need first to posit for its truth the secular (*Diesseitige*) powerful (actual) beings in order that being or the beyng-historical projecting-opening of its clearing can have a leap-off" (*M,* 170). Being has no need of a beyond, and therefore also no need of "this side" (*Diesseitige*), no need of the 'divine' and of the 'secular,' which means that its event remains in some dimension untouched by power and violence.

It is in the context of these remarks that Heidegger's insistence on the need to transform our relation to language gains broader philosophical and cultural significance. Understanding the parameters of this transformation is indispensible to following the distinct idiom of Heidegger's critique of power, violence, and sovereignty, where the poietic momentum of language—the word's faulting into signs—delineates the domain of the power-free, releasing signs from their implication in the operations of power. Similarly, the expectation for a turn in the essence of technology is tied to the possibility of letting be and releasement (*Gelassenheit*) brought about by language's transformation of thought, which indicates here the release from power into the free domain of poietic emergence. Yet this domain can be opened in its "silent force of the possible" only as the word's slide into signs, as language's reverberant envelope of stillness.

Heidegger hoped that the Janus-faced *Ge-stell*, the essence of technology, could potentially allow the disclosure of a different way of relating beyond the global *Machenschaft* (machination) of power. In the context of the information age, the transformation in relation to language would amount also to a transformation in relation to power, as it would shift the center of gravity away from humans and from their apparent or desired control over the operations of power, yet without giving such control over to computers and technological machines. Since the informational coding of language suggests that its primary function is to be of use in conveying and processing information, it gives the humans the position of those who aim to control and profit from this processing. This is why all that exists appears to be there *for* humans and their benefit, informational and otherwise, to be at their disposal, or at least at the disposal of power that humans aspire to control ever more efficiently. By contrast, in Heidegger's transformational view of language, humans find themselves always already responding to language, already claimed by it, as if engaged in its service. Rather than taking charge and exercising power, this response enacts an originary "responsibility" or responsiveness (*Verantwortung*) of humans toward the event, remaining engaged in the difficult possibility of bringing the event to language. This responsibility is of an ontological order, that is, with regard to being, and, as Heidegger makes clear, is not to be conceived in moral or ethical terms. In fact, it is only because, by their way of responding and being, humans are responsive and responsible toward the event, that there can be ethical or moral responsibility. Without the human capacity to be responsive to the event—a capacity that the event grants or dedicates to humans in the sense that Heidegger calls *Zueignung*— that is, without the human capacity to listen to and bring the word of being into signs, there would be no possibility of ethics.

The transformation that Heidegger seeks involves a critical shift in the world's relatedness, specifically from the relations operating in terms of power to relations engaged in the manner of responsiveness. This does not mean that power could be wished away but rather that its operations would be enveloped within responsiveness, that is, occur always already as an (en)counter to the event; its tone could perhaps be reset—in the Janus-like turn in the essence of technology—from machination and spiraling drive toward more power to the *Stimmung* of primary responsiveness to being's event, and thus of responsibility to beings. This responsibility for beings would not be "moral" but flow instead from thinking's correspondence (*Entsprechung*) and "adherence" or "dedication" to the event-like occurrence of being.

This critique of the enframing offered by Heidegger must be seen through the prism of two complementary yet also contesting terms, namely making (*machen*) and letting (*lassen*), sometimes linked to enabling (*vermögen*). In the 1930s and later, because of Heidegger's critique of Nietzsche's "will to power" and Jünger's notion of the worker, "making" became the shorthand for a constellation of terms having to do with production, positing, power, violence, and mastery. Letting or enabling, by contrast, both become associated with letting something be what it is, allowing it to unfold freely. This enabling, as Heidegger explains in "Letter on Humanism," "not only can achieve this or that but also can let something essentially unfold in its provenance, that is, let it be"(*BW*, 220). *Lassen* or "letting" involves then a distinctive acting or actuating that does not involve making, production, violence, or mastery, and that is, therefore, distinguished from action that requires bringing about in a way that makes, causes, or effects. As Heidegger remarks in *Four Seminars* about his lecture "Time and Being," "It is a matter here of understanding that the deepest meaning of being is *letting*. Letting the being be, this is the noncausal meaning of 'letting' in 'Time and Being.' This 'letting' is something fundamentally different from 'doing'"(*FS*, 59). By contrast with action, which entails making or producing (*Machen*) and thus power (*Macht*), the "middle voice" in which letting be happens instead enables something to become what it properly is. Such a letting be is never inaction or passivity, however, because it allows for and leads to an idiomatic way of relating released from power. It is a bearing that "bears on" and relates to a being without resorting to power and thus bears it, that is, both maintains and carries it, in a way that "gives birth" to or enables that being's capacity to be what it is. "If the emphasis is: *to let* presencing, there is no longer room for the very name of being. *Letting* is then the pure *giving*, which itself refers to the it (*das Es*) that gives, which is understood as *Ereignis*"(*FS*, 60). This letting be refers, for instance, to the characteristic way in which things bear world, as Heidegger describes it in "The Thing," holding it open in its proper spatiotemporal expanse of interwoven relations. It thus accomplishes or obtains—one of the senses of the

German verb *lassen*—by allowing and releasing, instead of making. As such, it does not have recourse to power, whether creative or dominating. While I have made this argument in more detail elsewhere, it is important to show here how this distinction between making and enabling recalls transversely the relation between power and the power-free, *Macht* and *das Macht-lose,* which comes to figure in Heidegger's reflections on the essence of technology in terms of the fold between the technic and the poietic.[7] The poietic, therefore, does not constitute simply the opposite of the technic or signify its negation but instead signals the subtle inflection of the enframing and its prevalent modalities of power from the active and power-ful to the "middle voice," power-free.

To the extent that it is neither without power nor powerful, *Lassen* as the poietic momentum of the word, opening up signs—often literally, sometimes invisibly inscribing a hyphen into signs—introduces a fault, perhaps even an interruption, into the workings of power. To let be does not mean to leave as is by not acting but instead to release into the potentiality to be, to actuate without making or forcing. Neither active nor passive, this letting is not "of" power, and this is why it can become easily miscognized in terms of power as merely a powerless interruption, woven back into the operations of power as an instance of the absence or lack of power. Yet the originative momentum of letting is more 'radical' in its release or freeing than any counterpower can be, precisely by virtue—Heidegger would probably say because of its dignity (*Würde*)—of the foregoing of power. In *Mindfulness,* Heidegger describes this foregoing and letting go of power as the "radicalism" beyond both a yes and a no. *Lassen* as letting and release radically abstains from either a yes or a no to power, indulging neither in power nor simply powerlessly ceding to a stronger force. It is also not a mere indifference to or a lack of concern for power, which would lead simply to abstaining from doing anything. Instead, the specific sense that Heidegger develops for the term *letting,* relying to a large extent on the connotation of the German term *lassen* as getting something done without making or causing it to happen, is meant to transform power beyond power and the absence of power (*Ohnmacht*), and do so not by force or compulsion but by release, that is, by allowing the power-free. This radicalism beyond "yes and no" opens power to a frequency or a tonality (*Stimmung*) of relations that is neither detectable to power nor merely registered or indexed within power relations. It allows experience to transpire differently, without being entirely circumscribed in power relations. Such radicalism refers to the stillness/silence of being, unheard-of within power, because it is the tonality of what Heidegger sometimes calls the silent force of the possible underwriting and evading power relations.

At issue in the power-free tonality (*Stimmung*) is specifically its ability to retune signs, so that their creative and subversive play, which can be said to function within the domain of power—its alterations, ruptures, and reformulations—comes to be inflected by the event. "Das Ereignis . . . , als welche die Kehre des Seyns stimmend sich ereignet und das Zeigen der Zeichen gewährt"—"The event . . . in whose guise the turning of beyng eventuates while disposing and bestows the showing power of signs" (*GA* 71, 173; *E*, 147). As the turn of being, the event brings beings into play, allowing them to become present through the showing accomplished by signs. This is why "Das Er-eignis ist der Schatz des Wortes" (The appropriating event is the treasure of the word, *GA* 71, 173; *E*, 147), and why, as such a treasure trove of the saying—that is, of the vectors spanning and crisscrossing the clearing—it forms "the treasure of the word (treasure as the origin of the 'vocabulary' of 'language,'" its lexical system (*der Schatz des Wortes als der Ursprung des 'Wortschatzes' der 'Sprache'* [*GA* 71, 172; *E*, 147]). As the treasury of words, being "is" a pre-scriptive event, since its clearing unfolds spatiotemporally into a grammar and a lexis of relations and their description by signs. And here the difficulty in Heidegger's approach to language becomes paramount. For this thinking of the event as the inceptive word goes against the metaphysical precepts of experience. Here language and word are no longer simply human, neither just human, nor even primarily and from the first "human." Moreover, being seen metaphysically as mute and therefore in need of language and expression, that is, as manifest and (becoming) present in order to be represented, is now thought in terms of (its being) language, that is, as a poietic "word" that calls forth the human response. Neither mute nor immediate, being is now the inceptual word, as Heidegger writes in *Das Ereignis* (*GA* 71, 172; *E*, 146), with its words marking the vectors of relations pre-scripted and echoed through the hyphenated prefixes into the writing, into the always already human language.

What is thus pre-scribed, and hopefully reverberates, in signs—via the *Stimmung* shaping their play—is the singularity (*Einzigkeit*) and the one-time occurrence (*Einmaligkeit*) of the clearing sketched out in its nonrepeatable play of time-space. This singular occurrence is what silently recedes, taking its leave (*Abschied*) from signs that operate on the principle of generalizable particularity. With regard to signs, at issue in transforming our relation to language is the capacity to register in the repeatability of signs the one-time giving characteristic of how "the event comes to word," the nonrepeatability that indelibly marks each moment and what comes to exist in it. The play of prefixes attempts to let this singularity remain outside the domain—and dominion—of signification, and at the same time to let it be outside the sign's lack of power to say the singular. How can the "word" of the always one-time singular "there is" be allowed to be heard in the already known and dominant meaning of the sign? The third difficulty involves the fact that, while it is possible to outline this transformation, writing about it does not in itself make it possible. Furthermore, even if successfully outlined or conceived, the transformation, whether its conception or "theory," cannot be willfully sprung into action. For this fabrication would amount only to the prolongation of metaphysical doing, which would continue to assign priority to making and effecting, while the transformation at issue here, as Heidegger makes clear, cannot be compelled or manufactured. In short, this transformation is not exclusively up to human doing, will, or power. Nonetheless, it does emphatically require human preparation, and it is in this sense that Heidegger conceives of his thinking from the 1930s onward as preparatory: a thinking that prepares for the possibility of letting the transformation occur and does so by opening the third way, as it were, between activity and passivity, namely, the letting be or releasement of the *Gelassenheit*. This preparation makes room for human participation, allows it to happen if called for, without human action being capable of procuring or assuring the occurrence of such a change. Yet even when we allow the term *Gelassenheit* the resonance befitting it, the metaphysical binary of doing and not doing, of action and inaction or indifference, must be loosened, admitting a distinct way of rendering possible. To experience being as saying, to let it give its word, is the prerequisite, or better the pre-scription, Heidegger is looking for.

The Nothingness as the "Poverty" of Being

The play of prefixes under-writing Heidegger's shift from philosophy toward poetic thinking, by critically opening up the possibility of the power-free relation to being, also offers a fresh taste of the nothingness constitutive to being's "quiet force of the possible." What imparts the momentum to the release from power and violence indicated by the hyphen in the terms *macht-los* and *gewalt-los* is the back draft characteristic of the event, that is, its *Abschied* (departure) or *Enteignis* (de-event). This back draft is precisely the pull of the nothingness, variously described by Heidegger as *Nichtung* or *Nichten*. However, the pull of this retraction, hovering over the abyssal non-ground (*Abgrund*), is what in the same gesture exposes the finitude of being and brings into play the "unprethinkable." *Nichtung* describes the "quiet force of the possible," which renders possible and enables precisely by "nihilating," that is by presenting what exists as instantiated each time over the nonrepeatable void, over the abyss that grants and guards impermanence. The openness brought into view by the event's back draft constitutes the power-free span, the "width" and the "while," as Heidegger refers to it, in which possibilities and impossibilities emerge, disposed in the mode of their momentary (dis)appearance.

This silent, power-free, yet overwhelmingly enabling span of the event calls for a radical transformation in the metaphysically conceived human mode of being, shifting the emphasis from the privilege of action, power, and accomplishment, to the postmetaphysical *Armut* or poverty: "Das höchste Eigentum des Menschentums, das nach der Überwindung der Metaphysik zur Inständigkeit im Da-sein bereit wird und so die Gründung der Wahrheit des Seyns übernimmt und so in die Geschichte des Seyns eingeht, ist zufolge diesem Eingang in das Ereignis die *Armut*" (*GA* 70, 132)—"The highest proper domain of humanity, which after the overcoming of metaphysics will be ready for the standing in Da-sein and in this way take over the grounding of the truth of being and thus enter the history of being, is, as a consequence of this entrance into the event, *poverty*." It is important to understand that in this context "poverty" indicates neither deprivation nor penury (for instance, lack of essentials required for existence), nor does it refer to the Christian ideal of poverty, but instead figures as "lacking nothing" in the sense of not missing anything (any being) and therefore "lacking" (missing, disregarding) the nothing(ness), that is, being seen nonmetaphysically as *Seyn*.[8] The term instantiates a denuding of the human into the most fundamental, "poor" openness to being, that is, to the poietic momentum of nihilation—which is how I read what Heidegger calls *das Nichthafte*, that which is "nothingness-like" or "like nothing"—continuously opening possibilities into the future, while marking the finite span of existence. Heidegger is quick to remark that this poverty is not a lack (*nicht Mangel*) but instead a perseverance in the simple and the singular: "die Inständigkeit (das Gemüt, die Gestimmtheit) im Einfachen und Einzigen: dieses aber ist die Wesung des Seyns" (*GA* 70, 132)—"the perseverance (the disposition, the attunement) in the simple and the unique: that is, though, the essencing of beyng." The denuding of *Mut* implied in the term *poverty* pivots, opening thought onto the gathered, underlying disposition, indicated by the term *Gemüt*. In this disposition, the human being becomes attuned to the singular unfolding, or to the simple essential occurrence, of being itself, rather than becoming preoccupied or distracted by whatever comes to influence one's mood or spirit.

The "simple" and the "singular" in this quotation recall the flash of the one-time occurrence (*Einmaligkeit*) of being mentioned in *Contributions to Philosophy*. The simple (*Einfach*) joins the array of prominent terms beginning with the prefix *ein-* and employed by Heidegger with regard to being

(*Seyn*) in order to underscore the most difficult simplicity with which being comes to pass each time only one time and always singularly or uniquely.[9] In this context, "poverty" indicates the only one-time, always already withdrawn and thus shot through with nothingness, giving of being: "Die Armut und die Schenkung—/ Die Gelassenheit in der Wesung der Er-eignung" (*GA* 70, 132)—"Poverty and donation—/ The letting be in the essencing of the event." On various occasions Heidegger coyly remarks that his thinking, for all its complexity and intricate language strategies, concerns itself with what remains the simplest, that is, with the simple of being. Yet this simplicity of being is what is most difficult to think, not because it is simple in the sense of not being complex but because the simple (*Einfach*) of being is singular and elementary, or perhaps elemental, and as such it does not bear repetition.

To develop Heidegger's point about the simple of being, we must look at the etymological composition to the term *Ein-fach,* which could be rendered literally as single-province, one-field, or single-trade. Related to activity or employment, *Fach* indicates trade, profession, business, or occupation, while with regard to territory it also denotes field, province, department, and so forth. Yet the primary meaning of the term implies division or compartmentalization, which, when combined with the prefix *ein-,* underscores the singleness and thus the simplicity of the fact that being is only and singularly in the business of "giving": *es gibt.* Being constitutes its own single province or department, and here *Einfach* becomes consonant with *Einfalt:* the one-as-in-fold. The simple of being constitutes the infold that opens as the one-fold of the event and language. This is why the simple (*Ein-fach*) is difficult, and exceedingly so, because it neither is one nor two but forms instead the peculiar and singular initial fold of the onefold of being. The "simple" that Heidegger has in mind here is what both envelops and inflects the movement of differentiation and the logic of identity and difference. At issue for Heidegger is letting this simple in-one-fold flash as singular and nonrepeatable in thinking, and then to hold thought attentive to this moment and its unprethinkable poietic momentum.

In the lecture "Die Armut," Heidegger patiently reinterprets the noun *Armut* (poverty), beginning with the usual sense of not having (*Nicht-Haben*) and being deprived of what is needed or necessary (*Entbehren des Nötigen, A,* 8). Richness, by contrast, means not doing without the necessary or having more than is necessary. Starting with these conventional meanings, Heidegger proceeds to invert the notion of poverty, stating that being truly poor means not lacking anything, except what is nonnecessary: "Wahrhaft arm seyn besagt: so seyn, dass wir nichts entbehren, es sey denn das Unnötige"— "To be truly poor means to be so that one is deprived of nothing except what is not needed" (*A*, 8; *P*, 6). The nonnecessary on which the notion of poverty comes to pivot is what does not come from need (*Not*), but it is disposed instead from the free domain (*aus dem Freien*)—that is, from what is also *das Macht-lose*, the power-free. In this context, freedom refers to that which is not used or useful and thus comes to be spared or safeguarded (*das Geschonte*). Bringing to the fore the composition of the term "necessity" in German (*Notwendigkeit*), Heidegger proceeds to explain that necessity is not the opposite of freedom but rather obtains from and in relation to freedom. Necessity is literally the turn within freedom toward need: *Not-wendigkeit*: "dann ist die Notwendigkeit keineswegs, wie alle Metaphysik meint, das Gegenteil der Freiheit, sondern einzig die Freiheit ist in sich die Not-wendigkeit"—"then necessity is not at all the opposite of freedom, as metaphysics assumes, but freedom is in itself solely turning unto need (*Not-wendigkeit*)" (*A*, 8; *P*, 7). One could say that what is necessary (for human beings) is guarding the openness of the free domain. This explication leads Heidegger to declare that the free is specifically what can invert necessity (*Not-wendigkeit*) and as the freeing sweep, that is, as what is not necessitated by need, the free is therefore the nonnecessary (*das Un-nötige, A*, 9). These inversions of phrases and words, combined with the insertion of hyphens, make it then possible for Heidegger to define being poor as surprisingly lacking nothing: "Armseyn heisst: nichts entbehren, es sey denn das Unnötige—nichts entbehren als das Freie-Freiende"—"Beyng poor (*Armseyn*) means lacking nothing except what is not needed—lacking nothing as the liberating free and open" (*A*, 9; *P*, 7, modified). It is, therefore, through poverty in the sense explained above that one can belong to the free and to the freeing momentum of the event's back draft, and do so through an idiomatic "sparing" of the unnecessary.

Heidegger's explanation of poverty, which keeps inverting the term from necessity and need to freedom, relies on the pivotal term *entbehren*, which usually means missing something or doing without it. Heidegger subtly shifts the emphasis in his discussion of the term from "doing without" seen negatively to "doing without" as "positive," that is, as indicating saving and sparing what one can do without, or not use. What one can do without is what precisely is not given to use: neither useless nor not useful but use-free, as it were, and what as use-free comes to be spared, sheltered in its use-free plangency. This freeing (from use) and foregoing are among the connotations of *entbehren*, which Heidegger amplifies and brings into resonance with the verb *schonen*, to spare, in order to highlight the capacity to shelter, that is, to hold open, preserve, or save. As he puts it, "when the human being spares the non-necessary, then man has become poor in the proper sense of the term" (*A*, 9; *P*, 8, modified). It is in this sparing and freeing gesture of "poverty" that

humans become "rich": "das eigentliche Armseyn ist in sich das Reichseyn"—
"The genuinely beyng poor is in itself beyng rich" (*A*, 9; *P*, 8, modified). Rich
here has nothing to do with possession, whether of things or goods, or of
abilities and power, over which one can have control. In other words, richness here is not thought from the essence of technology, or the enframing,
in terms of availability or possession and their relation to need or necessity,
but instead from the sense of a free and freeing sparing. "Indem wir aus der
Armut nichts entbehren, haben wir im vorhinein alles, wir stehen im Über-
fluss des Seyns, das alles Nötigende der Notdurft zum voraus überströmt"—
"As we are not deprived of anything because of poverty, we have everything in
advance; we reside in the overflowing of beyng, which overflows in advance
all needs that make us needy" (*A*, 9; *P*, 8, modified).

The singular simple of being that lights and lightens up the instant as
die Lichtung (the clearing) pivots open into the richness of the world: into
the profusion of beings, relations, phenomena, and occurrences. Poverty in
Heidegger's sense does not mean being poor as in lacking necessities or possessions; instead, it inverts into being open in the specific tonality of *Ar-mut*,
which transforms the human mode of being, freeing it from its metaphysical
capture in beings and from remaining engrossed in their possession, manipulation, and exploitation. As Schild suggests, poverty lacks nothing, were
it not the nothing as such, and therefore, being (*Seyn*).[10] The apparent richness
of beings, their possession, use, or manipulation, lacks the nothing(ness) as
being (*Seyn*), nothingness that comes to be covered over and forgotten under
the overwhelming dominion of beings and power. Yet from this lack with
regard to being, that is, from the everyday existence without attentiveness to
it, which disappears in our consuming preoccupation with beings, the verb
entbehren, when paired with *nichts* (nothing), is inverted by Heidegger to
indicate precisely the opposite of privation, namely "lacking nothing." Seen
this way, the verb *entbehren* shifts from "lacking" or "doing without" to not
lacking at all, that is, to being open and attentive to being, sparing its characteristic nothing(ness). It is in this sense that poverty becomes the new tone or
disposition (*Stimmung*) characteristic of the possibility of "the other beginning" (*der andere Anfang*) as the alternative nonmetaphysical attentiveness
to the freeing affluence of being. To put it simply, poverty in beings—that is,
breaking away from the hegemony of beings, things, or commodities—can
turn into the richness and abundance in being. It is important to note that
this "poverty in beings" is not thought here in terms of having or not having,
that is, not with regard to possession or satisfaction of needs. Rather, poverty
here is "ontological" in the sense of opening a transformed relation to being
(*Seyn*), which no longer proceeds through beings and beingness, thus becom-

ing engrossed exclusively in beings, but is capable of standing "poor" in the overflow of being, denuded of the drive to possess, master, or rule. At issue is not, therefore, simply the renunciation of possessions and assumption of mendicancy but a critical and liberating turn in our relation to beings: the shift from the technical, "enframing" relations of availability (for use, possession, consumption, manipulation, etc.) to a freer relation unfolding from the nonnecessary (*das Unnötige*), from what is not about need, necessity, usefulness, or possession.

In this interesting recasting of poverty, Heidegger allows his thinking to proceed again by literally listening to words. Here first to the turn constitutive of necessity and brought into the open by the hyphen (*Not-wendigkeit*), to the critical inversion of the tone from "doing without" to "sparing" in *entbehren*, and finally to the pivotal play of *nicht, nichts,* and *Nichts:* not, nothing, nothingness. The negative *nicht* (not) or *nichts* (nothing) appears first in relation to not having and "not lacking" (*nicht entbehren*), only to turn to "lacking not" verging on "lacking nothing" (*nichts entbehren*) and then to sparing the nothing(ness), that is, to being attentive to the nihilating momentum of being: *Nichts-entbehren.* "So wie die Freiheit in ihrem freienden Wesen allen das ist, was die Not zum voraus wendet, die Notwendigkeit, so ist das Armseyn als das Nichts-entbehren denn das Unnötige in sich aus schon das Reichsein"—"Just as freedom in its liberating ownmost is to everyone that which averts and circumvents the need, and is so a turning unto the need (*Not-wendigkeit*), beyng poor as being deprived of nothing [alternatively: as sparing the nothing(ness)] other than what is not needed is in itself already being rich" (*A,* 9; *P,* 8, modified). This whole explanation, which captures the upshot of Heidegger's transformation of the human into Da-sein, relies completely on the movement, inversion, and capitalization of the word(s) *nicht(s).* If the metaphysical notion of the human being is grounded in the first and fundamental possession, namely of *logos,* then the nonmetaphysically thought of human being is inverted and transformed through being-there into the poverty/richness of the possible attentiveness to the silent or still abundance of being. Quite dramatically, the human comes to be thought of no longer, and certainly not originarily, through possession but instead through the freeing nothing(ness) of being: from the concern with "not" (*nicht*), that is, with not having (things or beings), to the shift toward lacking nothing (*nichts*), which brings with it the freeing moment of openness to the nothing(ness) essentially occurring in being, and the decisive sparing and keeping attentive to this nothingness, now properly capitalized in German: *Nichts.* As Heidegger explains in *Four Seminars,* "The human is the placeholder of the nothing" (*FS,* 63), standing within the site (*Da*) where what holds sway is attentiveness to the nothing (*Nichts* or *Nichtung*) occurring essentially *as* being (*Seyn*).

The short lecture on poverty provides a snapshot both of how Heidegger's thinking works its inversions *through* language and how crucial the nothingness is to understanding the transformation at stake in Heidegger's project of the other beginning. This approach, which lets thinking unfold directly via words, manifests that the lecture does not begin with a preconceived idea of poverty or necessity, which it then proceeds to describe or expound, but that instead Heidegger literally essays to allow these notions to unfold from the words themselves, that is, by listening and allowing thinking to belong to language (*ge-hören*). The sense of the richness and abundance of the nothingness occurring as being is marked by withdrawal or refusal, whose back draft opens the clearing with the profusion of beings, relations, happenings, and so forth. As Heidegger explains in *Über den Anfang,* "beyng itself is however closely related to the nothing / Its nothingness is its poverty and this poverty is the richness of the simple of the beginning"—"Das Seyn selbst ist dagegen das Nichts-hafte. / Seine Nichtigkeit ist seine Armut und diese Armut ist der Reichtum des Einfachen des Anfangs" (*GA* 70, 175). The nonmetaphysical resonance of being (*Seyn*) comes from its occurrence essentially as "nothing": being occasions itself inverting into nothingness. This inversion, in the flash of one-time uniqueness, is what lets beings be. It lets beings be always as open in a manner of nihilation (*Nichtung*): open to the future, to being once (again) singular and one-time, and thus to the possibility of ceasing and not being at all. This nothingness, prior to any negation or affirmation, beyond a yes and a no, as Heidegger remarks in *Mindfulness,* constitutes the poietic momentum of being, its "silent force of the possible," unthinkable in terms of beings or through the prism of beingness. This nothingness occurring essentially as being (*Seyn*) is the disappropriation on the back draft of the event: *Nichtung* moves as *Enteignung,* as the unfolding of the event in its de-parting (*Ereignis* as *Abschied, GA* 70, 122). Perhaps the most poignant explanation of this inversion of being and nothingness appears in *Mindfulness:* "'Nothingness' is neither the negation of beings nor the negation of beingness, nor is it the 'privation' of being; it is not the deprivation [*Beraubung*] that simultaneously would be an annihilation [*Vernichtung*]. Rather, *'nothingness' is the foremost and highest gift of beyng* [*Seyn*], which along with itself and as itself gifts beyng as event unto the clearing of the prime-leap [*Ur-sprung*] as abyss [*Ab-grund*]" (*M,* 263, modified; *GA* 66, 294–295). The nothingness is the poverty of being as the donation (*Schenkung*) in the specific sense in which this momentum, while giving (into) beings, allows one to stay attentive to the always one-time occurrence of this giving. This is why, for Heidegger, being in its freeing essential occurrence as the nothingness that foregoes power (*macht-los* and *macht-frei*), never annihilates, because only power and violence, which target beings, can annihilate. On the contrary, the nothingness is being's "silent force of the possible," freeing and opening possibilities and impossibilities, without forgetting that the possibility to be involves and inevitably entails the possibility "not to be." As Heidegger explains in *Four Seminars,* the nothing is nothing negative and indicates "a nihilating nothing (*nichtendes Nichts*). The essence of the nothing consists in the turning away from beings, in the distance from them. . . . The nihilation of the nothing 'is' being" (*FS,* 57). Being's nihilation marks the span of finitude and Dasein's most own, nonrelational possibility: death. This is why the possibility "not to be" or "to cease being" unfolds as proper to the being's back draft of nihilation, which is not a matter of power, violence, or dominion. Here nihilation, disclosing its valence as *machtlos* and *gewaltlos,* that is, as power- and violence-free, comes into view as alternative to the metaphysical experience of being as machination or manipulative power (*Machenschaft*).

Rethought this way, nihilation is the highest gift in the sense that it allows the play of time-space to be instantiated each time as singular, experienced as properly one time. This experience of nihilation lets be in the specific sense in which *nichtig* and *Nichtigkeit* refer to a void and an emptiness, that is, to the clearing coming open in the wake of being's characteristic coming present through withdrawal, which can be sharply distinguished from annihilation as the deprivation of being. "It is essential to the participle form 'nihilating' (*nichtend*) that the participle show a determinate 'activity' of being, through which alone the particular being *is*. One can name it an origin, assuming that all ontic-causal overtones are excluded: it is the event [*Ereignis*] of being as condition for the arrival of beings: being lets beings presence" (*FS,* 58–59). What can be annihilated is precisely finitude as the possibility of the very experience of nihilation characteristic of Da-sein. Furthermore, it is precisely the *Nichten,* the nihilating *infolded* into being and ceaselessly unfolding its futural momentum of possibilities, that can, continuously inverting being into nothingness, release from power and violence, and forego manifesting being in these terms. Recast away from the notions of the nothing as absence or annihilation, nihilation instantiates the power-free, poietic momentum, rippling through technicity. The enframing as the essence of technology reveals everything in terms of its availability as a being, that is, as something that can be taken possession of, manipulated, or consumed. In this specific sense, the *Gestell* (enframing) blocks the experience of the nothingness, burying it under the staggering availability of objects and information, under the proliferation of beings and the possibilities for their control. Technicity thus provides the "spurious" richness of beings, while in fact it progressively impoverishes being and renders impossible the ontological experience of poverty as the opening onto the abundance of being (*Seyn*) through which alone the experience of the profusion of beings in their proper valence as beings can be possible.

What obtains (*Walten*) in being—what being "is"—is neither power nor violence (*Gewalt*) but nothingness, nihilation, and emptiness (*Nichts, Nichtung, Nichtigkeit*), which provide "the gentle bind" (*milde Bindung*) among beings, as Heidegger refers to it while writing about the clearing and its poietic momentum of unfolding. While commentators have remarked on the strident rhetoric of "struggle" (*Kampf*) in Heidegger's texts from the 1930s, not enough attention has been given to the astonishing hints of a radical transformation of this idiom into one of gentleness (*Milde*) and letting be (*Gelassenheit*), on which Heidegger's work in *Contributions to Philosophy* and onward relies and does so explicitly in transforming its approach to language and thought. This surprising—given the tone of *Introduction of Metaphysics*—idiom of gentleness and mildness becomes critical to understanding the event and its power-free occurrence. As Heidegger remarks in *Die Geschichte des Seyns,* "Event and the gentleness of the highest mastery, which does not need power and 'struggle,' but an originary confrontation. The violence-free reign"—"Ereignis und die Milde der höchsten Herrschaft, die nicht der Macht und nicht des 'Kampfes' bedarf, sondern ursprüngliche Auseinander-setzung. Das Gewalt-lose Walten" (*GA* 69, 8). The violence-free sway here, which bends power relations out of their habitual shape, is that of the nothingness occurring essentially in being and inverting it. The violence-free is not about fighting or struggle, power and powerlessness, but instead about an originative setting apart that would allow for the specific attentiveness to the event, required for the *Stimmung* of poverty. This setting apart and encountering (*Auseinander-setzung*) is the time-spacing opened by the hyphen in Da-sein, and its concomitant (en)countering of world and earth.

In *Mindfulness,* still speaking about the majesty (*maiestas*) of being, Heidegger reframes the notion of *Herrschaft* in terms of the mildness or gentleness (*Milde*) that informs being's "essentiality," its *Wesentlichkeit* (*M*, 306; *GA* 66, 343), contrasting it with the notions of mastery, rule, and sovereignty. *Die Geschichte des Seyns* deploys this idiom of gentleness several times, making an important juxtaposition between power, violence, and sovereignty, encoded into the complex and global scope of *Machenschaft,* on the one hand, and the gentle binds, event-like relations, which bind beings in the modality of *Gelassenheit,* on the other. Critical to understanding the gist and drift of Heidegger's thinking is once again not confusing this modality of gentleness and mildness (*Milde*) with powerlessness or absence of power. Heidegger is very clear in stating that this "gentleness" is *machtunbedürftig*: it has no need and no use for power. Having no need and no wish for power, this modality of gentleness resonates and binds 'beyond' the scope of power and being without power, or powerlessness (*Ohnmacht*). It is 'beyond' them in the sense of being unrelated to them, of indicating another order of relating, on the back side of power relations, as it were. Or perhaps it is power-free in the sense in that all instantiations of power come through as already inverting into nothingness, nihilated and emptied of power in the very moment of its actuation. This "gentle binding" does not constitute an actual beyond but remains within power and powerlessness as the unusual valence of the power-free. As Heidegger puts it, the power-free can never be disempowered (*M*, 168), because it is never a deficiency or lack of power. Rather, power and its absence are not fitting, apt or appropriate to the power-free. "... the name power-less [that is, power-free] should indicate that given its essence, beyng [*Seyn*] continues to be detached [*losgelöst*] from power. However, *this* powerless *is* mastery [*Herrschaft*]" (*M*, 170, modified).

In his later writings, Heidegger trades even this notion of *Herrschaft*, understood in the sense of majesty, for the notion of *Würde*, dignity or worthiness, which he explicitly juxtaposes and confronts with the idea of value, and thus also with use, consumption, and capital. *Herrschaft* remains too close to power and violence (*Gewalt*) and a different notion, that of the generosity of being's giving, understood also as its "dignity," comes to be associated with the idiom of gentleness and *Gelassenheit*. In his remarks in *GA* 74, Heidegger explains the stillness of being precisely by writing about this sense of gentleness: "The gentleness and stillness of beyng, the purity of its inceptual 'nothingness' lets human beings easily go astray with beings and become satisfied with this semblance"—"Die Milde und Stille des Seyns, die Reinheit seiner als anfängliches "Nichts" lässt den Menschen leicht sich an das Seiende verirren und am Schein sich genügen" (*GA* 74, 27). Pointing out how beings are only a "semblance" of being, that is, a form of beingness (*Seiendheit*), Heidegger underscores the fact that the stillness and gentleness intrinsic to being, its momentum of nihilation, becomes easily covered over and dissimulated by the precedence given to beings and their possibilities, which achieve dominance in everyday experience and dealings. To develop what Heidegger's turn to poetic thinking renders possible, we need to see stillness, nihilation, and gentleness, as manifesting the inceptual rift or fold of the event, which Heidegger designates as "pain" (*Schmerz*). Pain becomes the original disposition (*Stimmung*) of being, because it befits the (en)countering, gentle forms of relations: "The silent mildness of the exceptional pain in the event"—"Die stille

Milde des ungemeinen Schmerzes im Er-eignis" (*GA* 74, 29). The adjective *ungemein*, literally "uncommon," makes evident that "pain" here is neither psychological nor somatic but ontological and event-like, since it marks the vector of the event's abundant, each time singular and one-time, opening onto beings, relations, and occurrences.

Since the event is a soundless, still unarticulated (*lautlose*) word, this word—which unfolds into sounds and letters, giving in(to) signs, both granting signs and ceding its place to them, as it already recedes and refuses itself (*Versagen*)—is an "uncommonly painful," while also surprisingly gentle, experience of stillness, which envelops the bustle of existence and beings. This refusal, as Dastur elaborates, neither is a sign of weakness nor is it an index of the ineffable, but instead it maintains and supports being in its withdrawal, thus affording us an each-time singularly "true" relation to it.[11] It is in this sense that the silent word is gentle and forgoes power, as Heidegger explains: "The word compels nothing but *lets free* in the essential sense that—tuning—it first transposes into the tuned clearing, into the Free. *The word is the opening of freedom*"—"Das Wort verzwingt nichts, sondern *lässt frei* in dem wesentlichen Sinn, dass es—stimmend—erst in die erstimmte Lichtung, das Freie, versetzt. *Das Wort ist die Eröffnung der Freiheit*" (*GA* 74, 151). As the simple and singular beginning, the word's movement outlines the opening of freedom that comes to be experienced in the attunement of poverty as the profusion and overflow (*Überfluss*) of being.[12] As both "*Vorwort*" (*GA* 71, 252) and "*Anwort*" (*GA* 71, 313), as at once a pre-word or a fore-word, this releasement of the word gives beings to their being, while fore-wording them into signs. As essentially a one-time pre-word, this word does not exist—or come to presence—prior to signs, but expends and spends itself as the event's coming to word, in the same gesture leaving the scene to signs and meaning, to concepts, ideas, and statements. It exists neither before signs nor simply within them. Rather, the word "exists" only as the back draft bringing signs and language into existence. As the quotation that links the clearing, the *Stimmung,* and freedom indicates, *Stimmung* understood as the inceptual disposition must be thought of precisely in its momentum that opens freedom, that is, the vector of freedom's possibilities. Such word is "die anfänglich stimmende Stimme: das Wort"—"the inceptually disposing voice: the word" (*GA* 71, 171; *E,* 145). Neither language nor voice (speech or sound) to begin with, it carries (out) and decides the movement of the event into language, opening experience and lending it its initial pitch.

It is within this dispositive sense of the word that I locate the transformative momentum of thinking, momentum proper not only to language's movement but also—correspondingly, that is, by way of *Entsprechen*—to "poetic thinking" conceived as attentiveness to the event-like unfolding of language. The most significant and innovative aspect of this approach is the detaching of the essence and unfolding (*Wesen*) of language from the conception of the sign (*signum*). Withdrawn from the primacy of the sign and signification, language allows one to notice its own constitutive withdrawal and refusal, that is, the distinctive "back draft" of the event, without mistaking it all too easily for a defect of cognition or powerlessness of expression. Only within the expanse left open by this withdrawal can the nothingness essentially occurring as being be recognized as "the silent force of the possible." The poverty of this nothingness, the fact that it needs nothing, not a thing or a being, in order to give ceaselessly as the always singular occasion and one-time actuation, is what returns possibility to its essential play.

The event occurs, but it is carried out only with regard to human beings, that is, to the extent that it can be brought to language, albeit only as its silent back draft. This is the case because the event can be carried out only by coming to words. What must be recognized is that language in this essential occurrence is not human but takes place *with regard to* human beings, as it inescapably comes to be articulated through them into writing and speech. The event, Heidegger explains, has the momentum of *ostendere:* of manifesting and showing. Yet it "ostentates," if such a verb were possible, without being "ostentatious," and does so not only without showing off but, paradoxically, through withdrawal and holding back. The awareness of these complex and shifting movements at work in language, their essentially quiet occurrence on the back side of the eloquence of human languages with their complex grammatical and lexical systems, must be combined with attentiveness to the silent stillness (*Stille*) that envelops language, so that one could undergo an experience with language, which in turn can perhaps prompt a transformation in our relation to language on which the twisting free (*Verwindung*) of metaphysics depends. Heidegger's innovative approach to language stands apart precisely in its distinctive recognition of manifestation as an inceptual word (a *Vorwort* or an *Anwort*) whose force renders possible and, in the same stroke, inaugurates human language as a response to this initial, already departing, word. "Language speaks"; we (re)speak, say after, and (re)write it, but it is the event that thus "comes to word." This idiomatic wording of the event comes to refer to the vectors and the folds that bring beings into the open, link and relate them, and compose this continually emergent and shifting relatedness into a world.

What I have shown in this book is that this innovative sense of the word and language is indispensable to understanding and carrying forward the momentum of Heidegger's critique; not simply his critical assessment of metaphysics but equally his rethinking of difference and relation as well as of power and power's modern, technical modes of revealing and producing. Heidegger's conception of the enframing as the revealing at work in modern technology cannot be understood in its full impact without noting its poietic underside and recognizing its decisive role in (en)countering the technical. In the same vein, Heidegger's pioneering diagnosis and critique of planetary power, violence, and sovereignty, considered in their entwined macro- and microscopic scales of operation, and especially his claim about the possibility of a power-free (*machtlos*) momentum of possibility, will not register without attention to how his language changes the very manner of thinking from conceptual and propositional to poietic. The links between word and stillness, gentleness and *Gelassenheit*, become in turn crucial to avoiding the mistake of flattening the distinct "middle voice" disposition of Heidegger's late thought to simple passivity or mere indifference, instead of recognizing in it the possibilities opened by the poietic momentum of what may be called a power-free, "nothingness-related," (*Nichthafte*) doing. Without developing Heidegger's indexes of poetic thinking, it will be difficult to understand the possible political significance of his critique of power and action, which, even though not articulated expressly as such by Heidegger, extends to technicity and its intrinsically interconnected operations of capital(ization) and informatization. One way of beginning to evolve this political significance would be to note that, if it is the event that comes to word, and if language is initially, in its pre-word, nonhuman, then politics must begin each time also from the event, that is, from the world's fourfold, and not simply be approached at the outset from the point of view of humanity or, as is usual, be determined exclusively in terms of inter-human actions and relations. This is where the "politics of the event," in its post-Heideggerian inflection, would have to begin. Humanity would no longer be prioritized, from the beginning metaphysically ensconced in its *Herrschaft*, its mastery and sovereignty over beings, but instead approached and rethought from the event, that is, as part of the dimensioning of the fourfold, where humanity would be neither most important nor insignificant, but perhaps, to pun with Heidegger, of the "same" importance as earth, sky, and the possible experience of divinity.[13] In other words, a politics of the fourfold, of earth and sky, and only jointly with them, of humanity, life, and living beings, this is perhaps the twist in metaphysics that Heidegger has in mind. Instead of reconfirming the dominant perspective of mastery and possession of beings, or its twin, their creative manipulation and production, that is, of the conjoined glory and penury of knowledge, technology, capital, and, yes, culture—which always already constitutes an offspring of *techne*—we can try to evolve out of Heidegger a transformed view from within the "poverty" of being. This approach would evince attentiveness to what, as the abundance opening again and again from being's never-depleted and ceaseless force of nothingness, gives always singly, simply, and one-time, and thus makes all of the above possible: being in its no-longer-metaphysical valence of *Seyn*.

At issue in language "after" Heidegger is freedom given back to being, and through it, hopefully to beings: "The conversation of the saying of beyng is the *jointure* of the permissive, protective-dwelling releasement into freedom"—"Das Gespräch der Sage des Seyns ist die *Fuge* der lassenden, hütend-wohnenden Gelassenheit in die Freyheit. . . ." (*GA* 74, 163). Heidegger was convinced that only from the infinitely rich poverty and simplicity of this freedom, free beings—human and nonhuman, living and nonliving—could perhaps be allowed to be what they properly can be as beings. Freedom of being in the sense developed by Heidegger does not overlook freedom of beings but, conversely, releases and makes such freedom possible precisely with regard to its intrinsic, one wants to say, constitutive, nihilation. This freedom, which is approached in "Poverty" as the world-wise tending to and sparing of the nothingness of being, that is, as *Nichts-entbehren,* is the gift of language and can only be recognized inasmuch as language follows how the event comes to word. This word coming from the event is indeed the "word of freedom," for it does not force or compel but lets free or releases, disposing being in this manner and making experience possible (*Er-fahren lassen*). As a response to the word that disposes experience into its free span, language unceasingly, since it cannot desist manifesting and signifying, moves us to word-signs, articulating what is in the process of taking place *as* experience. This idiomatically presented fold between word and sign, between being and language, discloses the very relationality of the world and the occurrence of beings within it as a language-bearing movement, its emergent and shifting relatedness. While being is not language, it is being *only* with regard *to* language. This is why the giving, as that which we may say being comes to be experienced, constitutes already being's word, its fore-word to signs. This fold forces the difficult rethinking of the "earthiness" of existence beyond the convenient metaphysical divide into the sensible and the intelligible. Materializing as beings, the "word 'of' being" institutes the word-matter of language and its intelligibility. While language frames how "the event comes to word" in terms of the sensible and the intelligible, the event's fanning out into possibilities requires a thinking beyond these oppositional terms, a thinking nimble enough not only to demarcate the event's momentary, back-drafting plosion but also to render it into the transformative force in thought. To notice the distinctive quietness with which the word enables signs by taking leave of them, and to shape thinking in accord with this movement, is perhaps to let (thinking and beings) be free. Allowing this gesture of freeing to arise from the event, also means letting ourselves be free in the sense of staying open and attentive to the world's distinctive clearing, of standing always as if for the first time in the midst of beings in the manner of Da-sein, free as though "in advance" of the hustle and bustle of everydayness.

NOTES

Introduction

1. Critical responses to Heidegger have begun addressing his shift in the understanding of language in the mid-1930s, especially in the context of *Contributions to Philosophy*. It is significant that in the volume of proceedings from the 2004 colloquium on *Beiträge zur Philosophie,* no fewer than six essays are devoted to the problem of language: John Sallis, "The Manic Saying of Beyng" (75–84); Ivo de Gennaro, "Entmenschung und Sprache" (329–340); François Vezin, "Expérience de la parole, expérience de la traduction" (341–355); Jean-François Aenishanslin, "La logique, la pensée, le silence" (359–366); Ivan Kordić, "Das Sagen des Seyns und die Sprache" (367–382); Marco Casanova, "Die Sprache des Ereignisses" (383–392). All these essays share an emphasis on the critical need to (re)think language from the event, that is, as already "saying" and delivering itself to words. Although I return occasionally to these texts, my overall approach is informed by the same critical stance, emphasizing the importance of transforming (our relation to) language precisely from the event.

2. There are of course many earlier essays and book-length studies that predate the publication of these texts by Heidegger and pave the way for my study. Among them, I want to mention three that hold particular importance for my approach here, in order of their appearance: Bernasconi, *Question of Language,* my own *Inflected Language,* and Fynsk, *Language and Relation.* These studies share an understanding that language in Heidegger cannot be accounted for simply in conceptual terms, that is, presented as a theory or a philosophy of language, but that, taken beyond representation and expression, language comes to transform thinking, so that thought no longer "uses" language to present its findings but issues from language and responds to it. I also treated the issue of language in Heidegger in the two books that followed *Inflected Language* and several essays, not only on Heidegger but also on Heidegger and avant-garde poetry. Some of my intuitions about Heidegger's approach have been borne out, in particular by the publication of volumes 71 and 74 of the *Gesamtausgabe,* which allow us to comprehend better and develop the critical transformation of language sketched in *Contributions to Philosophy* and *Mindfulness.*

3. Robert Bernasconi emphasizes this notion of transformation in his essay "Transformation of Language at Another Beginning," where, rereading Derrida's critique of the "presence" of *phone* and *logos* in Heidegger's thinking on language, he instead draws parallels between the two thinkers, insisting that "The end of philosophy, or rather its closure (*Verendung*), takes place in both Heidegger and Derrida, therefore, only as a transformation of our relation to previous thinking" (205). Bernasconi, *Heidegger in Question*, 190–210.

4. My point here is that the publication of the series of manuscripts following from *Contributions to Philosophy* has made both possible and necessary the reappraisal of the manner in which Heidegger's thought proceeds from language, and thus from the event. Thus I revise and expand here my remarks about the poetic rigor of thinking and the relation of the "infold" (*Einfalt*) as constitutive to language in *Inflected Language*, 21–42. Fynsk is similar in his approach, as he frames his discussion of language as relation with regard to how in Heidegger "thought begins to proceed *from* language itself." Fynsk, *Language and Relation*, 4.

5. In *Inflected Language*, I emphasize the strangeness involved in the withdrawal or retraction of language from signification, the ways in which this retreat inflects meaning and helps change thought into poetic thinking; see 10 and 27–42. Fynsk makes a similar point about how Heidegger's account of language extends beyond the play of signification: "Thus Heidegger's target in his deconstruction of the traditional concept of language is the sign structure, conceived as the articulation of a phonic (or even written) substance and the meaning it would convey." See *Language and Relation*, 78. My approach differs importantly from Fynsk's in my emphasis on Heidegger's rethinking of difference in terms of nearness and departure (*Abschied*), and on the dependence of this account on Heidegger's critical distinction between words (*Worte*) and signs, or "dictionary words" (*Wörter*). The texts published in the *Collected Works* since 1999, especially GA 74, allow us to flesh out much more clearly Heidegger's position, especially his rethinking of the notion of the sign with regard to Heidegger's critique of difference, which I develop in chapter 2.

6. Two readings depart from this mold. Bernasconi shows in "Transformation of Language at Another Beginning" that Heidegger's essays on language, in particular "The Way to Language," already lead us toward the transformation of language away from its metaphysical conceptualization. It is instructive to reread Bernasconi's much earlier essay with the recent account of "The Way to Language" by Françoise Dastur, who foregrounds the difference of Heidegger's approach from the notion of language as *phone semantike* and as signs; see Dastur, *Heidegger*, 215–254.

1. Event | Language

1. The relation between *Entmenschung* and language, especially the critique of the subject-object and subject-predicate schemas, is discussed by Ivo de Gennaro in "Entmenschung und Sprache" and by Marco Casanova in "Die Sprache des Ereignisses."

2. My point is that the importance of this transformation has been insufficiently underscored or explored in Heidegger scholarship. One notable exception is Bernasconi's elaboration of the notion of transformation in "The Way to Language" in

chapter 11 of his *Heidegger in Question*, 190–210. Especially important is Berna-sconi's careful demonstration of how the transformation and the other beginning at issue in Heidegger complicate Derridean and more broadly post-structuralist accounts of Heidegger. For other discussions of transformation in language and thinking, see Christopher Fynsk, *Language and Relation*, and John Sallis, "The Manic Saying of Beyng."

3. In her 2007 study on Heidegger, Françoise Dastur insists on the fact that language is not just one of the topics in Heidegger but is coextensive with the ques-tions of being and of truth (*Heidegger*, 215).

4. "Sprache—was der Mensch hat—*Wesensbesitz*." *Zum Wesen der Sprache und Zur Frage nach der Kunst*, GA 74, 100.

5. "*Vernunft*—entsprungen dem stillhaltenden Achten auf das Seyn. . . . Aber dieser Ursprung—unerfragt, unerfahren und deshalb: nur *Vermögen im animal!*" GA 74, 133.

6. As Fynsk remarks in *Language and Relation*, Heidegger "proposes to think it [language] not in reference to humankind, as has been done throughout tradition, but in itself, and to think the essence of the human from the place of its advent" (17). It is perhaps more clear now that to think of language in this manner, that is, from and by way of language's own movement, language needs to be thought of in itself specifically *from* the event.

7. Two ways of notating Heidegger's archaic spelling of *Seyn* have been offered in English translations, "be-ing" or "beyng," in order to distinguish it from *Sein*, translated as "being" or "Being." While neither can reproduce the effect in German, I opt here for "beyng" simply for the sake of simplicity and consistency, except for a few citations. At the same time, in order to avoid adding to the clutter of a text already replete with unusual phrasings and words inherited from Heidegger and English translations of his texts, I use the English "being" most of the time, with the understanding that at issue in my comments is *Seyn* in its nonmetaphysical resonance evolved by Heidegger, not just *Sein* as already marked by *Seiendheit* (be-ingness). "Beyng" is used at times when the silent difference between *Seyn* and *Sein* needs to be underscored in my explanation, or else in translations of Heidegger's texts.

8. As Dastur shows as well, human beings are approached not on the basis of life but by way of their belonging to *physis* and *aletheia; Heidegger*, 161.

9. Writing about the fact that it is language that "speaks," Dastur indicates that language is neither human nor suprahuman; instead, humans are always already inscribed in language; see *Heidegger*, 246–249.

10. Two most significant Derrida texts in this regard are *The Animal That Therefore I Am* and *The Beast and the Sovereign*, vol. 1.

11. In "The Manic Saying of Beyng," John Sallis comments on the way in which this issue of the event is also the drawing of thinking into proximity to it and to its words: "The issue of Ereignis is to draw thoughtful saying into proximity to Being so that its words become those of Being" (79).

12. Vallega-Neu, *"Contributions to Philosophy": An Introduction*, 3.

13. See my discussion of the role of poetry in Heidegger's development of poetic thinking in *Inflected Language*, 23–33. Fynsk emphasizes this point as well in the chap-ters on Heidegger in *Language and Relation*; see, for instance, 39–47.

14. On this point, see also Ivan Kordić, "Das Sagen des Seyns und die Sprache," 378–379.

15. See Heidegger, *GA* 12, 230, note e.

16. See ibid., 231, note b.

17. In *Inflected Language,* I argue that understanding Heidegger on language involves an important shift from difference to infold, as well as a rethinking of the notion of relation through the prism of such infolding (33–42).

18. Fynsk discusses relation in a similar vein. He does not link this understanding of relation to a rethinking of *eigen.*

19. Fynsk provides a careful reading of the proper, *Brauch* and transformation in relation to language; see *Language and Relation,* 117–131.

20. Jean-François Aenishanslin lists tautology, parataxis, and nonpredicative expressions as part of Heidegger's unique style and turns of writing; see "La logique, la pensée, le silence," 365–366.

21. See Fynsk's discussion of *einsam* in *On the Way to Language;* Fynsk, *Language and Relation,* 116–117.

22. Vallega-Neu, *"Contributions to Philosophy": An Introduction,* 4.

23. Heidegger, *Off the Beaten Track,* 276.

24. Derrida, "Différance," in *Margins of Philosophy,* 27.

25. Vallega-Neu, *"Contributions to Philosophy": An Introduction,* 3.

26. On the difference between the saying of being and of beings, see Marco Casanova, "Die Sprache des Ereignisses," 387–390.

27. Dastur points out that Heidegger's tautological statements undermine the predicative structure, thus calling into question the separation into the "subject" and its "activity"; *Heidegger,* 249.

28. Heidegger, *Bremer und Freiburger Vorträge, GA* 79, 161. *Bremen and Freiburg Lectures,* 152.

29. Derrida sees in these remarks a forgetting of writing (*Of Spirit*); Diana Aurenque, by contrast, focuses on the connection between hand and acting (*Handeln,* handling), in "Literatur, Öffentlichkeit und Geheimnis," 22–23.

30. See Dastur, *Heidegger,* 246.

31. Aenishanslin points out that Heidegger's tautological statements zero in on what arrives in language without being spoken or said as such; see "La logique, la pensée, le silence," 363–365.

32. Ames and Hall, *Dao de Jing,"* 77.

33. See also Fynsk's illuminating explanation of the *Aufriss* in *Language and Relation,* 63–64.

34. Dastur explains that this monology of language arises not from the position of a self but as the con-ference, the relation, of being and humans as the very coming of language: "La monologie ne provient pas de la position d'un soi, mais de la con-férence(*Ver-halten*) de l'homme et de l'être come avènement du langage." *Heidegger,* 254.

35. In *Heidegger in Question,* Bernasconi underscores this point, indicating that human saying is preceded by the self-showing, forming part of Heidegger's displacement of "the metaphysical account of speech as a human activity" (201).

36. In the seminar in Le Thor, Heidegger speaks about "location of being" (*Ortschaft*) and of "truth as locality (*Örtlichkeit*) of being. This already presupposes, however, an

understanding of the place-being of place. Hence the expression *topology of be-ing* (Topologie des Seyns)." *FS*, 41.

37. See Malpas, *Heidegger's Topology*, 28–35.

38. "Essence, as we see, names the movement of the country, a movement of way-making that occurs properly in the speaking of language." Fynsk, *Language and Relation*, 76.

39. Dastur, *Heidegger*, 225. For Dastur's broader discussion of *Ortschaft* or locality in Heidegger, see 220–225.

40. In *Heidegger*, Dastur renders *Er-örterung* as *pensée localisante (218)*. She also points to the need in Heidegger to abandon the idea of explaining or grasping language in favor of attending to language's way of unfolding (*Wesen*). This is the case because explicative approaches to language conceive it as a being and explain it in relation to its being seen as its ground or reason, and thus as being-ness, while being brooks no grounds and unfolds as *Ab-grund* (243–245).

41. Such graphs can be found in many writings from the 1930s and abound in some. See, for instance, GA 66, 188 and 380; GA 69, 27 and 106; GA 71, 65, 78, 143, 272, and 305; GA 74, 111 and 163; GA 76, 142, 245–246, 260, 338, 344, 349, 370–371, and 376)

42. The complex discussion of the Open and the ways in which animals, plants, and humans belong to it can be found in Heidegger, "What Are Poets For?," *PLT*, 104–139.

43. Heidegger clearly notes this limitation to our ability to know how animals experience, speaking about at best going along with the animal. Heidegger, *Fundamental Concepts of Metaphysics*, 201–204.

44. Vallega-Neu defines the poietic with regard to the way in which thinking in *Contributions to Philosophy* proceeds from the event and allows language and thinking to appear as events; see *"Contributions to Philosophy": An Introduction*, 3.

2. Words and Signs

1. On Heidegger's approach to language in relation to the notion of language as the system of signs, see Vallega-Neu, *"Contributions to Philosophy": An Introduction*, 3.

2. Dastur elaborates this distinction between saying (*Sage*) and speaking (*sprechen*), which are not separated but form language as relation (*Ver-halten*); see Dastur, *Heidegger*, 254.

3. Dastur also emphasizes the fact that signs in Heidegger unfold from saying and writes about signs as constituting the imprint of the saying. See *Heidegger*, 246–247.

4. Fynsk, *Language and Relation*, 30.

5. Following Heidegger's remarks in "Language," Fynsk underscores the fact that "a *Verlauten* may be either speech or writing." See *Language and Relation*, 28.

6. Commenting on Heidegger's note referring to *"Laut und Schrift,"* Fynsk remarks that "this discussion of writing does not fall so immediately within the logic of phonocentrism," the point with which both Bernasconi and I agree. See Fynsk, *Language and Relation*, 99, footnote.

7. The translators render the line: "How words become words (*Wörter*)," which does not show the critical fold between *Worte* and *Wörter* on which Heidegger's argument depends.

8. *"Das Wort gründet nicht nur 'Welt,' sondern ist des Seyns und verwahrt verschwiegen die Lichtung des Da.* / Bedeutung und Lautung und Schrift schiessen ihm erst zu und sind nicht das 'Wesen.'" Heidegger, *GA* 85, 55.

9. "Das Wort be-dingt das Ding zum Ding." *GA 12*, 220.

10. Fynsk, *Language and Relation*, 61.

11. In "Transitional Breakdown of the Word," Jussi Backmann points out that the word in Heidegger's discussion of George "essentially evades naming" and links it specifically to Heidegger's remarks about transitional poets and transformation in relation to language (63).

12. For a short and eloquent discussion of this shift in Greek thinking about language from monstration to designation and the rise of the anthropological conception of language relying on the notion of *zoon logon echon,* see Dastur, *Heidegger,* 241–242. As Dastur explains, "Ce qui s'est donc fondé en fait de théorie du langage dans l'Antiquité grecque, c'est la théorie de l'équivalence ontologique des mots et des choses dans la même dimension de la présence subsistante . . ." (241).

13. "Die blosse physiologisch biologisch anthropologisch gesehene Ausstattung mit der Sprachfähigkeit, die man metaphysisch vom animal rationale her als das Erste nimmt, bedeutet für die Besinnung auf das Wesen der Sprache gar nichts, es sei denn die völlige Vermauerung jedes Weges in die Wesensbesinnung. . . ." (*GA* 74, 144).

14. With regard to Heidegger's specific remarks on Anaximander, this letting (*Lassen*) indicates a thinking attentive to and holding open the way in which all beings come to be in that they tarry, or stay awhile, always arising (*Enstehen*) only to disappear or go away (*Entgehen*) (*GA* 78, 133).

15. Heidegger, *Wegmarken,* 314.

16. Heidegger, *Vorträge und Aufsätze,* 173.

17. "Die weilende Weite kennt nicht die leere Einförmigkeit von Zeit und Raum. Fremd auch ist ihr die Einschränkung auf die blosse Ausdehnung des Körperhaften und des Ablaufs" (*GA* 74, 44).

18. Heidegger's most extensive discussion of the notion of the *Anfang* is in a Gesamtaugabe volume devoted to this notion: *Über den Anfang, GA* 70.

19. Derrida, *Of Grammatology,* 62 and 65.

20. Bernasconi, *Heidegger in Question,* 210.

21. Derrida, *Of Grammatology,* 50.

22. In "Language and Poetry," Lysaker underscores the role of language as the site of the dif-ference (*Unter-Schied*) of world and things: "In recalling us to the site/event where thing and world are disclosed or appear, both in their belonging together and their *dif-ference,* language, presuming we have learned to dwell in its speaking, exposes the basic scene of human being-in-the-world" (202).

3. Poetry and the Poietic

1. See Dastur, *Heidegger,* 165.

2. See especially Ziarek, *Historicity of Experience* and *Force of Art,* as well as "'Without Human Meaning.'"

3. "Mit der Metaphysik ended auch die 'Kunst'"; Heidegger, *Metaphysik und Nihilismus, GA* 67, 108.

4. Translations of both essays are in *Poetry, Language, Thought.*

5. The remark reads: "Das Denken und die *kunst-lose* Dichtung" (*GA* 67, 109).

6. Lyotard, *Inhuman*, 93.

7. See also Gennaro, "Entmenschung und Sprache," 339.

8. Fynsk develops the reflection on the sensible and the thingly element in language in a related but distinct manner: "Thus, Heidegger, is thinking the thingly character of language *by way of difference,* and in doing so he is aggressively avoiding an approach that takes human *Verlautbarung* as essential. But he is stepping back from the phenomena of phonetic articulation precisely in order to provide for a more concrete relation to language and a hearing that is not immediately hollowed out by the play of signification." Fynsk, *Language and Relation,* 79. I see as crucial, however, Heidegger refiguring, or perhaps, "disfiguring," of difference through departure (*Abschied*) and nearness (*Nähe*), discussed in chapter 2.

9. Ivan Kordić discusses the notions of reservedness (*Verhaltenheit*) and holding in silence (*Erschweigung*) in "Das Sagen des Seyns und die Sprache," 375–378.

10. For a more extensive discussion of Kim's work and the role of silence and its notation, see Ziarek, "Noting Silence."

11. I limit my discussion here to two publications by Myung Mi Kim, her volume *Dura* and a chapbook *River Antes.* In a substantially altered version—without fold-out pages—"River Antes" appears as a section of Kim's latest volume of poetry, *Penury.*

4. Language after Metaphysics

1. Dastur, *Heidegger,* 248.

2. In *Language and Relation,* Fynsk provides an illuminating discussion of another important prefix in Heidegger's German, *be-* (68).

3. Heidegger, *Basic Concepts,* 53.

4. In the original, "in den Wörtern der Sprache jeweils das Wort hört." Heidegger, *Das Ereignis, GA* 71, 173.

5. "Ce que Heidegger nomme *Ereignis* est donc spatialisant tout autant que temporalisant, mais il l'est de manière abyssale, car sa finitude ne peut lui donner aucune extériorité, ni ne lui procurer la figure d'aucun 'soi.'" Dastur, *Heidegger,* 225. Perhaps in the context of *Armut,* one can think of *Ereignis* as "poor" in self, in the sense in which the event de-emphasizes substantiality, dispelling the figures of self, identity, property to draw attention to the spatiotemporality of being's unfolding.

6. Heidegger, *Introduction to Metaphysics.*

7. See the more developed discussion of the relation between inventive, avantgarde poetry and use of language and the problematic of power in Ziarek, "The Turn of Art."

8. Schild, "Pauvreté," 79.

9. Schild discusses the link between poverty and the simple in Heidegger's work on Hölderlin published in *GA* 4, 132–133; see "Pauvreté," 70.

10. Schild, "Pauvreté," 79.

11. "Il n'est ni le signe d'une faiblesse, ni l'indice d'un ineffable, mais c'est ce *Versagen* qui soutient le retrait de l'être et est ainsi véritable rapport (*Verhalten*) à lui." Dastur, *Heidegger,* 228.

12. Dastur explicitly links *Versagen* with *Gelassenheit:* "Un autre nom de ce *Versagen* est *Gelassenheit,* où le *lassen* (laisser) parle à la fois à l'actif et au passif: on soutient le retrait de l'être en le laissant échapper." *Heidegger,* 228.

13. This transformed relation could lead, as Heidegger suggests, writing about "the last god" in *Contributions to Philosophy,* to an as-yet-unexperienced sense of divinity (see *CP,* 316–330). Giving proper due to Heidegger's notion of "the last god" and what it implies about human relation to divinity and its place within the non-metaphysical experience of the world, would necessitate a different study, one that would need to follow more closely Heidegger's remarks on "the heavenly" and the "unknown God" in his essays on poetry and Hölderlin.

BIBLIOGRAPHY

Aenishanslin, Jean-François. "La logique, la pensée, le silence. Un styl en transition." In Mejía and Schüssler, *Heideggers "Beiträge zur Philosophie,"* 359–366.

Ames, Roger T., and David L. Hall, trans. and commentary. *Dao de Jing: "Making This Life Significant": A Philosophical Translation.* New York: Ballantine, 2003.

Aurenque, Diana. "Literatur, Öffentlichkeit und Geheimnis. Die heideggersche Unterscheidung von geschrieben-ausgesprochenem und schweigend-hörendem Wort." In *Schreiben Dichten Denken: Zu Heideggers Sprachbegriff.* Ed. David Espinet. Frankfurt: V. Klostermann, 2011, 13–28.

Backmann, Jussi. "The Transitional Breakdown of the Word: Heidegger and Stephan George's Encounter with Language." *Gatherings: The Heidegger Circle Annual* (2011): 54–73.

Bernasconi, Robert. *Heidegger in Question: The Art of Existing.* Atlantic Heights, N.J.: Humanities Press, 1993.

———. *The Question of Language in Heidegger's History of Being.* Amherst, N.Y.: Prometheus Books, 1989.

Casanova, Marco. "Die Sprache des Ereignisses." In Mejía and Schüssler, *Heideggers "Beiträge zur Philosophie,"* 383–392.

Dastur, Françoise. *Heidegger: La question du logos.* Paris: Vrin, 2007.

Derrida, Jacques. *The Animal That Therefore I Am.* Trans. David Willis. New York: Fordham University Press, 2008.

———. *The Beast and the Sovereign.* vol. 1. Trans. Geoffrey Bennington. Chicago, Ill.: University of Chicago Press, 2009.

———. *Margins of Philosophy.* Trans. Alan Bass. Chicago, Ill.: University of Chicago Press, 1982.

———. *Of Grammatology.* Trans. Gayatri Chakravorty Spivak. Baltimore, Md.: Johns Hopkins University Press, 1974, 1976.

Fynsk, Christopher. *Language and Relation: . . . That There Is Language.* Stanford, Calif.: Stanford University Press, 1996.

Heidegger, Martin. *Basic Concepts.* Trans. Gary E. Aylesworth. Bloomington and Indianapolis: Indiana University Press, 1993.

——. *Basic Writings*. Ed. and intro. David Farrell Krell. New York: HarperCollins, 1977, 1993.

——. *Beiträge zur Philosophie: Vom Ereignis. Gesamtausgabe*, vol. 65. 1989, 1994.

——. *Besinnung. Gesamtausgabe*, vol. 66. 1997.

——. *Bremen and Freiburg Lectures: Insight into That Which Is, and Basic Principles of Thinking*. Trans. Andrew J. Mitchell. Bloomington: Indiana University Press, 2012.

——. *Bremer und Freiburger Vorträge. Gesamtausgabe*, vol. 79. 1994.

——. *Contributions to Philosophy (Of the Event)*. Trans. Richard Rojcewicz and Daniele Vallega-Neu. Bloomington and Indianapolis: Indiana University Press, 2012.

——. *Das Ereignis. Gesamtausgabe*, vol. 71. 2009.

——. *Der Spruch des Anaximader. Gesamtausgabe*, vol. 78. 2010.

——. "Die Armut." *Heidegger Studies* 10 (1994) 5–11.

——. *Die Geschichte des Seyns. Gesamtausgabe*, vol. 69. 1998.

——. *Erläuterungen zu Hölderlins Dichtung. Gesamtausgabe*, vol. 4. 1991, 2010, 2012.

——. *The Event*. Trans. Richard Rojcewicz. Bloomington and Indianapolis: Indiana University Press, 2012.

——. *Four Seminars*. Trans. Andrew J. Mitchell and François Raffoul. Bloomington: Indiana University Press, 2003.

——. *Fundamental Concepts of Metaphysics: World, Finitude, Solitude*. Trans. William McNeill and Nicholas Walker. Bloomington: Indiana University Press, 1995.

——. *Gesamtausgabe*. Frankfurt am Main: Vittorio Klostermann, 1975–.

——. *Introduction to Metaphysics*. Trans. Gregory Fried and Richard Polt. New Haven, Conn.: Yale University Press, 2000.

——. *Leitgedanken zur Entstehung der Metaphysik, der neuzeitlichen Wissenschaft, und der modernen Technik. Gesamtausgabe*, vol. 76. 2009.

——. *Metaphysik und Nihilismus. Gesamtausgabe*, vol. 67. 1999.

——. *Mindfulness*. Trans. Parvis Emad and Thomas Kalary. London and New York: Continuum, 2006.

——. *Off the Beaten Track*. Trans. Julian Young and Kenneth Haynes. Cambridge, U.K.: Cambridge University Press, 2002.

——. *On Time and Being*. Trans. Joan Stambaugh. Chicago, Ill.: University of Chicago Press, 2002.

——. *On the Essence of Language: The Metaphysics of Language and the Essencing of the Word; Concerning Herder's Treatise "On the Origin of Language."* Trans. Wanda Torres Gregory and Yvonne Unna. Albany: State University of New York Press, 2004.

——. *On the Way to Language*. Trans. Peter D. Hertz. New York: HarperCollins, 1961.

——. *Parmenides*. Trans. André Schuwer and Richard Rojcewicz. Bloomington: Indiana University Press, 1992.

——. *Poetry, Language, Thought*. Trans. Albert Hofstadter. New York: HarperCollins, 1971.

——. "Poverty." Trans. Thomas Kalary and F. Schalow. In *Heidegger, Translation, and the Task of Thinking: Essays in Honor of Parvis Emad*. Ed. F. Schalow. New York and Dordrecht: Springer, 2011, 3–10.

——. *Über den Anfang. Gesamtausgabe*, vol. 70. 2005.

——. *Unterwegs zur Sprache. Gesamtausgabe*, vol. 12. 1985.

——. *Vom Wesen der Sprache. Gesamtausgabe*, vol. 85. 1999.

——. *Vorträge und Aufsätze*. Pfullingen: Neske, 1954.

———. *Wegmarken.* Frankfurt: V. Klostermann, 1967, 1978.

———. *Zum Wesen der Sprache und Zur Frage nach der Kunst. Gesamtausgabe,* vol. 74. 2010.

———. *Zur Sache des Denkens.* Tübingen: Niemeyer, 1976.

Howe, Susan. *The Europe of Trusts.* Los Angeles, Calif.: Sun & Moon Press, 1990.

———. *Souls of the Labadie Tract.* New York: New Directions, 2007.

Gennaro, Ivo de. "Entmenschung und Sprache." In Mejía and Schüssler, *Heideggers "Beiträge zur Philosophie,"* 329–340.

Kim, Myung Mi. *Dura.* New York: Nightboat Books, 2008.

———. *Penury.* Richmond, Calif.: Omnidawn Publishing, 2009.

———. *River Antes.* Buffalo, N.Y.: Atticus/Finch Chapbooks, 2006.

Kordić, Ivan. "Das Sagen des Seyns und die Sprache. Zur Frage der Sprache in Heidegger's *Beiträge zur Philosophie.*" In Mejía and Schüssler, *Heideggers "Beiträge zur Philosophie,"* 367–382.

Lyotard, Jean-François. *The Inhuman: Reflections on Time.* Trans. Geoffrey Bennington and Rachel Bowlby. Stanford, Calif.: Stanford University Press, 1991.

Lysaker, John T. "Language and Poetry." In *Martin Heidegger: Key Concepts.* Ed. Bret W. Davis. Durham, U.K.: Acumen, 2010, 195–207.

Malpas, Jeff. *Heidegger's Topology: Being, Place, Word.* Cambridge, Mass.: MIT Press, 2006.

Mejía, Emmanuel, and Ingeborg Schüssler, eds. *Heideggers "Beiträge zur Philosophie": Internationales Kolloquium vom 20.–22. Mai 2004 an der Universität Lausanne (Schweiz).* Frankfurt: V. Klostermann, 2009.

Sallis, John. "The Manic Saying of Beyng." In Mejía and Schüssler, *Heideggers "Beiträge zur Philosophie,"* 75–84.

Schild. "Pauvreté." *Heidegger Studies* 26 (2010): 65–82.

Vallega-Neu, Daniela. *Contributions to Philosophy: An Introduction.* Bloomington: Indiana University Press, 2003.

Vezin, François. "Expérience de la parole, expérience de la traduction." In Mejía and Schüssler, *Heideggers "Beiträge zur Philosophie,"* 341–355.

Ziarek, Krzysztof. "Beyond Critique?: Art and Power." In *Adorno and Heidegger: Philosophical Questions.* Ed. Iain MacDonald and Krzysztof Ziarek. Stanford, Calif.: Stanford University Press, 2008, 105–123.

———. *The Force of Art.* Stanford, Calif.: Stanford University Press, 2004.

———. *The Historicity of Experience: Modernity, Avant-Garde, and the Event.* Evanston, Ill.: Northwestern University Press, 2001.

———. *Inflected Language: Toward a Hermeneutics of Nearness.* Albany: State University of New York Press, 1994.

———. "Noting Silence." *Critical Horizons* 11, 3 (2010): 359–377.

———. "The Turn of Art: The Avant-Garde and Power." *New Literary History* 33, 2 (2002): 89–107.

———. "'Without Human Meaning': Stevens, Heidegger, and the Foreignness of Poetry." In *Wallace Stevens Across the Atlantic.* Ed. Bart Eeckhout and Edward Ragg. Basingstoke and New York: Palgrave Macmillan, 2008, 79–94.

INDEX

ab-: back draft indicated by, 9; difference, new perspective provided by, 117–118; withdrawal indicated by, 9

Abgrund (abyss): *Ab-schied*'s relation to, 123; mortals opened to, 19; nearness as, 127; remoteness as, 127

Ab-grund (abyssal non-ground): momentum brought out by, 117; temporality of, 149

Abschied (departure): *Ab-grund*'s relation to, 123; being unconcealing as, 113–114; momentum brought out by, 117; *Unter-Schied* thought by way of, 119–123; *Verwindung* influenced by, 8–9

absence: opening onto, 192–193; and presence, 80

abyss. See *Abgrund*

actual: poietics revealing, 135–136; as standing-reserve, 133–134, 136; technicity revealing, 135–136

Adorno, Theodor, 177

Aenishanslin, Jean-François, 224n31

aletheia, 47–48

an-: connections established by, 77; role played by, 59

Anaximander, 38–39, 100–101

"Anaximander Fragment, The" (Heidegger), 38–39

Aneignung, 22

An-fang (beginning): another, 109; definition of, 106–107; discussion of, 226n18;

text on, 226n18; understanding of, 150–151

animals: communication, 20, 76; limits to knowing, 225n43; role of, 76

Anspruch (claim): *Aneignung* as, 22; cognitive science registering, 20; human beings answering, 58; *Vorwort* indicating pre-word status of, 59–60

Anstimmen (intoning or initial tuning), 93–94

anthropologization. See *Vermenschung*

Antigone (Sophocles), 196

Antwort (response): *Anwort* directed at, 58–59; speech as, 20–21; writing as, 20–21

An(t)wort, 60

An-wesen, 29

Anwort (oncoming word or word prior to words): *Antwort* in relation to, 58–59; coining of, 59; folding described by, 58–59; as pertinent to *Stimmung*, 93–94

Armut (poverty): definition of, 206, 207–208; necessity's role in, 207–209; as ontological, 209–210

"Die Armut" (Heidegger), 207–208

art: end of, 132–137; as language, 135; *Lichtung* as poietic dimension of, 135–136; metaphysics' relation to, 133, 136; as part or variation of *techne*, 136–137; as poetry, 134–135

KRZYSZTOF ZIAREK is a professor in the Department of Comparative
Literature at University at Buffalo, The State University of New York.
He is the author of *Inflected Language: Toward a Hermeneutics of Nearness*
(1994), *Historicity of Experience: Modernity, the Avant-Garde, and the Event*
(2001), and *The Force of Art* (2004).